Population in South Asia

Migration as a Survival Strategy

Population in South Asia
Migration as a Survival Strategy

Naveen Mishra

AUTHORSPRESS

First Published 2001
by Authorspress

E-35/103, Jawahar Park,
Laxmi Nagar, Delhi-110 092

e-mail: authorspress@yahoo.com
quantum_soul@mantramail.com

Typeset in NewCenturySchlbk by Chitra Computers

Population in South Asia: Migration as a Survival Strategy
ISBN 81-7273-066-7

Printed in India at Mehra Offset Press, Delhi.

Preface

The South Asian countries are facing explosive growth of population and have fallen further and further behind in all and every aspects of human development. The economic imbalances, poverty, environmental degradation, combined with the absence of peace and security, human rights violations and varying degrees of development of judicial and democratic institutions are the main factors of high-level migration rates in this region.

For individuals, migration is often a rational and dynamic effort to seek new opportunities in life. Migration is also prompted by push factors such as inequitable allocation of development resources, adoption of inappropriate technologies and lack of access to available land. Migration can have positive impacts on both the communities of origin and the communities of destination, providing the former with remittances and the latter with needed human resources. It also has the potential of facilitating the transfer of skills and contributing to cultural enrichment. However, migration entails the loss of human resources for many countries of origin and may give rise to political, economic or social tensions in countries of destination.

In South Asia, for the last two decades ahead, the population movements are likely to produce a further shift of rural populations to urban areas as well as continued high levels of migration between countries. These migrations are an important part of the economic transformations occurring around the world, and they present serious new challenges. Therefore, these issues must be addressed with more emphasis within population and development policies.

South Asian countries have pursued various strategies and actions to deal with the migration problems and their respective security implications. To be effective, migration policies need to take into account the economic constraints of the receiving country, the impact of migration on the host society and its effects on countries of origin. The long-term manageability of migration hinges on making the option to remain in South Asia a viable one for all people. Sustainable economic growth with equity and development strategies consistent with this aim are a necessary means to that end.

This book is a serious attempt to provide a comprehensive study of the interrelationship between migration and population in the South Asian context. Students researches, teachers, NGOs, besides educationists, planners, demographers and policy-makers will find this work informative and useful.

Naveen Mishra

Contents

1

Migration: An Introduction

Today, migration is becoming increasingly common as people move in search of security and a better livelihood: from villages to towns, from one region to another in their home country, or between countries and continents. Even those who do not migrate are affected as relative friends or descendants of migrants; or through experiences of change in their community a result of departure of neighbours or arrival of newcomers. Migration may contribute to further development and improve economic and social conditions, or alternatively may help to perpetuate stagnation and inequality. Much depends on the character migration and the actions taken by the governments and other stakeholders concerned. Migration helps to erode traditional boundaries between languages, cultures, ethnic groups and nation-states.

Migration means crossing the boundary of a political country in a certain minimum period.[1] Internal migration refers to a move from one area to another within one country.[2] International migration means crossing the frontiers which separate one of the world's approximately 200 states from one another.[3] Many scholars argue that internal and international migration are part of the same process, and should be analysed together. Rigid distinctions can be misleading: international migration may be over short distances and between culturally similar people, while internal migration can span great distances and bring together very different people. Sometimes the frontiers migrate, rather than the people, making internal migrants into inter national ones.

International migration arises in a world divided up into nation-states, in which remaining in the country of birth is still seen as a norm, and moving to another country as a deviation. That is why migration tends to be regarded as problematic: something to be controlled and even curbed, because it may bring about unpredictable changes. Problems of comparison arise not just because statistical categories differ, but because such differences reflect real variations in the social meaning of migration in differing contexts.

To improve control measures states divide international migrants into categories. They are:

i) *Temporary labour migrants*: Men and women who migrate for a limited period in order to take up employment and send money home.

ii) *Highly skilled and business migrants*: People with qualifications as managers, executives, professionals, technicians or similar, who move within the internal labour markets of transnational corporations and international organisations, or who seek employment through international labour markets for scarce skills.

iii) *Irregular migrants*: People who enter a country, usually in search of employment, without the necessary documents and permits. Many labour migration flows consist predominantly of undocumented migrants. In some cases immigration countries tacitly permit such migration since it allows mobilisation of labour in response to employer demands without social costs or measures for protection of migrants.

iv) *Refugees:* A refugee is a person residing outside his or her country of nationality, who is unable or unwilling to return because of a well-founded fear of persecution on account of race, religion, nationality, membership in a particular social group, or political opinion. Refugee organisations, especially the United Nations High Commission for Refugees (UNHCR), seek to distinguish clearly between refugees and migrants, but they do share many common characteristics with regard to social needs and cultural impacts in their place of settlement.

v) *Asylum-seekers:* People who move across borders in search of protection, but who may not fulfil the strict criteria laid down by the 1951 Convention. In many contemporary conflict situations in less developed countries it is difficult to distinguish between flights because of personal persecution and departure caused by the destruction of the economic and social infrastructure needed for survival.

vi) *Forced migrants:* This category includes not only refugees and asylum-seekers but also people forced to move by environmental catastrophes or development projects.

vii) *Family members*: Migration to join people who have already entered an immigration country under one of the above categories. Many countries, including the USA, Canada, Australia and most European Union (EU) member-states recognise in principle the flight to family reunion for legal immigrants. Other countries, especially those with contract labour systems, deny the flight to family reunion. In such cases, family members may enter illegally.

viii) *Return migrants:* People who return to their countries of origin after a period in another country. Return migrants are often looked on favourably as they may bring with them capital, skills and experience useful for economic development. Many countries have special schemes to make use of this development potential. However, some governments view returnees with suspicion since they may act as agents of cultural or political change.

International migration is an integral part of globalisation, which may be characterised as the widening, deepening and speeding up of worldwide inter-connectedness in all aspects of contemporary social life. The key indicator of globalisation is the rapid increase in cross-border flows of all sorts: finance, trade, ideas, pollution, media products and people. The key organising structure for all these flows is the transnational network, which can take the form of transnational corporations, global markets, international governmental and non-governmental organisations, global criminal syndicates, or transnational cultural communities.

The key tool is modern information and communications technology, including the internet, improved telephone connections and cheap air travel. Flows of capital and commodities are generally welcomed by the holders of economic and political power, but immigration and cultural differences are seen as potential threats to national sovereignty and identity, and many governments and political movements seek to restrict them.

The disparity in levels of income, employment and social well-being between differing areas is the most obvious cause of migration.[4] Differences in demographic patterns with regard to fertility, mortality, age-structure and labour force growth are also important. According to neoclassical economic theory, the main cause of migration is the individuals' efforts to maximise their income by moving from low-wage to high-wage economies.

However, causes of international migration are often quite complex. Movements may be initiated and regulated by powerful institutions, while state control of borders by states creates barriers to market forces. An alternative economic approach is provided by the new economics of labour migration, which argues that migration cannot simply be explained by income differences between two countries, but also by factors such as chances of secure employment, availability of capital for entrepreneurial activity, and the need to manage risk over long periods.

Migration decisions are made not just by individuals—they often represent family strategies to maximise income and survival chances. Use of remittances for consumption and investment can only be fully understood through a whole-household-economy approach. Thus there is no simple relationship between poverty and emigration. Departures from the very poorest areas may be rare, because people lack the economic capital needed to travel, the cultural capital needed to become aware of opportunities elsewhere, and the social capital needed to successfully find work and to cope in a new environment. However, in the event of a catastrophe, which destroys minimal subsistence levels, even the poorest may be forced to migrate, usually under very bad conditions.

Migration is thus both a result and a cause of development. Development leads to migration, because economic and educational improvements make people capable of seeking better opportunities elsewhere. Research shows that it is middle-income groups in developing areas that are most likely to depart. As incomes rise, emigration tends to decline.

The migration systems theory is found to be a useful approach to analyse the various factors causing emigration. A migration system is constituted by two or more countries which exchange migrants with each other. It is necessary to examine both ends of the flow and study all the linkages between the places concerned.

Migratory movements generally arise from the existence of prior links between sending and receiving countries based on colonisation, political influence, trade, investment or cultural ties. Typically migratory chains are started by an external factor, such as recruitment or military service, or by an initial movement of young pioneers. Once a movement is established, the migrants mainly follow beaten paths and are helped by relatives and friends already in the area of immigration.

Networks based on family or on common place of origin help provide shelter, work, assistance with bureaucratic procedures and support in personal difficulties. These social networks make the migratory process safer and more manageable for the migrants and their families. Migratory movements, once started, become self-sustaining social processes. Some people—both migrants and non-migrants—become facilitators of migration.

A migration industry emerges, consisting of recruitment organisations, lawyers, agents, smugglers and other middle-people. Such people can be both helpers and exploiters of migrants. The emergence of a migration industry with a strong interest in the continuation of migration has often confounded government efforts to control or stop movements. The links between migrant community and area of origin may persist over generations. Remittances fall off and visits to home may decline in frequency, but familial and cultural links remain. People stay in touch with their area of origin, and may seek marriage partners there.

Migration continues along the established chains and may increase dramatically at a time of crisis. In the long run, migrations may lead to international communicative networks, which affect economic relations, social and political institutions, and the cultural and national identity of all the concerned countries.

Warfare and formation of nations, states and empires have all led to migrations, both voluntary and forced. However, from the fifteenth century onwards, European nation-state formation, colonialism and industrialisation led to a rapid growth in migration. Colonialism involved overseas emigration of Europeans as sailors, soldiers, farmers, traders, priests and administrators. Colonial labour was provided first through forced migration of African slaves, and later through use of indentured workers, who were transported large distances within colonial empires. Industrialisation in Western Europe led to landlessness and impoverishment, which encouraged mass emigration to other continents.

International migration expanded in volume and scope, after the Second World War. More and more countries were affected by migration, while immigration countries received entrants from a broad spectrum of economic, social and cultural backgrounds. Two main phases can be distinguished. The first lasted from 1945 to 1973: the long boom stimulated large-scale labour migration to Western Europe, North America and Oceania from less-developed areas. In a second phase from the mid-1970s, capital investment shifted away from the old centres, and transnational forms of production and distribution reshaped the world economy.[5] The older industrial countries experienced new types of inflows, while new immigration countries emerged in Southern Europe, the Gulf oil countries, Latin America, Africa and Asia.

Comprehensive recent figures of migration have been provided by a study carried out by the United Nations Population Division, which gives estimates on migrant stock in 218 countries or territories. The UN figures show that the global migrant stock grew from 75 million in 1965 to 120 million in 1990. The 1990 figure was roughly equal to two per cent of the world's population.[6] The number of migrants grew slightly faster than world population as a whole, but the annual growth rate was not dramatic.

However, international migration appears to have grown more rapidly in the 1990s, reaching an estimated 135-140 million people, including some 13 million UNHCR-recognised refugees by 1997.[7] None the less, international migrants remain a fairly small minority, with most of the world's people remaining in their country of origin. Internal migration, by contrast, is much larger: for instance, the number of internal migrants in India in 1981 was some 200 million, more than double the number of international migrants in the whole world at the time.

One of the major significance of migration as a major factor in societal change lies in the fact that it is concentrated in certain countries and regions. The UN study shows that 90 per cent of the world's migrants were living in just 55 countries. In absolute terms, the most migration is between less-developed countries: in 1990, 55 per cent of all migrants were to be found in such areas. But in relative terms, the developed world has been far more affected by immigration: 4.6 per cent of the population of the developed countries were migrants in 1990, compared with 1.6 per cent in developing countries.[8]

As migratory chains develop, large proportions of the young men and women of specific villages or neighbourhoods leave, which may lead to local labour shortages as well as major changes in family and community life. In immigration countries, newcomers become concentrated in industrial areas and urban centres where there are chances of employment and where previous migrants can provide help with settlement. Typically, certain neighbourhoods become centres of immigrant settlement, marked by distinctive businesses, associations, social facilities and places of worship. Such neighbourhoods are the basis for ethnic community formation and cultural and linguistic maintenance.

Although women have always formed a large proportion of migrants, their share has gradually increased. By 1995 about 48 per cent of all international migrants were women, and they outnumbered male migrants in about a quarter of receiving countries.[9] More important was the shift in the character of female migration, with a trend away from movement as family members of male workers or refugees and an increase in the number of women who moved independently or as heads of households.

THEORETICAL BACKGROUND

Migration is too diverse and multifaceted to be explained by a single theory. Efforts at theory building should rather be evaluated by their potential to guide research and provide cogent hypotheses to be tested against empirical evidence, and by their contribution to a better understanding of specific facets, dimensions and processes of migration. Theory building in this realm is practically a matter of the second half of the twentieth century, and especially of its last third.

Most contributions prior to the 1960s are nowadays of only historical interest, except for a number of contributions to the vocabulary of migration and the epoch-making significance of a few outstanding forerunners. These include *The Laws of Migration* of Ernest-George Ravenstein, the undisputed founding father of the modern thinking about migration, and the seminal *The Polish Peasant in Europe and America* by William Thomas and Florian Znaniecki, probably the most impressive book ever written on the subject of migration. An array of new or renovated theories and conceptual frameworks has flourished in the last quarter of the century with the aim, mirroring the increasing relevance socially and politically accorded to the phenomenon.

During the third quarter of the twentieth century, rapid and sustained economic growth, the increasing internationalisation of economic activity, decolonisation, and emergent processes of economic development in the Third World, all brought about an intensification of migration, both internal and international. Thinking about migration at that time tended to mirror both the overall climate of the period and the characteristics of migration flows. It is hardly surprising that the major contributions to migration theorising in this period should come from the realm of economics.

The general primacy of economic motivations in migration had already been recognised by Ravenstein several decades before. Bad or oppressive laws, heavy taxation, an unattractive climate, uncongenial social surroundings, and even compulsion, all have produced and are still producing currents of migration, but none of these currents can compare in volume with that which arises from the desire inherent in most men to better themselves in material respects. Such a primacy was paramount in the third quarter of the century, after the hectic period of massive resettlement of displaced populations and accommodation to new borders that followed the Second World War.

W. Arthur Lewis's model of 'Economic Development with Unlimited Supply of Labour's an influential model of development in dual economies, in which migration plays a pivotal role. Dual economies are economies in development, usually in post-colonial contexts, in which a modern sector, connected with the outside world, coexists with a traditional one which relies on subsistence agriculture for survival. When the modern sector expands, it draws labour from the traditional sector, where its marginal productivity is zero.

Lewis estimated that a cliff of about 30 per cent was bound to exist between the wages of the two sectors, and that differential would suffice for workers to move. For the advanced sector, having at its disposal an unlimited supply of migrant labour makes it possible to expand while keeping wages low, thus securing a high rate of profit. For the traditional sector, out-migration is the only way to get rid of surplus labour and to proceed in the production function towards higher capital-output ratios, and thus constitutes the precondition to embark in a process of development, out of economic backwardness.

Therefore, in Lewis's model migration is a crucial mechanism of development for the economy as a whole, exploiting the potential of growth inherent in economic disparities, and both sectors, traditional and modern, sending and receiving, greatly benefit from it. Even though Lewis placed himself in what was known at the time as development economics, his model contained in a nutshell the basic elements of the equilibrium models which would dominate the social sciences, and migration theorising within it, at least in ensuring two decades.

Neoclassical Theory

The most influential theory about migration was the theory of migration that emanates from neoclassical economics, based on such familiar tenets as rational choice, utility maximisation, expected net returns, factor mobility and wage differentials. A paradigm so versatile, which has been applied to so many dimensions of human behaviour, and whose influences still spill over from economics to other social sciences, could hardly disregard migration, to which it seems to fit naturally. Simple, elegant, akin to common sense, it has the advantage of combining a micro-perspective of individual decision making and a macro-counterpart of structural determinants.

At a macro level, it is a theory about the spatial redistribution of the factors of production responding to different relative prices. Migration results from the uneven geographical distribution of labour and capital. In some countries, or regions, labour is scarce relative to capital, and its price—the wage level—correspondingly high, while in other countries or regions the opposite obtains. As a result, workers tend to go from countries or regions where labour is abundant and wages low to labour-scarce countries where wages are high. In so doing, they contribute to the redistribution of the factors of production and to the equalisation of wages between countries in the long run, redressing original inequalities. Therefore, in the neoclassical view, the origin of migration is to be sought in disparities in wage rates between countries, which in turn mirror income and welfare disparities.

The micro version of neoclassical theory explains the reason why individuals respond to structural differences between countries or regions and engage in migration. Migration is the result of individual decisions made by rational actors who seek to improve their well-being by moving to places where the reward of their labour will be higher than the one they get at home, in a measure sufficient to offset the tangible and intangible costs involved in the move. It is therefore an individual, spontaneous, and voluntary act, which rests on the comparison between the present situation of the actor and the expected net gain of moving, and results from a cost-benefit calculus. It follows that migrants will tend to go to the destination where a higher net return is expected, after pondering over all the available alternatives.

The predominance of the neoclassical persuasion was contested, with limited success, by a school of thought located at the opposite side of the ideological spectrum, which saw social processes in terms of conflict rather than of equilibrium. In the 1960s and 1970s, this historical-structural inspiration, with its strong Marxist overtones, was embodied in dependency theory, which posited that the evolution of capitalism had given way to an international order composed of core industrialised countries and peripheral agrarian ones linked by uneven and asymmetrical relations.

The advancement of the former rested on their exploitation of the latter, whose development was primarily hampered by their subordinate status. Underdevelopment was thus seen as a by-product of development. Dependency theory had little to say about migration, and that little was more about the rural-urban variety than about its international counterpart. The latter constituted one of the mechanisms through which inequalities between countries were perpetuated and reinforced.

However, the relative demise of the neoclassical explanation of migration in the course of the last quarter of the twentieth century was not caused by the rather ineffectual challenge of dependency theory, but by its own intrinsic shortcomings, magnified by the profound changes undergone by the nature and characteristics of international migration since the mid-1970s.[10] These changes have increased the heterogeneity and complexity of the phenomenon and have given rise to a migratory reality not very congenial with the neoclassical world. Contemporary problems of the neoclassical theory of migration do not stem primarily from its insufficiencies as a theory, but rather from its difficulties to come to terms with reality.

One important fact that runs counter to the neoclassical explanation is why so few people move, given the huge differences in income, wages and levels of welfare that exist among countries. This is clearly the achilles' heel of neoclassical theory. If migration flows between countries were to conform to the prescription of neoclassical theory, the number of international migrants should be many times higher than the one that obtains in reality. The theory fails to explain why some countries have relatively high out-migration rates, and others, structurally similar, do not.

These shortcomings of the neoclassical explanation of migration can be partly traced to the exclusion of the political dimension from the picture at a time in which it has risen to pre-eminence. Being in essence a theory of the mobility of factors of production in accordance with relative prices, the neoclassical theory is increasingly at odds, when not incapable to come to terms, with a world bristled with barriers which severely curtail the movement of labour.

The contemporary international system in which the free circulation of workers is the exception and restriction the rule, does hardly conform to the image of an ideal environment in which individuals move freely and spontaneously to pursue their own interest and maximise utility. Generalised restrictive admission policies reduce mobility and deter would-be migrants, in a proportion impossible to ascertain but likely to be very large.

In theory this factor—in the cases where there is a possibility of overcoming entry restrictions—could be included in the calculus of the would-be migrant, taken both as an additional cost and as an aggravation of the uncertainty of the investment implied by migration. But in practice its influence is so overriding that it deprives the theory of any use. It is true that almost everything can be translated into costs and benefits, and even that a value in monetary terms can be attached to it, but the price of such effort may often be the practical irrelevance, close to tautology, of finding that people move to enhance their well-being. In practice, the cost of overcoming entry obstacles is often so staggering that it dissuades the majority of those who might be candidates to migration if only economic considerations were at play.

In the cases when such barriers cannot be overcome, it would make little sense to explain the decision to stay on the basis of the neoclassical calculus. Therefore, political factors are nowadays much more influential than differential wages in determining mobility or immobility, and the selectivity of migration can be explained more in terms of legal entitlements, or of personal characteristics in the case of undocumented moves, than in terms of wage differentials. As a result, when applied to international movements in the contemporary world, the neoclassical explanation floats between the obvious and the unrealistic.

Obviously, a different matter is the explanation of internal migration, where mobility is normally unrestricted and the costs of cultural adaptation lower. The paradigm can also be successfully applied to the past, when entry barriers were less prominent than in the present. Yet, the insufficiencies of the paradigm do not stem only from restrictive entry policies. It is also be unable to explain reality even in spaces where mobility is unfettered.

The idea that migration only ceases when wage differentials have been reduced to the mere cost moving does not seem to hold. Neither does the correlative prescription of the theory that posits that migration will bring about an equalisation of levels of welfare between countries. The idea that international migration has brought about a significant reduction in economic disparities among sending and receiving countries in recent decades seems hard to sustain. Indeed, the neoclassical theory of migration has been often criticised on the grounds that it downplays non-economic factors—particularly cultural determinants, bound to be influential in such an existential decision as migration—that it mechanically reduces the determinants of migration, that treats migrants and societies as if they were homogeneous, and that its perspective is static.

Contemporary Theories

The last quarter of the twentieth century witnessed deep changes in international migration. During this period the flows have become more global and heterogeneous in composition. Asia, Africa and Latin America have replaced Europe as the major region of origin. Both the relative volume and the nature of labour demand in receiving societies have changed. New forms of migration based upon entitlements have become paramount. Undocumented flows and clandestine traffics have acquired an increasing saliency. Social integration in the receiving society has become less linear. Finally, transnational spaces and communities have emerged.

Since theories usually follow facts, these changes may have ushered in a new era in the ways of thinking about migration as well. The effects of such changes is compounded by the fact that thinking about migration seems to be presided over nowadays by the reality of international migration, while in the past it often mirrored internal migration. As a result of increasing interest in migration and the increasingly complex and different reality, an array of conceptual and theoretical approaches have either developed anew, or been invigorated with new air, or else brought to bear and adapted from other areas of human behaviour. Indeed, rather than new migration theories *qua se*, they are either modified versions of previous strands or adaptations of theoretical frameworks built for different purposes.

Economics of labour migration

The most migration-specific of all new theories is the new economics of labour migration. Associated primarily with the name of Oded Stark, it can be seen either as an inside criticism of the micro-version of neoclassical theory, or as a variant of it that refines and enriches it with a number of amendments and additions. It shares with the latter its básic cornerstone, rational choice, but differs from it in that the actor who seeks to enhance its utility is more the family or the household than the individual migrant.

Migration is a family strategy geared not so much to maximise income as to diversify sources of income, in order to minimise risks such as unemployment, loss of income, or crop failures—and loosen constraints, given the imperfections that usually plague credit and insurance markets in sending countries. In so far as migrants aim at maximising income, they do not necessarily do so in absolute terms, but rather relative to other households in its reference group, thus retaking the old notion of relative deprivation. From this it can be inferred that the more unequal the distribution of income in a given community, the more intensely relative deprivation will be felt, and the more incentives will there be for further migration to occur.

The new economics of migration lends attention to income distribution, contrary to the neoclassical explanation. It presents a number of improvements over neoclassical theory. To start with, the central importance accorded to wage differentials is considerably downplayed: they do not necessarily entail migration and they are not indispensable for migration to occur. In addition, it highlights the role of families and households, underlines the importance of remittances, and pays more attention to information and to the complex interdependence between migrants and the context in which they operate.

However, it is doubtful whether the disparate ingredients that make up the new economics of migration are sufficiently woven and logically integrated as to constitute a coherent theory, or whether it is no more than a critical, sophisticated variant of neoclassical theory. In any case, if anything detracts seriously from the value of the new economics of migration it is not so much its possible lack of theoretical autonomy as its limited applicability.

The contexts of migration it describes seem to be rather peculiar ones, characterised by decades long migration relationships. Indeed, although some of the evidence presented relates at times to other world regions, the new economics of migration seems to draw its inspiration as well as the bulk of the evidence on which it rests, from a small number of rural villages in Mexico. Its versatility *vis-a-vis* other, less established migration contexts—especially those that involve considerable degrees of societal disorganisation, not to speak of life-threatening circumstances—looks uncertain at best. It is not applicable either to the movement of complete households.

Migration networks

Migration networks can be defined as sets of interpersonal relations that link migrants or returned migrants with relatives, friends or fellow countrymen at home. They convey information, provide financial assistance, facilitate employment and accommodation, and give support in various forms. In so doing, they reduce the costs and uncertainty of migration and therefore facilitate it. Migration networks can be seen as a form of social capital, in so far as they are social relations that permit access to other goods of economic significance, such as employment or higher wages. This viewpoint was first suggested by Douglas Massey, drawing on social capital theory.

This larger framework might also accommodate, as it has been suggested, other intermediary institutions, such as struggling rings or benevolent, humanitarian groups, which, with different purposes and aims, assist migrants to overcome entry barriers. Yet, the inclusion of such institutions in the notion of social capital, which is made up of interpersonal ties, does not seem as straightforward as in the case of networks.

Migration networks have a multiplier effect, which is implicit in the formerly fashionable expression 'chain migration'. Moreover, the capital role that networks have usually played in migration flows is greatly enhanced nowadays in a world in which circulation is widely restricted. On the one hand, family reunion accounts for a substantial part of immigration flows in many countries. On the other, the importance of social networks is bound to increase as entry into receiving countries becomes more difficult, on account of their capacity to reduce the costs and risks of moving.

Networks are the main mechanism that makes migration a self-perpetuating phenomenon. They tend to grow ever larger and denser, as every move constitutes a resource for those who stay back, and facilitate further moves, which in turn widen the networks and the probability of their further expansion. The development of social networks may explain the continuation of migration independently from the causes that led to the initial movement. In fact, social networks may often be the foremost predictors of future flows. Due to this, migration networks may contribute to the explanation of differential migration.

Yet, experience shows that ever-expanding dynamics cannot go forever. At some moment a saturation point must be reached, after which deacceleration sets in. The dynamics of migration networks growth and stagnation constitute an area that calls for further investigation. Networks constitute an intermediate, relational level that stands between the micro level of individual decision making and the macro-level of structural determinants, thus contributing to bridge a gap that is one of the major limitations in migration thinking.

Dual labour market theory

The dual labour market theory of Michael Piore contributes to a better understanding of contemporary realities. It pays attention only to the receiving end of migration and places its explanation at the macro-level of structural determinants. According to it, international migration is caused by a permanent demand for foreign labour that stems from certain intrinsic characteristics of advanced industrial societies, which in turn result in the segmentation of their markets. For a number of reasons, highly developed economies require foreign workers to fill jobs that native workers refuse and that are no longer discharged—if they ever were—by women and teen-agers.

The merit of dual labour market theory lies in explaining in a complex and technical way why all this happens. Although structured in a different way, the theory explains why in advanced economies there are unstable and low productivity jobs; why local workers shun such jobs; why the local workers' reluctance to occupy unattractive jobs cannot be solved through standard markets mechanisms, contributes to a better understanding of contemporary realities; why foreign workers, from low-income countries are willing to accept such jobs; and, why such structural labour demand can no longer be filled as before by women and teenagers.

When the economies get advanced, there are unstable jobs due to the division of the economy in a capital-intensive primary sector and a labour-intensive, low-productivity secondary sector, which gives rise to a segmented labour market. Local workers shun such jobs because they confer low status and prestige and promise scant upward mobility, and because they entail motivation problems.

The local workers' reluctance to occupy unattractive jobs cannot be solved through standard market mechanisms, because raising salaries at the bottom of the occupational scale would require raising proportionately wages at the following echelons, in order to respect the occupational hierarchy, and that would result in structural inflation.

Foreign workers from low-income countries, especially temporary ones or those who entertain prospects of returning home some day, are willing to accept such jobs because low wages are usually high if compared with standards back home, and because the status and prestige that counts for them are the ones they have at home.

Such structural labour demand for entry-level jobs can no longer be filled as before by women and teenagers. This is because female work has lost its secondary, dependent status in favour of an autonomous, career-oriented one, and lower fertility and longer education have diminished the availability of youngsters.

The merit of dual labour markets theory lies in highlighting an important factor for the occurrence of international migration, namely, the structural demand for foreign labour that is inherent in the economic structure of contemporary advanced societies. It also provides cogent explanations for such demand—although certainly not the only plausible ones—which help to understand, among other things, the apparently anomalous coexistence of a chronic demand for foreign labour with significant rates of structural unemployment in a number of receiving countries.

Another merit is its contribution to dispel the idea that immigrant workers necessarily compete with native ones and affect the latter's level of wages and employment prospects. Indeed, as a general explanation of the causes of international migration, dual labour markets theory is far from flawless. In the first place, a theory that posits that all international migration is demand-driven and excludes altogether push factors cannot aspire to explain but a part of reality. Stating that most migrants end up finding employment at destination is one thing, and positing that migration flows are triggered by such demand is a different one.

Secondly, today's immigration flows do not seem to result primarily, let alone uniquely, from recruitment practices, especially in the advanced economies that the theory envisages. Recruitment was an important mechanism of immigration in those societies, in the decades that preceded the formulation of the theory, and it is still practised today, particularly in the Persian Gulf and Asia-Pacific regions. But in advanced industrial economies most migrants come on their own initiative, and not necessarily to fill pre-existing jobs. In many cases, immigrants constitute a supply of labour that creates its own demand, that is, jobs that would not exist without their previous presence.

World system theory

The conceptual cornerstone of world system theory is the notion of a 'modern world system' coined in the mid-1970s by historian sociologist Immanuel Wallerstein, a world system of European hegemony that took shape since the sixteenth century and which consists of three concentric spheres—core-states, semi-periphery and peripheral areas. The world system theory belongs in the historical-structural tradition that inspired dependency theory in the 1960s. It shares with it the view of migration as one more product of the domination exerted by core countries over peripheral areas, in the context of international relationships fraught with conflict and tension.

Kernel of the explanation of international migration has to be found primarily in the extension of the capitalist mode of production from core countries to peripheral ones, and the ensuing incorporation of new regions into an increasingly unified world economy. In the past this penetration was assisted by colonial regimes; in the present it is assured by neocolonial regimes and multinational corporations, and direct foreign investment plays a crucial role in it. In order to counteract a declining rate of profit as domestic wages rise, and to accrue additional benefits, core countries intervene in peripheral ones in search of raw materials and to profit from cheap labour.

This penetration, in combination with processes of modernisation and commercialisation of agriculture, entails the substitution of capitalist practices and process for traditional ones. A number of dislocations and disruptions ensue, including the displacement of workers who lose their traditional way of life. Typically a large labour surplus develops that the still small non-agricultural sector is incapable of absorbing. This leads to migration to the cities and to the swelling there of a traditional territory sector characterised by an extremely low productivity.

An uprooted proletariat, prone to move abroad, is thus first created and in turn siphoned to the core countries through the same channels that were opened by the economic penetration, and through the cultural, transportation and communication links that followed. In the core-countries migrants find employment in certain sectors which rely on cheap labour to maintain a high rate of profit.

The world system theory may shed light on the importance of past and present linkages between countries at different stages of development, and about some mechanisms of development which cause uprootedness. It also lends some flesh to the common sense empirical observation that migration often connects countries that were linked in the past by colonial bonds, on account of the many vestiges left by such bonds.

The world systems theory is a by-product of a univocal, reductionist and sense-loaded interpretation of history in which all countries pass through similar processes, as if following a grand script or some rigid laws of historical development. It is only applicable at the global level and migrants are little more that passive pawns in the play of big powers and world processes presided over by the logic of capital accumulation. It may provide a background for the study of specific migration relationships between countries, but not so much for its investigation, as it is an explanation given *ex ante*, and formulated in a way, that cannot be subject to empirical test. In addition, it seems difficult to reconcile with the increasing tendency towards the diversification of migration flows and paths, which runs parallel to the process of globalisation and questions the validity of one of the basic tenets of world system theory.

Systems approach

One fruitful, comprehensive framework of systems approach to migration was proposed by Akin Mabogunje, in his study of rural-urban migration in Africa. Migration systems are spaces characterised by the relatively stable association of a group of receiving countries with a number of areas of origin. Such association does not only result from migration flows, but is buttressed by connections and links of a varied nature. These linkages and the multiple interactions constitute the most appropriate context for the analysis of migration. Such a framework should ultimately be able to integrate the contributions of the remaining theoretical explanations, together with all the actors relevant in the process of migration, including networks and intermediary institutions, and some usually neglected dimensions, particularly the state.

The migration systems approach to migration, which aspired to draw on the analytic power of general system analysis is as yet no more than a desideratum which has never been fulfilled, at least as far as international migration is concerned. It has hardly gone beyond the identification of international migration systems, at a purely descriptive level. Moreover, such identification has confined itself so far to the most stable part of the system, the countries that stand at the receiving end. The same can be said about the enumeration of the elements that define the existence of a migration system, such as relative structural homogeneity, geographic contiguity or proximity, similarity of policies, and commonality belonging to supranational organisations.

Cumulative causation

Migration is a self-sustaining and self-perpetuating phenomenon. This idea was first put forth by Gunnar Myrdal several decades ago, under the label cumulative causation, in the context of the 'backwash effects' put in motion by uneven development in underdeveloped areas. Douglas Massey has recently retaken and enlarged the notion, identifying several factors and mechanisms that are responsible for the self-perpetuation of migration.

The basic idea is that migration changes reality in a way that induces subsequent moves through a number of socio-economic processes. The most important of them all is the expansion of networks. Other relevant mechanisms which stem from migration and which in turn induce further migration include relative deprivation, the development of a culture of migration, a perverse distribution of human capital, and the stigmatisation of jobs usually performed by immigrants.

Contemporary theories of migration contribute to a better understanding of the causes of migration, and of the mechanisms that contribute to its self-perpetuation. Yet, a number of clouds obscure the sky of migration theorising. The focus of existing theories may be somewhat misplaced. The first and foremost, often the only dimension of migration that theories have aimed at explaining is why people move, or variants of the same question. Theories of migration should not only look to mobility but also to immobility, not only to centrifugal forces but also to centripetal ones. The existence of centripetal forces that lead to staying has been generally ignored by theories, although there are signs of increasing interest towards them in very recent years. This implies that more attention than hitherto should be bestowed upon family types, kinship systems, social systems, and social structures in general.

Any theory built primarily with economic materials is bound to be in trouble in an international migration scene in which political considerations and the states intervene so prominently. In some of the most important contemporary migratory regions labour migration is severely curtailed—although a number of exceptions are generally recognised—and the largest migration flows result from legal entitlements, such as family reunion and asylum. Clearly, politics and the state are usually missing in theories of migration, and urgently need to be brought back.

Existing theories generally promise more than they deliver. They tend to be partial and limited, in the sense that they are useful to explain a facet, or a dimension, or shed light on a particular feature, or are applicable to certain types of migration in certain contexts and not to others. Most theories only explain labour migration, and this is a considerable limitation in a contemporary scene in which other forms of migration are prominent.

GLOBALISATION AND MIGRATION

Migration is a result of the integration of local communities and national economies into global relationships. At the same time, it is a cause of further social transformations in both migrant-sending and receiving countries. In traditional societies, many people spent their whole lives in their native village or neighbourhood. The phenomenon of international migration has changed the direction of public agenda of many countries. Economic, social and political problems have emerged from ethnic, religious and cultural differences between citizens and migrants. These factors have projected international migration into the public limelight, and receiving countries have been testing a number of strategies to reverse the trends.

We cannot study international migration without taking into account the growing pace of globalisation. The widespread use of a term does not always go hand in hand with a clear definition of its meaning. Globalisation is a multidimensional process characterised by the acceptance of a set of economic rules for the entire world designed to maximise profits and productivity by universalising markets and production, and to obtain the support of the state with a view to making the national economy more productive and competitive.

However, it is not the only process with a universal scope. Human rights is another equally important process. If the globalisation paradigm tends to emphasise transnational systems of exploitation and domination that undermine the potentially protective intervention of the nation-state, the human rights paradigm highlights the possibilities of empowerment in the international domain. Universal norms and enforceable minimum standards enshrined in international conventions provide mechanisms for curbing state power for transcending the particularisms of nationality and place, and for impinging on state structures to enforce internationally binding rights.

A combination of globalisation and human rights has an impact on international migration that social scientists specialising in the field and policy makers must address. To a large extent, theories on the causes of contemporary international migration tend to identify the links between such migration and some or all of the aspects of globalisation. Similarly, a significant portion of the policy recommendations of international organisations assume that a drop in international migration can be attributed to the adoption and implementation of policies that eliminate or, at least, reduce imbalances among countries.

From both a theoretical and a political standpoint, however, the extent to which human fights are respected in the country of origin and the receiving country undoubtedly affects migrants' motivations and decision to migrate. Receiving countries are required to respect the rights of migrants at the risk of moral and even political sanctions and international legal action. Analyses of policies relating to current and future trends in international migration must take into account both globalisation which has radically altered the economic, social, political and cultural arena, and the existence of ethical and legal regulations that protect individuals and groups, irrespective of nationality, race, ethnic group, religion, political beliefs and so forth.

Globalisation is a multidimensional process and the causes and consequences of migration in sending and receiving countries cannot be analysed from the standpoint of a single discipline; a multidisciplinary analysis is necessary in terms of both theory and practice. Since conceptualisation processes and explanations vary at least to a certain extent in different disciplines, and influence policies, conflicts often arise among researchers from different disciplines vying to influence public policy.

While identifying the main reasons of international migration, conferences and international organisations often emphasise poverty and the income gap between sending and receiving countries. Migration between developed and developing countries is thus seen as a consequence of the growing income imbalances between such countries, and within sending countries, that have been part of the story of globalisation.

The widespread acceptance of this premise can be found in Section 10.2 of Chapter 10 of the *Programme of Action of the International Conference on Population and Development,* which recommends poverty reduction as a suitable policy to prevent large-scale emigration from the least developed to the developed countries.[11] Given the importance and high profile of that Conference, we are justified in questioning whether current global trends in income distribution and poverty are consistent with international recommendations.

The 1999 edition of the prestigious and well-known *United Nations Human Development Report* provides a wealth of information on the topic.[12] The report shows that the current trends are heading in the opposite direction to a curb on migration between developed and developing countries. If there were indeed a linear relationship between poverty and migration, the recent trends that these figures, and others, reflect in terms of poverty and income should have boosted emigration from the poorest countries.

Extreme poverty effectively acted as a barrier to international migration, because the very poor lacked the financial and social resources to migrate. At intermediate income levels, however, migration propensities increased as families became able to opt for international migration as a strategy to diversify economic risks. At higher income levels, the propensity to migrate internationally declined. Indeed, this comes as no surprise to sociologists specialising in the migration theory. Many empirical studies confirm that international migrant workers come from the lower and middle strata of the countries with intermediate development levels, rather than from the lower strata of least developed countries. Emigration could increase from countries that are still relatively poor in comparison with developed countries, despite having reduced poverty in absolute terms.

Lack of a direct link between poverty and international migration brings us to the theory or theories on which policy recommendations are based in order to modify migration flows. Attempts to explain international migration, and to come up with general and specific policy recommendations, primarily adopt an economic standpoint, in terms of neoclassical economics and related areas, or a historical and structural focus with a neo-dependence slant. A neoclassical economic analysis of the problem, essentially based on differences between labour supply and demand, suggests that international migration is part of an adjustment process in the world economy which, rather than posing a problem, contributes to the global efficiency of production and should therefore not be hampered by restrictive policies or distorting incentives.

A large number of historical and structural migration theories also end up regarding migration as a consequence of the expansion of capitalism and, in particular, the internationalisation of markets and transfers of capital, technology, and profits. The practical suggestion that can be derived from these macro-theories is that no policy makes sense unless it changes the world economic system. Paradoxically, diverging economic theories are at one in not recommending that public policy be used to alter international migration flows.

The economic theories can be criticised in two respects. First, they focus primarily on permanent individual migration, to the detriment of other actors and other types of migration. Second, they ignore institutional historical links, as well as differences between gender and ethnic groups. Historical and structural theories, however, are criticised for disregarding the cultural factors that affect the assimilation of migrants and national policies. Furthermore, focusing on the economic dimension generally means ignoring the fact that economic growth does not necessarily go hand in hand with social development.

According to *UNDP's Human Development Report 1999*, of the 174 countries included in the Report, only five had equivalent GDP per capita and human development ratings, while 92 ranked higher on human development than GDP per capita and 77 ranked lower on human development.[13] Inconsistency between the two aspects of development is the rule, and this must be taken into account in any comparative studies on migration processes.

If international migration is going to be examined in the context of globalisation and if the aim is to improve current policies, the social sciences must develop theoretical frameworks capable of unravelling the links between the macro-trends of the globalisation process and other intermediate and micro-trends which determine migratory movements or affect their consequences in countries of destination and of origin, deciding the political response to the problem as well.

Until recently, the few economic and demographic or sociological and demographic studies on international migration could not compete with sophisticated conceptual frameworks available to analyse other socio-demographic problems, such as changes in fertility and the abundance of interdisciplinary empirical research on this topic. Finding ways of breaking disciplinary barriers and fostering joint efforts to develop more comprehensive focuses that can also be verified empirically is a major challenge for research on international migration in the social sciences. There are two problems that must be resolved to face this challenge.

First, a solution needs to be found to conceptual differences within and between disciplines. This is no easy task, given the long list of failures of similar attempts in the past. Nevertheless, the search for new avenues to achieve the goal of interdisciplinary cooperation is experiencing a rebirth. One of these avenues is the development of general theoretical models of migration. The second avenue, related to the first, involves outlining multidisciplinary research projects based on a common framework to be defined and enhanced when analysing the results obtained. The third avenue consists in addressing a policy problem and organising interdisciplinary teams of researchers and policy analysts to explore its overall consequences. The choice of an avenue will be influenced by personal preferences and comparative advantages, but whatever avenue is picked as a starting point, it must be followed by the other two at a later stage.

Another major problem involved in linking globalisation and international migration is the increasing coincidence or super-position of different forms of population mobility in the same place and at the same time each with different socio-economic causes and effects.[14] Clarifying such super-position and seeking a solution to the problems it presents means once again broadening the disciplinary spectrum to include an analysis of social processes, such as the creation and operation of social networks, the consequences of imbalances in social capital, etc.

Super-position problems will be resolved more easily by developing a multidisciplinary focus, but at the same time this may also serve as a means of identifying them. At the same time, since they affect the clarification of very concrete social processes, we could probably make faster progress in solving such problems conceptually and empirically than in seeking a general development model. Efforts to define such a model will necessarily require spelling out links and interrelationships which have traditionally lain within the purview of different disciplines and hence will be increasingly subject to power struggles among disciplines.

International migration constitutes a challenge for public policy. Social scientists cannot ignore this challenge if they want to help prevent these policies from being based on preconceptions and misconceptions, which will only worsen the situation or, at best, fail to resolve the problems. The ability of social scientists to help meet this challenge depends on the relevant knowledge available and the existence of channels that allow this knowledge to become part of the decision making process. Knowledge of migration trends and their causes and effects will have to be bolstered for the social sciences to play a part in formulating international migration policies.

It is possible to identify the following categories of relevant knowledge for international migration.

a) *Descriptive knowledge* of migration trends and processes in countries of origin and receiving countries: This category uses different sources to quantify legal and illegal migration and the characteristics of migrants and their changes over time. It also comprises descriptive studies on legal and administrative migration regulations and on the status and rights of migrants, together with their social and cultural characteristics.

b) *Knowledge leading to the definition of migration* as a problem. This category can include studies on how levels, trends and different types of international migration affect individuals, families, geographical communities, social groups and the nation at large. Studies on the impact of migration, in countries of origin and receiving countries, on social well-being, labour markets and culture are just some examples of knowledge leading to the definition of migration as a problem. In this case, cooperation is essential between demography and at least one other discipline.

c) *Explanatory, quantitative and qualitative knowledge* at the macro-, meso- and micro-levels of factors and processes that affect migration trends. This category provides the bulk of theoretical debate in the field of international migration. This is the basis of knowledge for the formulation of policies and programmes whose objectives are explicitly related to migration.

d) *Evaluative knowledge* of the impact of public policies and programmes on international migration and its consequences.

The descriptive knowledge serves as a factual basis for other types of knowledge. It is the only type of knowledge that cannot be replaced by information on other countries or regions of the world. This is not the case with knowledge leading to the definition of migration as a problem or knowledge of the causes of migration. While it is indeed preferable to possess empirical knowledge in order to pinpoint problems in the country or countries for which policies are to be formulated, most countries fall far short of adequate knowledge of these issues.

The use in policy formulation of ready-existing knowledge in the country or countries concerned is another important aspect. We must realise that the state has lost part of its clout in policy making as a result of supranational agreements, its former key role in economic and social policy now being shared with enterprise and private institutions.

Recurring themes include decentralisation, reform of the state and democratic management practices; new state-civil society relations aimed at strengthening civil society; changes in the role of parliament and the judiciary; a greater regulatory role for the state in public and private activities and, lastly, changes in the decision-making process, making decisions more technical.[15]

The uses of knowledge can be subject to both internal political processes and external power struggles.

Many of the policies affecting international migration are economic or social policies that have not explicitly considered these effects. As a consequence, potential users of social science knowledge work in different ministries and government agencies. As is often the case with cross-functional policies, communication problems and organisational and political infighting hinder the exchange and joint use of relevant information on migration.

There are at least two countries involved in the international migration process.[16] This means that both are affected by the decisions the other may take. In the event of conflicts of interest, knowledge and information must be shared equally among the countries involved to resolve such conflicts peacefully. However, here, as always, knowledge and the use of knowledge are empowering. We should therefore not be surprised to find *de facto* and *de jure* barriers to the free circulation of relevant knowledge on international migration.

Available knowledge can be used in a conceptual or instrumental manner. Policies depend on a conceptual framework that serves to define specific events as problems and to select the most appropriate general ways of dealing with them. Such frameworks are based in part on preconceptions and common sense, but also on more systematic assertions about society, many of which are nowadays directly or indirectly derived from the social sciences.

Empirical research has in fact found that social science theories, methods and results play a core role in helping the general public and policy makers identify problems. To illustrate this, a historical analysis of the evolution of international migration policy in Latin America has identified five different conceptual frameworks.

The first conceptualises the problem on the basis of the need to provide labour force for the regional economy. This framework apparently dates back to the colonial era but was influential until the early twentieth century.

A second conceptual framework focuses on the need to populate what was considered empty land and it was apparently prevalent in the period from independence to the early twentieth century.

A third conceptual framework is based on the need to protect political, ethnic and cultural characteristics viewed by the elite as part of the 'national soul'. This is still a valid framework for many.

A fourth framework centres on the protection of the national workforce, supposedly threatened by large-scale migration, and spans the period from the 1930s to the present day.

Finally, a new conceptual framework is reportedly being constructed around the idea of regional and sub-regional integration.

All these frameworks keep on including arguments in favour of selective migration policies, backed by knowledge considered valid and reliable at the time. Social science thinking is no doubt still being used, consciously or otherwise, to construct these conceptual frameworks.

Nowadays, the prime consideration is the dominant discipline and what the most influential theoretical and methodological framework is within the discipline. A more multidisciplinary conceptual framework would undoubtedly lead to new and more varied policies. The use of such knowledge for policies related to international migration is part of a complex process that includes individual, organisational and political actors in several countries. The main users are political leaders and government decision makers. But another important category of users is certainly made up of those influencing the use made of knowledge by the former: technical advisory committees, independent academic centres, private consulting firms, specialists in ministries, and so forth.

Most individuals are sufficiently attached to their land and to their country to keep living there as long as they can be assured of a decent standard of living. Without hope of improving their circumstances, individuals can be tempted or compelled to consider leaving their country.[18] The more salary and employment opportunities differ from one country to another the more the tendency to migrate is strong, all things being equal.

Migration is an individual or family solution to poor living conditions. One can thus contrast the socialist, proletarian model, which sees social progress being achieved through collective action by the working class, with the liberal, individual model which permits an enterprising individual to escape from higher background. The link between migration and development is to be explained in substantially different terms. It is not disparities in living standards that give rise to a migratory movement, nor is it the most deprived who leave.

The nineteenth-century transo-oceanic migration began in countries where the industrial revolution had already begun. The beginning of a development process, whether it be the penetration of the market economy or a national development strategy, bring about a radical change in demographic economic balances which in the long run, fosters workforce mobility and modifies the expectations of individuals, who begin to envisage an improvement in their well-being which would make it possible to defray the cost of moving.

All these factors increase the number of potential emigrants, whose hopes have greater chances of being realised in that there is a demand for workers in the most developed countries. Without minimising the impact of migration policies in the receiving countries, economic analysis, confirmed by the observation of migratory processes, thus highlights the vital importance of market forces, in particular the conditions governing the labour market in the countries of origin and in the host countries. Structural changes and the interaction between conditions governing supply and demand on the labour market explain the emergence of migratory movements, but once the migratory process starts, the differences in the living standards and the migration networks which have been formed sustain the impetus towards migration.

Economists see migration as a process of allocating resources between two geographical areas that have allotments of different factors and accordingly different factor payments. Individuals who leave the area where labour is more plentiful boost the marginal productivity of those who stay, and salary transfers from those who have left help raise the living standards of families remaining in the home country. The end result of migration is to reduce the disparities that gave it birth.

The complexity of migratory phenomena and the crucial importance of the historical, institutional, economic and demographic context in which they take place lead to contrasting approaches that make generalisations risky. We must identify the short-term positive effects on the income of the members of the migrant families and the consequences for the rest of the population, and establish whether migration has a significant impact on development factors, especially the accumulation of capital and technical progress.

In fact, other analyses stress the cumulative destabilising mechanisms sustained by migratory flows. Also remittances, inasmuch as they are used to improve the well-being of the migrants' families in the present, which is the main reason for the departure of a family member, have only a limited impact on development factors. Besides, the transfers of funds have a twofold effect. In the short term, they retain in the home country the families of those who have left and, in the longer term, they encourage new departures of other family members and of families which had up to then been uninterested in migration.

The history of migration shows that the positive association between emigration and development requires the existence in the country of origin of efficient institutions and markets—for work, goods and credit—which are generally lacking and whose absence is precisely the root cause of emigration; it also needs an appropriate development policy to enable the most to be made of migrants' remittances.

For the last few decades, migratory movements have been taking place within a new paradoxical context. The industrialised countries have reaffirmed their policy of controlling migratory movements. These restrictions are being enforced at a time when the developing countries, which have generally started their demographic transition, are seeing their workforce and the proportion of their working-age population rise sharply without a corresponding increase in employment.

With the worsening of economic disparities between the countries of the north and the south the causes of migratory movements are reinforced. This has led to the resumption of illegal immigration and the development of new channels of entry, in particular through requests for asylum, significantly blurring the distinction between economic migrants and refugees. At the same time, the speeding up of the process of globalisation has been marked by a greater opening up of frontiers to trade, a considerable increase in capital flows and an internationalisation of the processes of production.

The quality of statistics on migration rules out a full assessment of transborder movements of population for all countries worldwide. The data available, over the last 30 years, have shown an increase in the number of migrants, rising from 77 million people in 1965 to 111 million in 1990.[19] But the proportion of migrants in the world's population as a whole has remained more or less stable over the period. These data do not include temporary migratory movements or most illegal immigration. If these had been included a slight increase over the period would have emerged.

While the proportion of migrants is dropping in developing countries, it is rising noticeably in developed countries. The highest proportions of foreign-born individuals are observed in the countries where immigrants are allowed to settle. On the other hand, it is now in Europe that the foreign workforce is the largest and that the increase in their proportion of the workforce has been the greatest.

The relative proportion of people from developing countries in the total immigrant population of developed countries has changed quite noticeably. The change is radical, particularly in countries where immigrants are allowed to settle. The proportion of immigrants from the least developed countries rose from 33 per cent to 77 per cent in the United States from 1960 to 1994, and from eight per cent to 80 per cent in Canada from 1961 to 1992. New migratory movements have emerged between countries with no particular links; thus large numbers of Sri Lankans, Filipinos and Moroccans are found in Italy.

The problem of the alternative to migration should be considered in a more realistic way now. First, the closure of borders to migrant workers, which had initially been a temporary measure linked to the energy crisis and to the deterioration of the employment situation, has become a permanent feature of immigration policy. Secondly, whereas the new international division of labour could be interpreted as a way for developed countries to circumvent criticism from the south of their unilateral closure of borders, the latest attempt to offer an alternative to migration is being made within the context of the new development strategy of the countries of origin, which involves abandoning self-sufficiency and import substitution policies.

In the process of regional integration tendency towards the equalisation of factor prices, which should have the effect of reducing population mobility between the countries involved, would at the same time attract more migrants from other countries not party to the preferential agreements. Furthermore, the level of equalisation and the time needed to achieve it cannot be inferred from a comparative static model. And the duration of the process is a decisive factor when potential migrants opt between the hope of a permanent improvement in their living standards at some unspecified time in the future thanks to free trade, and the immediate, if transitory, improvement brought about by temporary emigration if they decide to emigrate.

Reducing disparities in earnings between countries requires a strong and stable growth in poor countries over a long period. The most optimistic assessment would be 50 years of over six per cent annual growth before[20] there could be a significant reduction in the disparities. The choice between these two approaches is fundamentally altered, however, by any uncertainty about the political and economic stability of the country of origin. The fact remains that if there are no restrictions on the movement of goods or of the factors of production, the theory does not make it possible to forecast whether the specialisation of a country well-endowed with the labour factor will take the form of labour-intensive exports or of an outflow of workers.

Although we may be able to predict that in the long term factor price equalisation will weaken the motivation to emigrate, in the meantime what may represent several decades structural changes in the economy will strengthen it. In the presence of features such as a deliberate policy of settlement immigration, or a demand for labour linked to the segmentation of the labour market, as is currently the case in Western Europe, the outflow of labour is increased by a growth in production in the regions of origin.

The development process requires and encourages the working population to be willing to move from one geographical area or sector of the economy to the other. Population transfers to the secondary sector, in particular construction, increase money earnings, helping to defray the cost of migration, and make employment very vulnerable to fluctuations in the sector concerned, and higher levels of education and urbanisation reduce cultural disparities. All these factors tend to encourage emigration.

Economic liberalism can only be a substitute for migration if it alters significantly the parameters of the decision to emigrate in a particular way and within an acceptable period for individuals and their families. The economic decision making model postulates simple modes of behaviour. Individuals, all things being equal, will only consider emigrating, whether on a temporary basis or for good, if there is some prospect of improving their well-being and that of their group—the family or any other extended unit—within a fixed timeframe, which could be a period of a few years, a lifetime, or perhaps even the lifetime of their descendants.

We consequently expect a positive link between disparities in real income and the intensity of migratory movements. The direction of the migratory movements observed from developing countries towards the developed countries confirms the expected link, but the model's predictive capacity is weak. First, the existence and the persistence of income disparities between countries is not necessarily associated with migratory movements and, secondly, the decrease in income disparities between two countries—following the beginning of development in the poorer country—often results in the emergence of, or increase in, outflows and not in their decline.

Economic analysis of the decision to emigrate attempts to reconcile the model's predictions with situations observed in reality. Once one has identified the institutional, cultural or psychological factors that prevent individuals from settling in the country of their choice or take too high a psychological toll, behaviour variables need to be specified. An initial series of arguments relates to the cost of the move and to uncertainty as to whether anything is to be gained from it. No one can leave their home country unless they are able to pay for the move, the costs of which can be met either by drawing on support networks, primarily the family, and/or by spreading out the payment over time.

The nature and weighting of different factors determining migration depend on the period of time the emigrant expects to stay in the host country. To simplify, in *ex ante* temporary migration, what counts is the earnings differential and the possibility of employment; in *ex ante* permanent migration, prospects of social and professional mobility are as important as the immediate differences in remuneration.

Temporary migration means that members of the same household live in two different places. The strategic approach would mean that the family, as a decision-making unit, chooses to disperse its members in space for specific periods, depending on the comparative advantage which a given place confers on each member. Calculation of the expected gain involves not only real income differentials but also price differentials. The decisive factor is in fact the migrant's ability to save and, through salary remittances, increase the purchasing power of those remaining in the home country. Given a particular income, temporary expatriation results in far greater financial gain for the household as a whole than does permanent emigration. Furthermore, unlike permanent migration where there is no escape from the parameters of the decision, in temporary migration the net costs or benefits of the move depend, to a large extent, on the migrant, him/herself, who can decide how large a proportion of his/her income to spend in the host country and how much to send back home.

The anticipated duration of the move has interesting and paradoxical implications as regards the effectiveness of immigration policies. A decision by the host country to restrict the employment of migrants to a limited period of time in fact makes emigration a viable possibility for some who could not have envisaged permanent expatriation.

IMPACTS ON SOCIAL DEVELOPMENT

For the last few decades internal as well as international migration has grown considerably, and taken on forms which were not anticipated by governments and planners. This poses new challenges for societies and policy-makers all over the world. The most important question for countries of origin is whether migration assists or hinders development. Migration may hinder development by siphoning of qualified personnel, removing dynamic young workers and reducing pressures for social change.

Migration often involves a transfer of the most valuable economic resource—human capital—from a poor country to a rich one. The family, local community and state of the place of origin have borne the costs of upbringing of the migrant to young adulthood. The immigration country will reap the benefits of this investment, and the migrant will often return home after completing his/her working life to once again be the responsibility of the country of origin. It is only worthwhile for the emigration country if the gain in human capital through working abroad can be productively utilised upon return and the transfer of income from immigration to emigration country outweighs the costs of upbringing of the migrant.

Many countries actively encourage emigration for employment. This may mean actual government involvement in non-recruitment and deployment of workers, regulation of non-governmental recruitment agencies, or simply laissez-faire with regard to spontaneous movements. Some Asian governments have set up special departments or agencies to manage tabour emigration, such as the Bureau of Manpower, Employment and Training (BMET) in Bangladesh, or the Office of the Protector of Emigrants within the Ministry of Labour in India. However, regulation of emigration from less-developed countries is often ineffective, as the large number of irregular migrants demonstrates.

Global migrant remittances increased from US $2 billion in 1970 to US $70 billion in 1995.[21] Orderly transfer of remittances is essential if the potential benefits are to be realised—otherwise remittances will be transferred in irregular ways, often in the form of cash or consumer goods. Money which goes through the banking system may be more conducive to investment than cash transfers. Realistic exchange rates, low bank charges, and availability of reliable financial services in both area of employment and area of origin are vital. Special investment schemes to encourage migrants to combine their savings to set up companies or carry out infrastructure projects in the home community could play a part.

Emigration countries have policies to prevent abuse or exploitation of their citizens while abroad, and to provide assistance in case of illness, accident, death, trouble with the law, disputes with employers or other emergencies. However, measures and services for the protection of emigrants are frequently ineffective. They are not available to the irregular migrants, who may face the worst problems. The number of consular officials is often far too small to cope with the case-load. Even legal migrants are so dependent on finding and keeping employment abroad that they hesitate to complain about abuses.

Most returning migrants are left to their own devices and

frequently face difficulty in finding employment commensurate with the skills they have acquired abroad. They may end up running small unproductive businesses which often fail. Savings may be spent on consumption and dowries rather than investment. The experience of returnees is thus very uneven, but there is sufficient experience to permit some policy-relevant conclusions. Adequate counselling and information both before and after return, as well as help in obtaining investment credits are factors conducive to successful re-insertion and maximisation of positive effects on development.

To ensure orderly migration and to enhance the contribution of migration to development, international cooperation could be developed. However, efforts and outcomes so far have been disappointing. The main reasons for this are lack of long-term strategies by both emigration and immigration countries, and the reluctance of immigration countries to take steps which might increase the cost of migrant labour to employers.

Major elements of an international regulatory framework already exist in International Labour Organisation (ILO) Conventions No. 97 of 1949 and No. 143 of 1975, and in the 1990 United Nations Convention on the Rights of Migrant Workers and Members of their Families.[22] These standards need to be linked together in a comprehensive framework to regulate the rights and conditions of migrant workers. However, the main problem is that relatively few countries have ratified these instruments. Action is needed to persuade more countries to sign up and implement the Conventions.

Nowadays, most countries lack effective systems for monitoring international migration. Effective monitoring and comprehensive and internally comparable statistics are essential for effective multilateral action. Trends of regional economic integration and political cooperation in many parts of the world often include consideration of labour migration. Some regional bodies have highly developed policies with regard to movements between the member countries.

Common policies on migration, both from member states and from third countries, should be seen as an essential part of regional integration, and should be linked to policies on international cooperation and development. Emigration countries frequently seek to make bilateral agreements with immigration countries on the regulation of migration and the rights and conditions of their citizens. Such bilateral agreements played a major role in labour migration to Western Europe in the 1960s and 1970s, and did much to improve the social security and tights of migrant workers and their families.

More recently, immigration countries have been reluctant to conclude such agreements. International efforts should be made to encourage bilateral cooperation, by showing that it can bring benefits for all parties concerned. The migrants would gain through enhanced protection and greater social security. The emigration countries would gain because-such agreements could facilitate transfer of remittances and make it harder for agents and recruiters to cream off profits from migration.

For immigration countries, the key question is whether immigration will lead to settlement, formation of ethnic communities, and new forms of ethnic and cultural diversity. It seems that migration almost inevitably leads to settlement of a certain proportion of the migrants, whatever policy-makers expect. This is partly due to the social nature of the migration process, which is sustained by informal networks once it gets started. Another factor is the increasing strength of human rights safeguards.

Immigrants may come from different types of societies with different traditions, religions and political institutions. They often speak a different language and follow different cultural practices. They may be visibly different, through physical appearance or style of dress. Some migrant groups become concentrated in certain types of work and live in low-income residential areas. The position of immigrants is often marked by a specific legal status: that of the foreigner or non-citizen. The social meaning of ethnic diversity depends to a large extent on the significance attached to it by the populations and states of the receiving countries. Culturally distinct settler groups almost always maintain their languages and some elements of their homeland cultures, at least for a few generations.

Where governments have recognised permanent settlement, there has been a tendency to move from policies of individual assimilation to acceptance of some degree of cultural difference. The result has been granting of minority cultural and political rights. Governments which reject the idea of permanent settlement also oppose pluralism, which they see as a threat to national unity and identity. In such cases, immigrants tend to turn into marginalised ethnic minorities. Whatever the policies of the governments, immigration may lead to strong reactions from some sections of the population.

Immigration often takes place at the same time as economic restructuring and far-reaching social change. People whose conditions of life are already changing in an unpredictable way often see the newcomers as the cause of insecurity. Migrations and minorities are seen as a danger to living standards, life styles and social cohesion.

Migration is one of the forces eroding the power of the nation-state. One area in which this is particularly apparent is that of border-control—which is usually seen as a crucial aspect of nation-state sovereignty. Indeed the very fact that large numbers of people have to go abroad to seek a reasonable livelihood exposes the inability of the state to bring about economic development and may lead to a crisis of confidence.

Where the state of the country of origin is unable to provide effective protection to nationals abroad, this may lead to a public outcry.

Barriers to mobility contradict the powerful forces which are leading towards greater economic and cultural interchange. In an increasingly international economy, it is difficult to open borders for movements of information, commodities and capital and yet close them to people. Most states welcome tourists and students, and favour international labour markets for highly skilled personnel, yet seek to limit flows of manual workers, family members, and asylum-seekers. Such distinctions are hard to enforce and millions people move irregularly. They are aided by a transnational 'migration industry' consisting of recruiters, labour brokers, travel agents.

The nation-state is premised on the idea of cultural as well as political unity. In many countries, ethnic homogeneity, defined in terms of common language, culture, traditions and history, has been seen as the basis of the nation-state. This unity has often been fictitious, but it has provided powerful national myths. Immigration and ethnic diversity threaten such ideas of the nation, because they create a people without common ethnic origins. Democratic states tend to integrate immigrants by offering them and their children citizenship. However, the failure of assimilation policies and the growth of ethnic communities mean that the new citizens are often not nationals.

The emergence of multicultural societies creates major challenges to national identities. Institutions are likely to change in response to diverse values and needs. The classical countries of immigration have been able to cope with this situation most easily, since absorption of immigrants has been part of their myth of nation-building. But countries which place a common culture at the heart of their nation-building process have found it very difficult to resolve the contradiction. Asian states have tended to adopt quite restrictive rules on naturalisation and citizenship, and find it very difficult to accept the possibility of integrating new immigrant populations.

The recent trend to development of transnational communities is a further challenge to the nation-state: modern forms of transport and communication make it possible for immigrants and their descendants to maintain long-term links with the ancestral homeland or with diaspora groups elsewhere.

REFERENCES

1. Seligman, Edwin R.A. and Alvin Johnson (eds), *Encyclopedia of the Social Sciences,* New York, The Macmillan Company.
2. Marie L. Borgatta and Edgar F. Borgatta (eds), *Encyclopedia of Sociology*, Volume 3, 1984, Macmillan Company, New York.
3. Julius Gould William L. Koeb (eds), *A Dictionary of Social Science*, New York, The Free Press, 1967.
4. Peter Berton, 'International Sub-systems: A Submacro Approach to International Studies', *International Studies Quarterly* (Detroit-Michigan) Vol. 13, No. 4, 1969.
5. Ibid.
6. Ibid.
7. Louis J. Cantori and Steven L. Spiegel, 'International Relations: A Comparative Approach to Five Subordinate Systems', *International Studies Quarterly*, Ibid.
8. Ibid.
9. Ibid.
10. Ibid.
11. P.C. Mathur, Virendra Narain and M.V. Lekhi, 'Intra-Regional Relations: A Study in Infrastructural Determinants', in S.P. Verma and K.P. Mishra (Ed.), *Foreign Policies in South Asia* (Jaipur, 1969) pp. 91-106.

12. Ibid.
13. *Economic and Political Weekly*, Vol. 7, No. 8, 1972 pp.471-5.
14. *Quarterly Newsletter*, December 1995, SAARC Chamber of Commerce and Industry, Karachi, p.2.
15. *SAARC SCAN*, December, 1996.
16. *The Tribuze*, May 9, 1996.
17. *Indian Express,* December 10, 1984.
18. *Indian Express,* November 6, 1990.
19. Ibid.
20. *The Tribuze,* November 12, 1992.
21. Ibid.
22. Ibid.

2

Population Movements in South Asia

Today, refugees and displaced people are high on the list of international concerns, not only because of the humanitarian importance, but also because of the impact on peace and security. It is no longer sufficient to discuss the subject of forced migration within a narrow national context as a strictly humanitarian problem requiring humanitarian solutions. Despite this recognition of the underlying political nature of refugee movements and of the strategic effects of forced migration, surprisingly little systematic research has come out to explain the interrelationships among foreign policy factors, international security concerns and population movements.

The concept of national security has changed dramatically and has acquired a new and complex significance by the end of the cold war. Considerations of national security have expanded from traditional military-political issues at the interstate level, such as protecting the inviolability of a country's borders or the continued existence of state from external threats, to many new concerns including refugee and migration flows. In recent years, religious, ethnic or communal tensions in Africa, former Soviet Union, the Middle East and parts of the Asia subcontinent frequently result in the spillover of conflict or of internal human rights crises into neighbouring countries, resulting not only in the outflow of refugees, but also in the exacerbation of interstate tensions and the destabilisation and overthrow of governments.[1]

Certain kinds of government actions, ranging from decrees and overt use of force to more covert persecution, intimidation, discrimination and inducement of an unwanted group to leave, generate refugee flows.[2] Most states are ethnically plural societies in which individual national or communal groups have their own separate identities, rooted in common history and culture and often language.

Mass displacements of people frequently occur when multinational governments seek to form or reconstitute homogeneous and united populations by forcible means. Sometimes a dominant group tries to marginalise further or expel minorities; sometimes a government seeks cultural and political homogeneity in the form of a new national identity; or sometimes ruling regimes impose a substitute ideology in place of nationalism in order to unite diverse peoples for state building. A large proportion of the world's displacements also occur as a direct result of political and social revolutions. Revolutions are uniquely powerful refugee-generating events because they involve a deliberate attempt to transform social and economic relations and to construct a radically different political system.

Refugees are often viewed both as a challenge to the integrity and security of sending and receiving states and as a source of tension and conflict between states. In some instances, forced migrants may present a military threat to a host country. Mass migrations are frequently employed as foreign policy tools and as instruments of warfare and military strategy.

During the 1980s, the strategic and political interests of the West and its allies, to maintain pressure against and to destabilise revolutionary states in the Third World, and through them, to raise the costs to their patron, the Soviet Union, were served by the continued military use of refugees. The emergence of armed groups of exiles, the so-called 'refugee warriors', symbolised for the West the popular rejection of communist governments and served to legitimise the resistance movements. The former Soviet Union likewise allied itself with governments and opposition groups, providing them with arms and logistical support.

An increase in military intervention in local Third World conflicts by other outside powers such as South Africa, Cuba, Israel, Vietnam, China, Syria, Iraq and India among others, was also evident, in some cases acting as proxies for the USA or the former Soviet Union, either supporting regimes causing major refugee flows or refugee warrior groups seeking to overthrow or destabilise governments. The mass influx of refugees also influences domestic politics, particularly in the developing world.

The presence of refugees accelerates existing internal conflicts in the host countries. Refugee warriors invite military retaliation, complicate relations with other states, and threaten the host states and the security of their citizens. As a result, host countries have often been unwillingly drawn into conflicts with their neighbours. Tensions between Rwanda and Zaire over the issue of sanctuary for Hutu militia, and the destruction wreaked on south Lebanon in Israel reprisals for Palestinian raids are but two illustrations of the consequences for the security of host nation during the last decade.[3]

A great majority of the refugees seek safety in the world's poorest states. Even when the international community provides assistance, forced migrants make demands on the host country's resources, in particular on water, food, fuel and arable land. The strain on a host population's social services and physical infrastructure and the distortion of local economic conditions can destabilise many weak developing states. In countries with a precarious balance between ethnic or religious populations, the influx of people with ties to a particular group may change the population balance and pose a threat to the existing power structure.

The mass migration is a threat for communal identity and culture by directly altering the ethnic, cultural, religious and linguistic composition of the population and the integrity of their countries. In addition, there are increasing tensions between migrants and their host communities over education, religion and culture. Population movements can also be perceived by governments to enhance their security and well-being.

Sending states may use migration for the purposes of asserting either formal sovereignty or *de facto* control over a territory. This policy involves governmental encouragement of civilian rather than military movement into claimed territories for the purposes of establishing effective control. Sending states can also actively use population movements or 'push-outs' as tools in their foreign policies. The export of refugees can also be used as a bargaining chip in interstate negotiations over trade and bilateral political recognition. Typically in such situations the sending state possesses considerable leverage in the bargaining process. By pleading an inability to control the population outflow, or by demonstrating a willingness to manipulate it, the sending state is in a position to extract foreign policy and strategic concessions from the receiving state.

Population movements are seen as contributing to the host state's power base, national self-confidence or dominant ethnic community. Population influxes can also augment or increase the size of the receiving state's defence capabilities or military establishment. Security can no longer be viewed as an independent national problem based on limited self-interest, and that problems of forced migration can no longer be viewed from the limited humanitarian perspective has significantly broadened the agenda of international relations.

The UN Security Council's Summit Declaration of 31 January 1992 acknowledged that threats to international peace and security can originate from non-military sources of instability in the economic, social, humanitarian and ecological fields, and that such conflicts fall within the Security Council's sphere of action.[4] The declaration also welcomed election-monitoring, human rights verification, and the repatriation of refugees as integral parts of the Security Council's efforts to maintain international peace and security. These expanded notions of what constitute threats to international security have resulted in new international actions to deal with human rights violations which generate forced migration on a large scale.

The South Asian region is emerging as the poorest, the most illiterate, the most malnourished and the least gender-sensitive region in the world. The causes of the exoduses of 1947-48 and 1971, can clearly be identified as violent communal conflict associated in both cases with the process of state formation. The other involuntary movements mentioned above can broadly be ascribed to human rights violations, resulting from the existence of elite-dominated political systems and a pervasive climate of religious and ethnic intolerance reinforced by high levels of poverty, landlessness and unemployment. Unless there are determined efforts to address the causes of mass displacement, South Asia could well be the scene of further refugee exoduses in the years to come. Meaningful political reforms are needed to ensure that violence both by the state and by non-state actors is uncompromisingly subordinated to the rule of law.

As well as increasing in scale, the geographical scope of forced displacement can also be said to have widened in recent years. But this trend is not a simple one. During the past decade, a number of conflicts and associated problems of forced displacement have been resolved. At the same time, however, new crises have exploded in regions which were previously unaffected by the problem of forced displacement or where involuntary population movements did not come to the attention of the international community. South Asia, which is rarely recognised as a 'refugee-affected' region, has in recent years witnessed a succession of cross-border movements: from Bhutan and Tibet to Nepal; from Myanmar to Bangladesh and Thailand; and from Bhutan, Sri Lanka and Tibet to India. According to one recent estimate, moreover, the 750,000 people in South Asia who are currently protected and assisted by UNHCR constitute less than half of all the displaced people in the subcontinent.[5]

In a number of locations around the world, whole 'neighbourhoods' of states have become affected by interlocking and mutually reinforcing patterns of armed conflict and forced displacement. This phenomenon can be observed in the Caucasus, for example, a region which includes no fewer than six entities which have produced refugees and displaced people: Abkhazia, Armenia, Azerbaijan, Chechnya, North and South Ossetia. It can also be seen in Central Africa, where forced population displacements have recently taken place within and between nine contiguous states: Angola, Burundi, Central African Republic, Congo, Rwanda, Tanzania, Uganda, Zaire and Zambia.

As these examples suggest, forced population displacements are becoming increasingly complex. Movements of refugees and internally displaced people now often criss-cross each other, collecting and discarding people on the way. At the same time, there would appear to be a growing number of situations in which people are repeatedly uprooted, expelled or relocated within and across state borders, forcing them to live a desperately insecure and nomadic existence.

During the past few years, a growing proportion of the people who have succeeded in escaping from their own country have found that their new situation is just as—if not more—insecure than the one they left behind. Paradoxically, in an era when so many people have become the victims of ethnic cleansing and other forms of mass expulsion, many others have found it impossible to escape from their own country and to find refuge elsewhere. In some case cases, as in Sri Lanka, for example, their departure has been blocked by government or opposition forces who wish to maintain control over the civilian population. Diaspora communities, many of which are themselves the product of forced population displacements, have played an important part in maintaining the volume and determining the direction of such migratory movements. The Tamil who decides to leave Sri Lanka, will almost invariably make use of information, resources and contacts provided by compatriots in Europe or North America in the bid to leave his or her homeland.

A number of trends appear to have contributed to the growing scale and speed of forced displacement in various parts of the world: the emergence of new forms of warfare, entailing the destruction of whole social, economic and political systems; the spread of light weapons and landmines, available at prices which enable whole populations—including their youngest members—to be armed; and, perhaps most significantly, the use of mass evictions and expulsions as a weapon of war and as a means of establishing culturally or ethnically homogeneous societies.

The large scale of some population displacements and migratory movements can be attributed to a form of mass desperation, provoked by very rapid processes of social, political and economic change. Commenting upon such developments, the UN High Commissioner for Refugees has observed that "the forced displacement of minorities, including depopulation and repopulation tactics in support of territorial claims and self-determination, has become an abominable characteristic of the contemporary world."[6]

Forced displacement in general, and rural depopulation in particular, have also become increasingly common weapons of war, even in armed conflicts where ethnic cleansing is not a specific objective of the parties involved. In some countries, the tactic of rural depopulation has been used to permit the theft of cattle, property and other assets, whereas in other situations, such as Afghanistan, Sri Lanka, civilian populations have been forcibly dispersed or relocated for primarily political reasons, so as to deprive rebel movements of their natural supporters. The present conflict may result in the flight of Mujahirs to India. This is evident from the mood of the people coming from Pakistan these days, who now blame the partition for their plight and express preference for returning to India as they do not expect to get justice and fair treatment in Pakistan.

There is the developing situation in Myanmar, after the release of the leader of the Democracy Movement Aung San Suu Kyi in July 1995. The thrust of her statements has been that the political crisis of democracy in Myanmar be resolved through talks and national reconciliation. This could also be the wish of Myanmar's present and future foreign investors. However, the sticking point between the Democracy Movement and the military regime—the State Law and Order Reorganisation Committee (SLORC)—is that military must have an important constitutional position in Myanmar's political system. This is not acceptable to the leaders of the Democracy Movement. If an amicable way out is not found to this problem, the revival of conflict between the SLORC and the Democracy Movement, and the reintensification of insurgency and ethnic conflict may generate refugee flows from Myanmar to its neighbours including those in South Asia.

The emerging ethnic and regional tensions in Nepal would be absorbed and accommodated with the demographic framework of polity but if not, then any outbreak of conflict on these divisive lines would produce refugees. India would be the only destination of these refugees, particularly from the Limbuwan region because of socio-cultural identities of Rais, Limbus, Magars and Gurungs across the border in India where there is concentration of Indian Nepalis in North Bengal and Sikkim. Democratic politics in Nepal promises to play a positive role in diffusing ethnic tensions by channelising them through political parties, media, non-governmental organisations and even parliament.

There is, no scope for complacency as some regions of Nepal are not free from regional and ethnic problems, and similar developments in India tend to activist-sectarian identities which cut across national boundaries of the two neighbours. In addition to these potential conflicts becoming a source of refugees in South Asia, there are also prospects of economic migration increasing in the region in the years to come. The UNHCR reported a return of 103,000 refugees from Pakistan to Afghanistan during 1994, even in the midst of reintensified conflict.[7] This could be possible, perhaps because the fighting was confined mostly to Kabul and its vicinity, and the refugees belonging to other areas could go back. Similarly, the Bangladesh government, with the help of the UNHCR could help 82,860 Rohingyas return to their villages in Myanmar during the later half of 1994.

There has been a significant shift in South Asia since the mid-sixties, in the context of repatriation. Earlier there was a greater willingness to accept refugees and rehabilitate them without making efforts for their repatriation. This was clearly the case with regard to the refugees that crossed Indian and Pakistani borders in 1947 and later on.[8] India also accepted refugees coming from Sri Lanka and Myanmar during the early sixties.

During partition, it was accepted by both the countries that that the displaced people were the responsibility of the host country, notwithstanding the fact that India had not endorsed the two-nation theory that sought to divide states on the basis of religion. India, also, it seems had either accepted its moral responsibility or found it politically prudent in the aftermath of conflict with China to rehabilitate the refugees from Myanmar and Sri Lanka. India and other South Asian countries had also accepted refugees coming from Tibet since the early fifties, possibly, as a result of political decision to make use of them strategically in their relations with communist China.

Gradually, the South Asian countries have become more and more unwilling to accept refugees coming from their neighbours. Even when Pakistan has made a strategic use of the Afghan refugees and India of the East Pakistan and Sri Lankan refugees, the efforts have been to send them back soon after the strategic value of the refugees was lost and the burden of their presence became an economic, administrative and political liability. Now the shift in the global attitude towards the refugees, of "keeping would-be refugees at home" has also strengthened the South Asian attitudes, not only to resist the incoming refugees but also to send those living for long time, back as soon as possible. It may be mentioned in this regard that almost every South Asian country—India, Pakistan, Bangladesh and Nepal—have even used force, either to stop refugees from coming, or to send them back, or in both the circumstances.

Under a bilateral agreement with India, the Bangladesh government promised "a 16-point repatriation and reintegration package that included financial assistance worth some $250" per individual, but on actual verification of conditions on ground, it was found that "less than half of the financial aid promised" had been given and other conditions had not been created for the repatriates to "settle in their places of origin."

The South Asian countries have pursued various strategies and actions to deal with the refugee problems and their respective security implications. At the local level two broad patterns of settlement adopted for the refugees are evident in South Asia. The host state has either kept the refugees in well defined camps at one place or kept the movements of the refugees somewhat restricted. Such settlement pattern, if maintained and regulated properly, may give rise to least difficulties, keeping the security implications manageable. Alternately, refugees have been dispersed to different areas, farther from their points of entry, and even among the local populations that do not share much of the socio-cultural identities with the asylum seekers. In such cases, refugees have also enjoyed a greater freedom of movement and activity, including seeking jobs and organising themselves politically.

The settlements of Afghan refugees in Pakistan and the Tamils of Sri Lanka in India may be mentioned here. Security risks and instances of instability caused by tensions between the local population and the refugees have been the largest and the most severe in such cases. In relation to the external dimension of the refugee question, the general and most natural strategy adopted by the host state has been to engage the home state in direct negotiations to resolve, and/or moderate the implications of the refugee presence.

The experience in South Asia shows that this strategy has been considerably successful in terms of its costs and results. Bilateral and negotiated agreements between India and Sri Lanka on the Tamil issue, the Myanmar and the Bangladeshi governments on the Rohingyas, and between India and Bangladesh on the Chakmas, may be mentioned in this regard. Such agreements have not been perfect and their implementation has often been tardy and cumbersome, resulting in slow and delayed resolution of the problem at hand.

The Indian military intervention in arming the Mukti Bahini, and fighting a full-scale war with Pakistan which enabled the ten million and odd refugees to return to Bangladesh was initiated after the failure of other options. The then Prime Minister of India, Indira Gandhi, had clearly warned that "Pakistan cannot be allowed to seek a solution of its political or other problems at the expense of India and on the Indian soil". The strategy of intervention and war was also evident in dealing with the crisis of Afghan refugees in Pakistan. The US, Western powers, their allies and China had all joined hands with Pakistan to force the Soviet military out of Afghanistan and thus create conditions for the return of refugees.

The qualitative difference in this situation with that of the Bangladesh conflict of 1971 was that while the intervention and war in Afghanistan was a part of the global Cold War and Sino-Soviet rivalry, in the 1971 conflict the host state alone was motivated into action to defend its interests. The burden of the global rivalries in fact lent support to the home state, Pakistan, in 1971. The third instance of this drastic strategy in dealing with the refugee-generating conflict in South Asia was India's intervention and pressure on Sri Lanka. The Agreement of July 1987 aimed not only at securing conditions for the repatriation of refugees but also at resolving the ethnic conflict through a fair accommodation of Tamils' fights and interests.

In all the instances of the use of war and intervention as a strategy to deal with the refugee issue, we must reiterate that return of the refugees was only one of the many objectives and motivating factors. This involved political use of refugees by the host state in pursuance of broader and diverse interests. It may also be kept in mind that this strategy only partially resolved the refugee-related concerns. In the case of the emergence of Bangladesh, an unassessed number of refugees did get lost and were eventually absorbed in the vast Indian heartland, mixing with its teeming millions. The hopes of a very amicable relationship between India and Bangladesh also vanished after initial years when India started facing the pressure of economic and illegal migrants from Bangladesh.

In Afghanistan, the arms and militia forces raised during the war of attrition precipitated yet another internecine conflict which has not allowed all the refugees to repatriate. And in Sri Lanka, the 1987 Agreement and the political and military arrangements envisaged under this, ran into rough weather due to changing political dynamics in the two countries.[9] The conflict in Sri Lanka has also been reintensified, leaving the unrepatriated refugees in the lurch.

Besides the partial and constrained efficacy of the strategy of war and intervention, this option is also not available to all. The weak and small countries are incapable of pursuing such a strategy either in relation to each other or *vis-a-vis* a strong and powerful neighbour.

Thus a country like Nepal cannot take resort to this strategy either against Bhutan where negotiated solution does not hold much promise, at least for the time being, or against Tibet. Nepal is also not in a position to exercise pressure against India to stop the inflow of economic migrants. Nepal's repeated attempts to get the Indo-Nepal border movements regulated has not evoked any desirable responses from India.

The only South Asian regional organisation, SAARC, does not permit 'bilateral and contentious issues' to be brought on its agenda and as most of the refugee issues are bilateral and contentious in nature, SAARC cannot address them. There is a pressure for liberating SAARC from this disability of not discussing bilateral and contentious issues, particularly from countries like Pakistan, Bangladesh and Nepal. But this is a politically motivated pressure, not sincerely concerned with the resolution of problems and evolution of mutually accommodative solutions.

Notwithstanding this debate on the acceptance of 'bilateral and contentious issues', the fact remains that the SAARC forum and frequency of meetings at various senior bureaucratic and political levels have exercised a benign influence on the resolution of bilateral conflictual issues, including those related with the refugees.

The Indo-Sri Lanka dialogue on the Tamil ethnic conflict during the 1986 SAARC Summit may be recalled. Similarly, talks between Nepali Prime Minister Koirala and the Bhutanese King on the question of the Bhutanese refugees in Nepal, during the Dhaka SAARC Summit in 1994, paved the way for bilateral negotiations between the two countries.[10]

Almost all the South Asian states are afflicted by the refugee problem and in some cases, the refugee issues affect more than two countries. The Bhutanese refugees, for instance, are an issue both in India and Nepal. The Bangladeshi economic and illegal immigrants are present in India, Nepal and also Pakistan. There are also Bihari Muslims in Bangladesh who have proclaimed their loyalties to Pakistan but have not been able to go to their cherished land.

In addition, the security implications of refugee movements involve drug trafficking and terrorism, the areas which are already covered under a regional SAARC convention. Above all, if the refugee question is denuded from the political and strategic use of the refugees by either the home or the host state then much of its contentious and conflictual aspects will get moderated.

On the lines of the SAARC Convention on Suppression of Drug Trafficking and Terrorism, a regional understanding on refugee-related issues may be evolved. Under the umbrella of such an understanding, security and other implications of the refugee movements may be more effectively addressed even in the bilateral context.

The real answer to the refugee problem lies in working at the national level to resolve such conflicts or diffuse such situations that produce refugees. For example, a resolution of ethnic conflict in Sri Lanka and Bhutan, or the ending of the power struggle in Afghanistan with the establishment of a stable political order, will make it far more easier to repatriate the refugees produced by all these conflicts. It is interesting to recall that the Indo-Sri Lanka Agreement of 1987 devoted considerable attention to the action on the part of the Sri Lankan government at the national level for resolving the ethnic conflict that had produced refugees.[11]

The Indo-Bangladesh understanding on the Chakma refugees repatriation also expected national action on the part of Bangladesh government whereby Muslims settled in CHT in the Chakma areas were to be shifted away. Failure of the envisaged national actions both in Sri Lanka and Bangladesh vitiated the expectations on repatriation. But then, there may be no guarantee that such conflicts will not be created anew by the state and nation-building processes in South Asian countries.

Throughout the centuries, people have been obliged to flee from their own country or community as a result of persecution, armed conflict and violence. And in part of the world, governments, armies and rebel movements have resorted to moving people by force in order to attain their political and military objectives. The people most seriously affected by the problem of forced displacement are often the most marginalised members of society: minority groups, stateless people, indigenous populations and others who are excluded from the structures of political power. Persecuted by their governments or by other members of their society, many find themselves living in a state of constant insecurity and uncertainty.

MIGRATION TRENDS OF SOUTH ASIA

In South Asia, the migration trends has two main periods of direct outflow and a third period of secondary movement. The first period is dominated by the Indenture movement. Indenture took place within the British imperial system but indenturing workers from British India was adopted in Dutch and French colonial territories as well. This period stretched from 1834 to 1920. The second main phase is that of the post-war period of free market migration. This movement affected Britain in particular, but also the United States, Canada, some European countries and the Middle East. The third movement overlaps the last and shares with it many of the destinations. This is the secondary migration, often forced, of the descendants of the first phase of migration. The most spectacular of these movements was the expulsion of Asians from East Africa, but there were also expulsions or repatriations from Burma (now Myanmar) and Ceylon (now Sri Lanka) and political flights of South Asians from Surinam and Fiji.

The timing of its inception, just after the 1833 emancipation of slaves in the British Empire, is not accidental: indenture replaced direct slavery. In the West Indies, sugar plantations were still being established in Trinidad and in British Guiana in the 1830s. The Dutch, at a later date, were engaged in similar developments in their part of Guyana (Surinam) and the French in the islands of Martinique and Guadeloupe.

Indenture was started in the French and Dutch colonies shortly after they abolished slavery. The French banned slavery in their colonies in 1848 and recruitment from their

Indian colonies started in 1854 and from British India in 1861. The Dutch banned slavery even later, 1863, and started recruiting 'Hindustanis' in 1873.[12]

The banning of slavery by the British government, coupled with the rejection by Afro-Caribbeans of plantation work, made the West Indian planters search for new labour sources. Similar searches took place in Natal, Mauritius, Fiji and elsewhere.

Land-hungry India provided the source. Indentured migration must therefore be seen as part of the imperialist and capitalist core-periphery relationship. In East Africa and Malaya, they went as railway builders and as administrators. In South Africa, they worked in the coal mines as well as on sugar and cotton plantations. Nor was indenture the only scheme of recruitment.

Under the *Kangani* and *Maistri* systems, an Indian returning home was commissioned as a middleman to recruit labourers from his home district. The *Kangani* system of labour recruitment was particularly important and replaced indenture in Malaya after that system was abolished there in 1910. There was also considerable movement of free migrants, traders, doctors and lawyers ('passenger Indians') to areas where South Asian communities were settled. Seamen had been important migrants since the days of the East India Company and Lascar sailors had formed the nucleus of Bengali settlement in the East End of London. Finally, one should not overlook the importance of student movement and the settlement of scientists, doctors and academics in Britain.

Indenture generally required the emigrant to apprentice himself or herself to a master for five years, although a range from three to ten years is found. There were often additional conditions. In the case of Trinidad, the worker was indentured for five years but was obliged to work for a further five before he/she was eligible for a free return passage.

At the end of this period he could either retire, passage paid, to his homeland or else take a piece of land to cultivate as his own in the overseas territory. These contractual promises were not always fulfilled. The Protectors, who were appointed by the Indian government, seem to have been fairly powerless. For whatever reasons, the return flow of formerly indentured workers was generally small. For example, of the 143, 939 Indians who migrated to Trinidad under indenture, only 33,294 eventually returned to India.[13]

A considerable number of repatriated indentured migrants signed on for further periods in Trinidad. However, in Martinique and Guadeloupe, just under a third of the immigrants seem to have been repatriated and a similar rate is true of Surinam.

The agreements between governments which controlled these contracts required women to be included in the indentured group in the ratio of 4 : 10. Women also seem to have had a shorter period of indenture—three rather than five years. The communities which resulted from indenture thus tended initially to have a skewed sex-ratio. 'Passenger Indians', on the other hand, tended to have a much more balanced structure so that in South Africa, for example, although passenger Indians constituted only 10 per cent of the migrants, their descendants now form 30 per cent of the current South Asian population in that country.[14]

In Mauritius, Fiji and Guyana they came to constitute a majority, but only in Mauritius has that demographic fact been turned into democratic political control. In Fiji, the Constitution created by the British on independence guaranteed native Fijian control.

Coups in 1988 subsequently have kept the South Asians out of power. In Guyana, after a brief period of power under Cheddi Jagan in the late 1950s and early 1960s, British and American machinations against his Marxist-inspired government ousted the Indian leadership and encouraged politics to split along ethnic rather than class lines. East Indians were rural land workers.

In Sri Lanka, their position was even poorer. Whereas in Guyana and Trinidad, East Indians had citizenship and had achieved landownership and some degree of upward mobility through education, in Sri Lanka they were stateless estate labourers.

In African countries where they had settled, South Asians, on the other hand, formed a middle class elite between the indigenous African population and the white rulers. In South Africa, whites tried at first to disenfranchise them and later (in the 1980s) to co-opt them to bolster the white position against the African population.

In East Africa, the removal of white colonial rule left them in an exposed position. Non-citizens were first forced out of civil service occupations in Kenya and Uganda.

During British rule, South Asians also formed a middle class in Myanmar but independence brought ethnically exclusionary policies and forced many of them (the skilled service occupation sector in particular) out of the country. Only the poor South Asians continued to live there, keeping a low profile, adopting Myanmar dress and language in public. Even here, however, Muslims along the border with India and Bangladesh were being forced out of the country in 1992.

There is no clear findings to what extent the origins of the overseas South Asians reflect the balance of the population of the subcontinent. In the subcontinent, about three-quarters come from the Aryan north and about a quarter from the Dravidian south. Northerners (Punjabis and Gujaratis) are dominant in Britain, Canada and the British Caribbean. Tamils are prominent in the settlement of Malaysia, Singapore, and also in the French territories. Gujaratis and Punjabis were prominent in the East and South African settlements. Northerners, from Uttar Pradesh in particular, predominate among the Trinidad East Indians.

However, Bengalis seem curiously under-represented in the overseas movements. Given that Calcutta was the main port of India for a long time, that Bengal was desperately overpopulated, and that there was a tradition of sailing on British merchant ships, surprisingly few Bengalis migrated.

Muslims and Sikhs are probably over-represented relative to Hindus, but their proportions differ in different countries. For example, Sikhs form about two per cent of the Indian population but probably about 11 per cent of the East African Asian population and a quarter of the Indian ethnic population of Britain.

Muslims form about a third of the population of the subcontinent, but just under half of the South Asian ethnic population in Britain. Likewise, the position of Christians is not clear although they seem over-represented among the migrants to Britain. In addition, significant conversions have taken place among the East Indian communities in the Caribbean.[15]

Distance from the subcontinent of the areas of settlement had quite profound effects. In many of the East African countries and Burma, proximity was sufficiently close for some migrants to leave their families in the subcontinent and not have family settlement. Even if families were settled, distances were not so great as to prevent return to the homeland in the search for brides or grooms for their children.

Under these circumstances, the maintenance of traditional values and practices was relatively easy, particularly for the richer classes. In the Caribbean, on the other hand, social renewal through arranged marriages with the homeland was not a practical proposition. This led to greater reduction in traditional caste divisions, if marriage was to be kept within the South Asian population.

Distance was not the only factor in this consideration. The size of the community was important also. With relatively small communities at considerable distance from the subcontinent, adoption of English as the *lingua franca* (or French in the French territories) became more likely. In effect, there was a tendency for small isolated communities to become more homogeneous.

Caste is thought by some to have become profoundly changed or to have disintegrated in almost all of these proletarian overseas communities, while its influence has remained much stronger in urbanised and middle-class societies.

The absence of precise occupational specialisation, precise ritual roles, and inter-caste dependence in the new setting, the confusion of purity and pollution notions due to caste co-residence and commensality on estates must have contributed to the reformulation of subcastes into larger groupings. Sceptics have pointed out that more Brahmins seem to have disembarked in Port of Spain than embarked in Calcutta. High caste status certainly survived in Trinidad as is evidenced by Naipaul in *The Middle Passage*. However, among the urban-based merchants and civil servants, caste-based interaction and exchange ceased to function.

If colonialism brought into existence the indentured colonies in South Asia overseas, decolonisation contributed substantially to their secondary dispersal. Decolonisation unleashed the xenophobic forces of the indigenous populations into which the immigrant indentured workers and passenger migrants had been introduced.

In some cases, Indians were unable to take up citizenship of the newly independent countries; in other cases, they were unwilling to do so. In Sri Lanka, for example, most of the Indian Tamils resident in the country were made non-citizens by the citizenship laws introduced shortly after independence.

In 1964, about 134,000 Indian Tamils, less than 10 per cent of the total, had gained Sri Lankan citizenship. In 1964, by the terms of an agreement reached between Sri Lanka and India, it was decided that 525,000 'stateless' persons of Indian origin in Sri Lanka would be repatriated to India and 300,000 persons would be given citizenship in Sri Lanka over a period of 15 years. The position of the remaining 150,000 was left undecided at the time.[16]

In Myanmar, resentment against the Indian migrants and settlers seems to have been of long standing. Although Indians formed only eight per cent of the total work force in Myanmar in the 1930s, they were concentrated in key positions which made them appear conspicuous.

When the Japanese invaded Burma in 1941, about half a million Indians fled the country. Both the British and the Myanmar resisted Indian attempts to return to Myanmar after the war, and with Myanmar independence, there began the familiar process of restricting Indian access to citizenship, reduction of their economic livelihoods and finally expulsion after 1962 when General Ne Win seized power. After independence in 1948, there were about 800,000 Indian and 100,000 Pakistani resident aliens in Myanmar.

With independence in Kenya and Uganda came a process of Africanisation. Indians formed the middleclass entrepreneurial elite in these countries. On independence, they were able to acquire citizenship, but there was a considerable reluctance to do so, except among the Ismaili minority. This 15,000 strong minority in Uganda did so *en masse*. At independence in 1962 there were 77,400 Asians in Uganda. Between 1969 and 1971 their numbers fell to 50,000. After Idi Amin staged a coup and came to power in 1971, he accused the Asians of being socially and economically exclusive (failing to inter-marry and controlling the economy). He informed the governments of Britain, India, Pakistan and Bangladesh that they would have to take back all of their nationals, the first plane-load of expellees arriving in Britain in 1972. As Amin's ruthlessness grew, even the Ismailis who held Ugandan citizenship found that their claims were not recognised and fled the country.

The Surinam ethnic position was much closer to that of Guyana or Trinidad than to East Africa. Indians and Javanese were at the bottom of Surinamese society and although they held political power in the early 1970s they were ousted by the Creoles. Fear of Creole domination and the loss of Dutch citizenship after independence in 1975 precipitated a huge flight to the Netherlands before the effective date. By 1964 the 'Hindustanis' (as South Asians were known) were just slightly less numerous than the Creoles: 38.5 per cent as against 39.3 per cent; the Indonesians numbered a further 16.6 per cent. However, political power lay with the more urbanised Creole population.

The prospect of Creole domination precipitated a panic flight which affected the Hindustani and Indonesian population disproportionately. Between 1970 and 1975, 80,583 Surinamese migrated to the Netherlands. This is the equivalent of about a quarter of its 1980 population. Indeed, the United Nations Centre for Human Settlements indicates a decrease in Surinam's population between 1970 and 1980. Cross and Entzinger estimated that about 40 per cent of the 200,000 Surinamese present in the Netherlands in the mid-1980s, about 80,000 were Hindustani. Subsequent coups have precipitated further flights of population.

Beginning just before the secondary movement, but overlapping it, is the second major movement from the subcontinent. The migration has taken place largely since 1947. These movements have been concentrated in areas strongly affected by the upheavals of the 1947 Partition, but the causes of movement are not directly related to that event. It is mainly a movement to the industrialised world and particularly to the UK, USA, Canada, and Australia.

At the beginning of the 1990s, there were about 1.5 million South Asians living in Europe, about 0.75 million living in the USA and Canada and over 100,000 living in Australia and New Zealand. However, since 1973, there has also been a major movement to the oil-rich countries of the Gulf.

At the beginning of 1990, this population numbered about 1.4 million (about the same size as that living in the much larger population of Europe) but the 1991 Gulf War produced a major upheaval. The effects of flight and reflux are not yet clear but some indication of their scale is given later in this chapter.

By far the most important single destination for South Asians living in the developed world is the United Kingdom. Of the 1.5 million living in Europe, 1.2 million live in the UK. The USA with five times the population of the UK has only about one-third of the number of South Asians. The reasons for this concentration are bound up with the post-war labour shortage in Britain and the Commonwealth membership of the successor states of British India. This made the citizens of these countries simultaneously citizens of the United Kingdom.

Up to the enactment of the British 1962 Commonwealth Immigrants Act, this gave them the right of entry and settlement in the UK. The 1962 Act controlled worker immigration and successive legislation further restricted the access of dependants. However, the movement to Britain should not be seen as a fortuitous outcome of a historical colonial tie.

The British demand for labour was a particular example of a general Western European phenomenon. Germany, France and Britain sucked in labour and dependants. Even the socialist countries of Eastern Europe had miniature *Gastarbeiter* labour movements from Vietnam, Angola and Mozambique.

France drew a foreign population of four million from Italy, Spain and Portugal and its former North African territories of Algeria, Morocco and Tunisia, and also drew population from sub-Saharan Africa.

Germany drew its four million *Gastarbeiter* and dependent population from the southern and eastern quadrant, from Italy, Yugoslavia and Greece, but above all from Turkey. Austria and Switzerland showed a rather 'German' pattern in their foreign workers while Belgium showed more of a 'French' pattern.

West Indian movement to Britain was marked by a very close adjustment between British economic cycles and migration. The movement began effectively in 1948, peaked in 1961 and was over by 1973. The correlation coefficient for net West Indian immigration against British unemployment was $r = -0.65$ for the period 1955-74.

Movement from South Asia was tied less closely to British economic conditions. The movement started about eight years later than that from the West Indies and was more disrupted by British political legislation.

The correlation coefficient for the relationship between British economic indicators and Indian and Pakistani immigration is neither as large nor as significant as that for the West Indian movement but does, nevertheless, show the importance of economic motivation. The movement from India slightly preceded that from Pakistan, while that from Bangladesh was even further behind. The peak period of arrival for west Indian-born persons living in Britain in 1987 was 1955-64, for the Indian- and Pakistani-born it was 1965-74 and for the Bangladeshi-born 1980-84.

The gross movement from Bangladesh, perversely, shows a direct rather than a negative correlation with unemployment in Britain. It has been said that West Indians in Britain face an 'Irish' future while Asians face a 'Jewish' future. By this it is implied that West Indians will remain concentrated in blue-collar occupations, council housing and with low educational qualifications, while Asians will move more to entrepreneurial activities and self-employment in white-collar jobs with owner occupation and higher educational certification.

In Great Britain, during 1987-89, the Indian male occupational structure was very close to the white population and above it at the top end. For example, 11 per cent of Indian men were in professional occupations compared with seven per cent for the white population; 19 per cent were employers or managers compared with 20 per cent for the white population and 16 per cent were in other non-manual occupations compared with 18 per cent for the white population. The comparable figures for the combined Pakistani-Bangladeshi population were five per cent, 16 per cent and 11 per cent respectively.

However, as with most generalisations, this hides many contrary examples. Perhaps, as far as the Asian population is concerned, the most serious qualification is that it hides major differences in housing tenure characteristics between the national origin groups. The Indians and Pakistanis have the highest housing tenure profile while the Bangladeshis are, in some ways, closer to the Caribbean model. Indian households were 77 per cent owner occupiers in Great Britain in 1983-85; Pakistani households were 74 per cent owner occupiers while the proportion for the white population was 59 per cent and that for Bangladeshi households, 35 per cent.

Recent estimates of the South Asian ethnic population of Britain is that Indians number 779,000, Pakistanis 433,000 and Bangladeshis 111,000.[17] These figures include direct migrants from the subcontinent, secondary migrants from third countries, mainly East African, together with children born in the UK.

The recent figures which disaggregate the proportion of children born in the UK to individual national origin groups, refer to 1985. At that time, 241,000 out of the then total Indian ethnic population of 689,000 (35 per cent) had been born in the UK. For the Pakistani population 177,000 out of 406,000 (44 per cent) were UK born, while for the Bangladeshi population, 28,000 out of 99,000 (28 per cent) were UK born.

Of the Indian ethnic population 39 per cent had been born in India and 20 per cent in East Africa. About one per cent of the Pakistani ethnic population was East African born. Most East African Asians are classified as 'Indian' and roughly 20 per cent of the Indian ethnic population of the UK is East African in origin.

One of the effects of the massive redistribution of world wealth in the aftermath of the 1973 petroleum price rise was the huge increase in demand for labour in the Gulf. The South Asian population in the Middle Eastern oil-rich countries grew from about half a million in 1975 to nearly two and a half million in 1985.

The Gulf crisis from August 1990 to early 1991 produced a major upheaval for contract workers from India, Pakistan and Bangladesh in Iraq and Kuwait. At the beginning of 1990, there were about 366,000 such workers in the two countries.

THREATS TO SECURITY

The *World Refugee Survey, 1994*, shows that the number of refugees from Bhutan increased in India and Nepal by 10,000 and 1,300 respectively.

The Bhutanese government continues to assert that these are not Bhutanese refugees and most of them have been hired to the refugee camps from among the Nepalis living in India or Nepal, either through the temptation of UNHCR roles or though sheer coercion of the leaders of dissident Nepalis.

Conflicts in Sri Lanka which was hoped to be resolved following a fresh bold approach by President Chandrika Kumaratunga's peace process initiated soon after her impressive electoral victory in November 1994 got reintensified. The Tamil militant group, LTTE, broke the peace process on 19 April 1995 and took recourse to arms.

In response, the Sri Lankan government has also decided to deal with the LTTE militarily, while still maintaining that the problem cannot be resolved except through political negotiations to ensure legitimate rights to the Tamil community. As the conflict widens, and military operations like 'leap forward' are undertaken by the Sri Lankan forces and counter-operations are launched by the LTTE, movement of refugees will increase.

There are reports of hundreds of thousands of Tamils vacating from the conflict-ridden areas and moving to safer places within Jaffna. Though most of them have become internal refugees, within the northern and the eastern provinces as also elsewhere in Sri Lanka, revival of the refugee trickle into India has also been noticed.

Conflict arising out of a power struggle among the erstwhile Afghan refugee groups was intensified when Afghanistan's President Burhanuddin Rabbani refused to transfer power in December 1993, as agreed among various groups. This power struggle was further intensified by the induction of a new Islamic militia force called Taliban, nurtured by Pakistan, with suspected US blessings, ostensibly to create order in Afghanistan and open its land routes for trade with the Central Asian members of the Commonwealth of Independent States (CIS). Before the entry of the Talibans, the conflict was broadly confined to Kabul and its surrounding areas, but the Talibans widened the conflict to the southern regions of Afghanistan as they entered the conflict from the Pakistan side. This strengthened the flow of refugees into Pakistan. According to one estimate, some 75,000 refugees came to Pakistan in 1994, and as the conflict continues, so does this flow.

During the last two decades, conflict for Tibet's autonomy and Tibetan rights has been revived. The refugees generated from this conflict are showing their numbers in India and Nepal where the strength rose by 2,000 and 4,000 respectively, over their 1993 estimates according to the figures available for the year 1994. Since the Tibetan refugees complete their journey through the Himalayas, it is possible that some of those entering Nepal would also eventually end up in India. The possibilities of the Tibetan conflict getting intensified already exist. With the hopes of any reasonable compromise between the Dalai Lama and the Chinese authorities being dashed to the ground, the Tibetan movement for autonomy is picking up strength with the help of the West. This was evident in the convening of World Parliamentarians' Convention in March 1994 and repeated expression of concern for the plight of Tibetans in the US Congress and European capitals.

The persisting tensions between the US and China on trade, human rights and strategic issues, including those of Taiwan and supply of Chinese missiles to Pakistan and other developing countries, may encourage many in the US establishments and outside to fan the Tibetan conflict. New potential conflict situations are emerging that may become serious sources of refugee generation, in addition to the revival and reintensification of the persisting conflicts.

The conflict in Pakistan's Sind province between the government and the Mujhahir Quami Mahaz (MQM) is another thratening issue. The MQM represents those Urdu-speaking Muslims who migrated from India as a result of partition in 1947. These people have been complaining against discrimination for a very long time and since 1978, they have initiated a movement to protest against this discrimination. The revival of democracy in Pakistan since 1986-87 gave them a chance to show their electoral strength, and they established their dominance in Karachi and other urban areas of Sindh. For many years, the movement has taken a violent turn, with the help of surplus Afghan resistance weapons that are easily flowing to Karachi and Sindh. The government's efforts to suppress their movement has not succeeded so far. In some of his recent statements, the leader of the movement, Altaf Hussain, who is living in exile in London, has debunked the two-nation theory which created Pakistan and has warned that if a peaceful solution of the Mujhahirs' grievances does not emerge, not only that he will ask for the creation of a separate province for the Mujhahirs, but Pakistan may face prospects of yet another break-up, on the lines of 1971, when Bangladesh was created due to the failure of the resolution of the problem of the Bengalis of East Pakistan. His views have been supported by the former President of Pakistan, Nawaz Sharif. The present conflict, if it further intensifies, may result in the flight of Mujhahirs to India. This is evident from the mood of the people coming from Pakistan these days, who now blame the partition for their plight and express preference for returning to India as they do not expect to get justice and fair treatment in Pakistan.

There is the developing situation in Myanmar, after the release of the leader of the Democracy Movement Aung San Suu Kyi in July 1995. The thrust of her statements has been that the political crisis of democracy in Myanmar be resolved through talks and national reconciliation. This could also be the wish of Myanmar's present and future foreign investors.

However, the sticking point between the Democracy Movement and the military regime—the State Law and Order Reorganisation Committee (SLORC)—is that military must have an important constitutional position in Myanmar's political system. This is not acceptable to the leaders of the Democracy Movement. If an amicable way out is not found to this problem, the revival of conflict between the SLORC and the Democracy Movement, and the reintensification of insurgency and ethnic conflict may generate refugee flows from Myanmar to its neighbours including those in South Asia.

The ethnic situation that emerged in Nepal during the mid-seventies has started becoming troublesome with the ushering in of democracy in 1990. Marginalised hill ethnic groups like the Rais, Kirats, Limbus, Magars and others are becoming conscious of their identity and rights and are getting mobilised along ethnic lines for the redressal of their grievances. The emerging ethnic and regional tensions in Nepal would be absorbed and accommodated with the demographic framework of polity but if not, then any outbreak of conflict on these divisive lines would produce refugees.

India would be the only destination of these refugees, particularly from the Limbuwan region because of socio-cultural identities of Rais, Limbus, Magars and Gurungs across the border in India where there is concentration of Indian Nepalis in North Bengal and Sikkim. Democratic politics in Nepal promises to play a positive role in diffusing ethnic tensions by channellising them through political parties, media, non-governmental organisations and even parliament.

Communal and regional forces suffered serious setbacks at the 1991 and 1994 elections may not be underestimated. There is, however, no scope for complacency as some regions of Nepal are not free from regional and ethnic problems and similar developments in India tend to activist-sectarian identities which cut across national boundaries of the countries.

Besides these potential conflicts becoming a source of refugees in South Asia, there are also prospects of economic migration increasing in the region in the years to come. This is because of the growing thrust of economic liberalisation and integration/harmonisation of regional economy encouraged by the post-Cold War international economic trends and the IMF/ World Bank-sponsored structural adjustment programmes. There is a sudden spurt in the transport of capital goods and services from one country to the other in the region. In the event of this trend gaining momentum, the spurt in the movement of labour cannot be avoided. Such movement of labour would depend upon the nature of economic activity and the extent of employment openings created.

According to UNHCR there is a return of 103,000 refugees from Pakistan to Afghanistan during 1994, even in the midst of reintensified conflict. This could be possible, perhaps because the fighting was confined mostly to Kabul and its vicinity, and the refugees belonging to other areas could go back. Similarly, the Bangladesh government, with the help of the UNHCR could help 82,860 Rohingyas go back to their villages in Myanmar during the later half of 1994. India succeeded in repatriating 8,150 Sri Lankan Tamils to Sri Lanka and 5,200 Buddhist Chakmas to Bangladesh during 1994. In doing so, while India sought the good offices of the UNHCR in the case of Sri Lankan refugees, the repatriation of Chakmas was worked out on the basis of rehabilitation and financial incentives from the government of Bangladesh. India also managed to send back 'forcibly', nearly 2,000 Chin-Myanmar from Mizoram, where they were living in refugee-like circumstances.

Since the mid-sixties, in the context of repatriation, there has been a significant shift in South Asia. Earlier there was a greater willingness to accept refugees and rehabilitate them without making efforts for their repatriation. This was clearly the case with regard to the refugees that crossed Indian and Pakistani borders in 1947 and later on. India also accepted refugees coming from Sri Lanka and Myanmar during the early sixties. The obvious reason behind India's responses was that during partition, it was accepted that the displaced people were the responsibility of the host country, notwithstanding the fact that India had not endorsed the two-nation theory that sought to divide states on the basis of religion. India, also, it seems had either accepted its moral responsibility or found it politically prudent in the aftermath of conflict with China to rehabilitate the refugees from Myanmar and Sri Lanka.

India and other South Asian countries had also accepted refugees coming from Tibet since the early fifties, possibly, as a result of political decision to make use of them strategically in their relations with communist China. Gradually, the South Asian countries have become more and more unwilling to accept refugees coming from their neighbours. Even when Pakistan has made a strategic use of the Afghan refugees and India of the East Pakistan and Sri Lankan refugees, the efforts have been to send them back soon after the strategic value of the refugees was lost and the burden of their presence became an economic, administrative and political liability. Now the shift in the global attitude towards the refugees, of "keeping would-be refugees at home" has also strengthened the South Asian attitudes, not only to resist the incoming refugees but also to send those living for a long time, back as soon as possible.

Almost every South Asian country—India, Pakistan, Bangladesh and Nepal—have even used force, either to stop refugees from coming, or to send them back, or in both the circumstances. UNHCR interventions and the pressures from various NGOs as well as refugee groups themselves have at times slowed down their repatriation not based on voluntary choice, but the hardened attitude that the refugees must return has continued. As a result of such attitude, refugees, like the Sri Lankan Tamils, have preferred to return and stay in the rehabilitation camps within their country, in the absence of propitious conditions in their traditional places of residence.

The persisting conflicts in Sri Lanka and Afghanistan may be mentioned in this regard. Even refugees that have gone back, like the Sri Lankan refugees, have mostly remained confined to internal refugee camps, because their villages and towns are still the theatres of conflict and there is no immediate possibility of their destroyed homes and farms to be reconstructed or repaired.

More so in the case of Afghan refugees where neither their own government, nor international relief agencies are in a position to be of much help. Even where help and assistance have been promised, it has not been delivered to the satisfaction of the returnees. For instance, under a bilateral agreement with India, the Bangladesh government promised "a 16-point repatriation and reintegration package that included financial assistance worth some $250" per individual, but on actual verification of conditions on ground, it was found that "less than half of the financial aid promised" had been given and other conditions had not been created for the repatriates to "settle in their places of origin".

South Asian countries have pursued various strategies and actions to deal with the refugee problems and their respective security implications. At the local level two broad patterns of settlement adopted for the refugees are evident in South Asia. The host state has either kept the refugees in well defined camps at one place or kept the movements of the refugees somewhat restricted. Such settlement pattern, if maintained and regulated properly, may give rise to least difficulties, keeping the security implications manageable. Alternately, refugees have been dispersed to different areas, farther from their points of entry, and even among the local populations that do not share much of the socio-cultural identities with the asylum seekers. In such cases, refugees have also enjoyed a greater freedom of movement and activity, including seeking jobs and organising themselves politically.

The settlements of Afghan refugees in Pakistan and the Tamils of Sri Lanka in India may be mentioned here. Security risks and instances of instability caused by tensions between the local population and the refugees have been the largest and the most severe in such cases. In relation to the external dimension of the refugee question, the general and most natural strategy adopted by the host state has been to engage the home state in direct negotiations to resolve, and/or moderate the implications of the refugee presence.

This strategy has been considerably successful in terms of its costs and results. Bilateral and negotiated agreements between India and Sri Lanka on the Tamil issue, the Myanmar and the Bangladeshi governments on the Rohingyas, and between India and Bangladesh on the Chakmas, may be mentioned in this regard. Such agreements have not been perfect and their implementation has often been tardy and cumbersome, resulting in slow and delayed resolution of the problem at hand. The difficulty with the strategy of bilateral negotiations is that it does not always work smoothly.

In the cases where antagonism and incompatibility between the interests and objectives of the home and the host states are sharp and deep, this strategy may not yield the desired results. At times the benign influence of international agencies and the third parties like the UNHCR may help break the ice and facilitate the evolution of an agreement but this is not always the case. The case of the Bhutanese refugees in Nepal may be mentioned here.

Bilateral negotiations have not yet shown signs of success, particularly because Bhutan is not even willing to accept the dimensions of the problem. But there lies no other better alternative than to continue to negotiate in the spirit of mutual accommodation and compromise. Similarly, Bangladesh has not even been willing to accept formally that there has been illegal migration of its nationals into India in search of economic opportunities.

There is, however, an informal acceptance on the part of Bangladesh that the problem exists and that it should be resolved amicably. It may therefore be advisable that the two sides continue to discuss this question bilaterally. After all, sustained and sincere negotiations did produce positive results on the question of Chakma refugees.

The repatriation of Chakmas has been stalled due to the difficulties in the execution of promises on the part of Bangladesh, but this in no way reduces the importance of negotiations and accommodation. The failure of negotiations to resolve the refugee-generating conflicts has led South Asian states to try drastic strategies, involving armed hostilities, war and intervention. This was evident in India's approach to the problem of East Pakistan which eventually led to the emergence of Bangladesh in 1971.

The Indian military intervention in arming the Mukti Bahini, and fighting a full-scale war with Pakistan which enabled the ten million and odd refugees to return to Bangladesh was initiated after the failure of other options. The then Prime Minister of India, Indira Gandhi, had clearly warned that "Pakistan cannot be allowed to seek a solution of its political or other problems at the expense of India and on the Indian soil."

The strategy of intervention and war was also evident in dealing with the crisis of Afghan refugees in Pakistan. The US, Western powers, their allies and China had all joined hands with Pakistan to force the Soviet military out of Afghanistan and thus create conditions for the return of refugees.

The qualitative difference in this situation with that of the Bangladesh conflict of 1971 was that while the intervention and war in Afghanistan was a part of the global Cold War and Sino-Soviet rivalry, in the 1971 conflict the host state alone was motivated into action to defend its interests.

The burden of the global rivalries in fact lent support to the home state, Pakistan, in 1971. The third instance of this drastic strategy in dealing with the refugee-generating conflict in South Asia was India's intervention and pressure on Sri Lanka.

The Agreement of July 1987 aimed not only at securing conditions for the repatriation of refugees but also at resolving the ethnic conflict through a fair accommodation of Tamils' fights and interests. In all the instances of the use of war and intervention as strategy to deal with the refugee issue, we must reiterate that return of the refugees was only one of the many objectives and motivating factors. This involved political use of refugees by the host state in pursuance of broader and diverse interests. It may also be kept in mind that this strategy only partially resolved the refugee-related concerns. In the case of the emergence of Bangladesh, an unassessed number of refugees did get lost and were eventually absorbed in the vast Indian heartland, mixing with its teeming millions.

The hopes of a very amicable relationship between India and Bangladesh also vanished after initial years when India started facing the pressure of economic and illegal migrants from Bangladesh.

In Afghanistan, the arms and militia forces raised during the war of attrition precipitated yet another internecine conflict which has not allowed all the refugees to repatriate.

In Sri Lanka, the 1987 Agreement and the political and military arrangements envisaged under this, ran into rough weather due to changing political dynamics in the two countries. The conflict in Sri Lanka has also been reintensified, leaving the unrepatriated refugees in the lurch. Besides the partial and constrained efficacy of the strategy of war and intervention, this option is also not available to all.

The weak and small countries are incapable of pursuing such a strategy either in relation to each other or *vis-a-vis* a strong and powerful neighbour. Thus a country like Nepal cannot take resort to this strategy either against Bhutan where negotiated solution does not hold much promise, at least for the time being, or against Tibet. Nepal is also not in a position to exercise pressure against India to stop the inflow of economic migrants.

The only South Asian Association for Regional Cooperation (SAARC) does not permit 'bilateral and contentious issues' to be brought on its agenda, and as most of the refugee issues are bilateral and contentious in nature, SAARC cannot address them. There is a pressure for liberating SAARC from this disability of not discussing bilateral and contentious issues, particularly from countries like Pakistan, Bangladesh and Nepal. But this is a politically motivated pressure, not sincerely concerned with the resolution of problems and evolution of mutually accommodative solutions. Notwithstanding this debate on the acceptance of 'bilateral and contentious issues', the fact remains that the SAARC forum and frequency of meetings at various senior bureaucratic and political levels have exercised a benign influence on the resolution of bilateral conflictual issues, including those related with the refugees. Indo-Sri Lanka dialogue on the Tamil ethnic conflict during the 1986 SAARC Summit may be recalled, similarly, talks between Nepali Prime Minister Koirala and the Bhutanese King on the question of the Bhutanese refugees in Nepal, during the Dhaka SAARC Summit in 1994.

Almost all the counties in South Asian are afflicted by the refugee problem and in some cases, the refugee issues affect more than two countries. The Bhutanese refugees, for instance, are an issue both in India and Nepal. The Bangladeshi economic and illegal immigrants are present in India, Nepal and also Pakistan. There are also Bihari Muslims in Bangladesh who have proclaimed their loyalties to Pakistan but have not been able to go to their cherished land. In addition, the security implications of refugee movements involve drug trafficking and terrorism, the areas which are already covered under a regional SAARC convention.

If the refugee question is denuded from the political and strategic use of the refugees by either the home or the host state then much of its contentious and conflictual aspects will get moderated. On the lines of the SAARC Convention on Suppression of Drug Trafficking and Terrorism, a regional understanding on refugee-related issues may be evolved. Under the umbrella of such an understanding, security and other implications of the refugee movements may be more effectively addressed even in the bilateral context. The real answer to the refugee problem lies in working at the national level to resolve such conflicts or diffuse such situations that produce refugees. For example, a resolution of ethnic conflict in Sri Lanka and Bhutan, or the ending of the power struggle in Afghanistan with the establishment of a stable political order, will make it far more easier to repatriate the refugees produced by all these conflicts.

It is interesting to recall that the Indo-Sri Lanka Agreement of 1987 devoted considerable attention to the action on the part of the Sri Lankan government at the national level for resolving the ethnic conflict that had produced refugees. The Indo-Bangladesh understanding on the Chakma refugees repatriation also expected national action on the part of Bangladesh government whereby Muslims settled in CHT in the Chakma areas were to be shifted away. Failure of the envisaged national actions both in Sri Lanka and Bangladesh vitiated the expectations on repatriation.

As we enter into the 21st century, we must ensure that humanitarian organisations have the ability to respond quickly and effectively to complex emergencies and other situations in which people are forced to flee for their lives. But we must also recognise that such a capacity is of limited value unless it is accompanied by vigorous advocacy and longer-term action on behalf of victimised and dispossessed populations.

REFERENCES

1. Mahbub Ul Haq Human Development Centre, Islamabad, *Human Development in South Asia*, 1999.
2. *Economic and Political Weekly,* 5 June 1999.
3. Ibid.
4. Ibid.
5. Ibid.
6. Ibid.
7. *The Hindu*, 6 March, 1996.
7. World Bank, *World Development Report,* 1995.
9. *SAARC SCAN,* April 1996.
10. Ibid.
11. *Economic Times,* 19 May, 1997.
12. *The Pioneer,* 9 May 1996.
13. *Weesing's Contempory Archives,* Vol. XIV, 20038.
14. *POT*, September 30, 1997.
15. Ibid.
16. *Economic Times,* 14 December 2000.
17. Ibid.

3

Colonialism and Migration

The relationship of colonialism with migration, however, is not a mechanical or deterministic one. The terrain of empire is a contested site, where contradictions between imperatives of exchange and sovereignty, and conflicts between domination and resistance, are played out. These contradictions and conflicts inject indeterminacy and instability into the questions of migration and immigrant identity. Within the general context of an empire, the determinants and processes of migration in the modern world are multiple, as borders are porous, identities are flexible, and sovereignties are malleable. Moreover, compatibility of the immigrant with sovereignty, nation, and state is always partial, contingent, and unstable.

The immigrant puts at issue the inviolability of borders, territoriality of sovereignty, particularity of jurisdiction, and uniformity of citizenship—fundamental characteristics of the modern state.[1] The immigrant calls into question cultural homogeneity, linguistic commonality, shared history, sense of belonging, and security of identity—the key ideologies of the nation.[2] These assumptions and postures warrant a re-examination of some fundamental questions that surround the phenomenon of migration: Are causes, sources, and processes of colonial migration uniform and predictable? Is the post-colonial immigrant amenable to sovereignty's demand of complete allegiance? Can the immigrant partake of the pre-existing imagined community, the nation? Is the immigrant compatible with institutional designs of the state?

Is immigrant identity commensurable with the requisites of citizenship? While these were not the only migrations triggered by colonialism within and from India, they highlight this article's central thesis that international imaginations of the immigrant must take account of the relationship of empire, and that within the context of this relationship, causes, processes, and results of migration, and the accompanying constructions and deployments of identities. are multiple, diverse, and even contradictory.

This examination of the colonial encounter aims not simply to document its record of exploitation and domination, but also to track its failures and silences, in order to focus on displacements and transformations produced by its functioning. Implicated in this study are not only the successfully implemented designs of colonialism, but also its accommodations, ambivalences, and breakdowns. Centrestage here are not only the strategies of colonial power but also native designs of resistance. The three migrations are:

i) one of the product of colonial design,
ii) one of anti-colonial resistance, and
iii) and one of the collapse of colonial rule.

They substantiate that migrant identities are constituted both by operations of power and strategies of resistance. Then there is the question of construction and deployment of post-migration identity of the immigrant in postcolonial settings. This part narrates a brief story of post-migration existence of a particular South Asian community, in order to draw conclusions about the relationships of the immigrant with the nation, the state, and citizenship. Whether the immigrant is privileged or marginalised in the national imagination is not so much the result of the fact of migration, but rather of specific political conjunctures that determine the extent to which the nation may be reimagined, the state reordered, and norms of citizenship restructured.

In the modern world two basic features of system furnish the essential framework within which there are the determinants and operations of migrations and immigrant identities. These features are the incorporation of different parts of the world into a single division of labour of the capitalist world economy and the construction of political units under the organising principle of the sovereign nation-state. As a result of these two features, the modern world system exhibits two dominant impulses: that towards establishing sovereignty and that towards expanding levels of exchange.[3]

The fundamental tension between these two tendencies has crucial implications for questions of migration and identity. The sovereignty impulse locates the citizen within firm territorial boundaries, constitutes individual and collective identities, privileges a homogeneous subjectivity eligible for political recognition, and posits identities of ineligible others. In contrast, the exchange impulse encourages flows of capital, commodities, and labour power, and thus demands the dilution of specifications of eligible subjectivities and relaxation of territorial boundaries.

The conflict between exchange and sovereignty comes in sharp relief around questions of identity and location of the self. It involves a priority either of maintenance of order and control within bounded spaces or of relaxation of territorial control in order to facilitate circulation and exchange. However, the relationship between sovereignty and exchange is not one of simple opposition.

The sovereignty and exchange impulses can be either antagonistic, mutually reinforcing, or relatively autonomous. The interplay between exchange and sovereignty in the context of the colonial encounter has a particular bearing on questions of migration, identity and political eligibility. While conventional discourse on migration remains imprisoned within the territorial imperative of the sovereign nation-state, re-imaging the question necessitates an accounting of the colonial encounter and the traces of that encounter. Locating a subject outside the imaginary of the territorial state requires specific genealogical recoveries which denaturalise those boundaries and thereby destabilise discursive hegemonies attached to spatial configurations associated with the system of state sovereignty.

Between 1834 and 1937, 30 million Indians left India as part of the global division of labour, and just under 24 million returned.[4] Most of this migration formed part of the 'coolie system' that came into existence in the early nineteenth century, whereby Asian labour, primarily from India and China, was dispatched to European colonies in the tropics to work on plantations, mines, railroads, canals, and similar projects.[5]

The 'coolie system' was a mixture of various labour systems that stood somewhere between slavery and free wage labour, and constituted 'an anomalous necessity' of the early stage of global expansion of capitalist production and the resulting articulation of different modes of production. The abolition of slavery in the early nineteenth century caused an immediate crisis in tropical plantation colonies of Europe, whose economies rested upon a critical ratio between abundant land and cheap labour, a ratio which slavery had served well and which after abolition needed to be replaced by 'a new system of slavery'.

The early consensus was that the tropical plantation owners had found in the meek Hindu a ready substitution for the Negro slave he had lost. This system of commodified labour remained in place for nearly one hundred years and occasioned forging of a whole ensemble of enabling discursive and institutional structures and construction of corresponding identities. The linkages between constructions of identities with exigencies of the plantation economies, and the interconnections of unstable and shifting identities of different labour groups, are central to this story of migration. Besides providing cheap labour, the Indian workers were to be the medium through which planters would reassert control over African workers.[6]

The unfolding of this stratagem was accompanied by enabling constructions of identities of both the African and Indian labour. Planters' claims that African labour available to them was inadequate numerically and morally became orthodoxy: African workers were portrayed as lazy, unreliable, untruthful, and unable or unwilling to understand or honour a contract.[7] The reports of parliamentary and royal commissions appointed to investigate the condition of the sugar colonies in almost every decade into the twentieth century reproduced and sanctified these portrayals.

The significance of the genealogy of these unfavourable representations of African labour both for the introduction of indentured labour from India and for the subsequent emergence of distinctive communities and strained relations among them is considerable. Disparaging characterisations of African labour were critical to the construction of identity of Indian labour in the plantation colonies. The Indian workers were extolled for their docility, industriousness, familiarity with agriculture, strong family ties, respect for authority, and the sanctity of contracts. These constructions, however, did not last very long. Once the Indians were on the plantations and adopted strategies of self-preservation and resistance, the planters' praises were leavened with distaste and dissatisfaction.

The Indians, they now observed, were steadier workers than the Africans, but they were also avaricious, jealous, less robust, not to mention dishonest, idolatrous, filthy, etc. As the catchment area of Indian labour expanded, corresponding with the territorial expansion of colonial rule in India, planters began to distinguish among labour from different parts of India. As dissatisfaction with Indians spread among the planters, and as they began looking into opportunities to recruit workers from China, the Indians came to be increasingly and unfavourably compared with the Chinese, who were portrayed as "fully alive to the necessity of authority for their regulation and control ... generally tractable and manageable", strong, tough, and "not averse to foreigners"... "highly intelligent and discerning, steady labourers, and well versed in the tillage of the soil". The crucial role of the migrations triggered by the indenture system in the forging of an Indian identity substantiates the point that colonialism is not only territorial and economic, but inevitably also a subject-constituting project. Indentured labour transported from colonial India became 'Indian' in the context of its sandwiched placement between European colonisers and the natives.

Identity is always related to what one is not—the other; identity is conceivable only in and through difference. Spatial identities are powerfully shaped by the accompanying processes of deterritorialisation and displacement. In pre-colonial India, identities coalesced around religion, caste, ethnic, linguistic and regional differences. In the indenture system the diverse and heterogeneous labour drawn from India found itself similarly positioned by this regime of colonial economy.

Institutional and discursive practices accompanying the coolie system reconstituted this heterogeneity as a singularity. Differences were also downplayed by the indentured as they forged a collective identity in resistance to a shared experience of a singular form of colonial oppression. Indian identity, thus, became a field of possibility through suppression of internal difference, at least temporarily, occasioned by similarities of conditions created by the colonial regime of labour.

In the 1920s, nearly a hundred thousand Muslims from north-western India moved through the Khyber Pass bent on crossing the border from colonial India into Afghanistan, ostensibly to fulfil their religious duty to migrate from a *Dar al-Harb* (house of war) to a *Dar al-Islam* (house of Islam).[8] This episode, known to the history of colonial India as the *hijrat* (migration) movement, offers a unique context within which to examine the interrelated questions of migration, identity, and politics. Implicated in this use of migration as an instrument of political protest are interpretations of Islam, the conjuncture of anti-colonial movement in India. This migration as resistance deployed constructions of sovereignty, nationhood, and statehood incompatible with those forwarded by modern Eurocentric discourse of the sovereign nation-state.

In the process, the migrants posited and deployed identities autonomous of both the sovereignty and exchange imperatives of the modern world system. This migration also involved a passionate deployment of religion as politics in a mode inaccessible to modern discourses of enlightenment and rationality. The Muslim elite and *ulama*, having been associated with the ruling classes of India for many centuries, had a difficult time reconciling to their removal from positions of political and cultural pre-eminence. To ameliorate their situation as a political and cultural minority, many Indian Muslims sought to reaffirm their Islamic identity through movements of religious revival. By a curious mix of temporal realities and spiritual beliefs, many Muslims of India considered the Turkish Sultan, in his capacity as the Khaliph, to be the symbolic head of the universal Muslim *ummah.* Here was a case of fractured sovereignties and ambivalent identities, whereby many Indian Muslims concurrently acknowledged the temporal and territorial sovereignty of the British colonial rule and the spiritual, extra-territorial sovereignty symbolised by the *Khaliph.*[9]

Following the First World War, Muslims of India demanded that the Turkish Sultan, as the Khaliph of the Muslims, must retain control over the Muslim sacred places, and that the Arabian peninsula must remain under Muslim sovereignty. During the same time nationalist resistance to colonial rule was activated in the aftermath of the Rowlatt Act, the Amritsar Massacre and the Hunter Commission Report. The cause of Indian self-governance and that of Khilafat were joined, and in August 1920, the Khilafat Movement under Gandhi formally launched the non-cooperation movement. It was in this general context that the question arose whether in the circumstances where their rulers were endangering the Khilafat, Muslims should leave the *dar al-harb* of British India and go to some other land under Muslim rule. Like lay Muslims, the *ulama* were deeply divided on the question, and a public controversy among the *ulama* ensued.

Finally, a noted religious leader and scholar, Abul-Kalam Azad, supplied the much-needed *fatwa*, holding that, under the circumstances, *hijrat* had become an important part of the political duties of Indian Muslims.[10] Armed with the *pro-hijrat fatwa,* an active *hijrat* campaign began in earnest. Efforts were made to familiarise the masses with the religious aspects of *hijrat*, propaganda leaflets were widely distributed and preachers were appointed to spread the campaign.

A significant part in the mobilisation campaign was played by rumours regarding the cities of Mecca and Madina in Arabia, home to the holy shrines of Muslims. These rumours ranged from the bombardment of the two cities, to their occupation, destruction, and desecration. An important part of the campaign was attractive accounts of life in Afghanistan. The people were told of the great receptions awaiting them; that the Amir of Afghanistan had promised them tracts of fertile land, that they would be taken care of by their Afghan co-religionists. While the *hijrat* movement can be comprehended only within the context of India's encounter with colonial rule, its two exceptional aspects need to be highlighted: one, that it was relatively immune from both the exchange and sovereignty impulses of the modern world system; and two, that its notions of sovereignty, nationhood, and state constituted subjectivities not available for colonial subjugation.

The global division of labour borne by colonial rule had very little, if anything, to do with *hijrat.* The centre of gravity of the movement was in extreme north-western India, an area where British colonial rule reached late and remained tenuous. More significantly, *hijrat* constituted a refutation of the territorial grounding of modern Eurocentric notions of nation, state, and sovereignty.

The migrants considered themselves part of the universal community of the Muslim *ummah,* and the only state worthy of their fidelity was the one organised to facilitate commands of a transcendental divine sovereign. The *hijrat* movement was an assertion that political borders are not territorial, but rather moral, ones that individuals and collectivities carry with them. While territory is the fundamental currency of geopolitics, *hijrat* in its complete rejection of territorial demarcation of identity asserted a subjectivity beyond the reach of geopolitics.

Finally, *hijrat* was a moment of resistance to colonial domination, conducted by assertion of identities almost incomprehensible to the colonial order; in this manoeuvre, *hijrat* refutes the claim that "resistance is never in a position of exteriority in relation to power". The long-term outcomes of the *hijrat* movement were varied. It inaugurated explicit uses of Islam as a political rallying cry in colonial India. It entrenched anti-colonial sentiments among the Pathans and facilitated the inroads made by the Indian National Congress in this predominantly Muslim area.

Between August 1947 and April 1951, the month that opened borders between the two new states were finally closed, some 14 million people moved between the two countries.[11] About eight million Muslims migrated from India to Pakistan and about six million non-Muslims migrated from Pakistan to India.[12] The partition, and the mass migration it triggered, was the result of two broad trends characteristic of colonialism in general and of India's colonial encounter in particular: one, the classic colonial governance technique of 'divide and rule,' when practised in the demographic complexity of India, culminated in divide and quit; and, two, the nationalist elites adopted the modern Eurocentric concepts of the 'nation-state' and indivisible sovereignty, that could be reconciled with the heterogeneity of India only by fracturing it. The regional, cultural, linguistic, religious, and political heterogeneity of pre-colonial India furnished a fertile ground for colonial governance strategy of 'divide and rule'. Operational dualities were quickly developed and institutionalised under colonial rule.

The most salient political divisions in India created and consolidated by the British were: an administrative division between directly governed areas and the indirectly governed princely states; the division between uniform colonial laws for the public sphere and religion-based customary laws for the private sphere; and the construction and institutionalisation of political identities based on diverse religious affiliations. The distinctive characteristic of communalism is the belief that a group of people, who have one ascriptive identity in common, say, religion or language, also shares common interest in all other fields of collective life.

A collective communal identity is not a given primordial social fact, even though it is often thought useful to seek the sanction of history. The activation of distinctive boundaries between social groups takes place in a process of social identification, a dialectic of inclusion and exclusion. In mass politics communities emerge in a dynamic of group solidarities, when political actors mobilise one or another structure of identification.

The emergence of communalism means, then, that one particular set of social boundaries is deliberately activated and imbued with a new meaning at the cost of other possible identities. Religion is one possible variable of communal identity. The decision of the colonial government to introduce religion as the fundamental category for administrative and electoral classification infused a particular political meaning into concepts like Hindu and Muslim, and privileged the religious aspect of identity at the expense of other aspects. These classifications and constructions of identities were the fruits of the colonial projects of knowledge geared at making the colony susceptible to certain kinds of governance; projects that specialised in the particularising and dividing of things oriental into manageable parts.

One of the most lasting contributions of the orientalist knowledge about India was the essentialisation of the Hindu-Muslim opposition and its institutionalisation in political representation. The primary instrument used by colonialism in India to demarcate political identities along religious communal lines was the system of so-called 'separate electorates', which provided for reserved seats in legislative bodies for religious minorities to be filled by elections within the respective minority.

The system was introduced in 1909 for Muslims and in 1919 extended to other religious minorities. The scheme of separate electorate illustrated the resolve of the colonial power to use the "existence side by side of these hostile creeds as one of the strong points in our political position in India". By setting up the "election framework for two party-systems—not for a two-party system"—based on religious divisions, this system transformed Hindu and Muslim religious affiliations into fixed political identities and positioned them antagonistically.

The end of colonial rule became imminent. This created an unprecedented political problem for the nationalist elites The problem was the incompatibility between assumptions and implications of separate electorates and imperatives of the basic operating principle of colonial India, i.e., indivisible sovereignty in the geographical unity of India. What made British colonial rule unique in Indian history were its discursive and institutional designs that reconstituted geographical India into a centralised political unity based on the notion of a singular and indivisible sovereignty. The nationalist elites in colonial India, both Hindu and Muslim, were the products not only of the general milieu of the colonial encounter, but had developed in close proximity to the colonial state apparatuses and, as such, formed part of what Alavi terms the 'salariat'. It was their proximity to the colonial state apparatuses, and their having internalised aspects of European public culture, that furnished the bases of their elite status. As such they were well versed with the modern interplay of sovereignty, state, and nationhood.

They were thus alert to the classic nationalist project in the colonies that eligibility for self-determination and independence required articulation of the 'nationhood' that was to inherit the colonial state apparatus, and thereby exercise its sovereignty. The Indian National Congress took the position that all inhabitants of India, regardless of religious and cultural differences, constitute a single nation entitled to a sovereign unified state. This scheme did not leave much room for the Muslim elites, who increasingly felt secure in their communal identities institutionalised through the system of a separate electorate.

The Muslim League took the religious-communal political identity a step further and advanced the so-called 'two-nation theory'. Using religion as the primary determinant of political identity, this theory posited that there were two nations in India, the Hindus and the Muslims, and that, therefore, both had a right to have their separate sovereign states, with the Muslim state to be carved out of the Muslim majority areas of the north-west and north-east. Some commentators have strongly argued that the 'two-nation theory' was not a blue-print for partition, but formed part of a strategy to win a larger share of power for the Muslims at the all-India level on the basis of their combined numerical majorities in the north-west and the north-east. The problem was that this posture rested on an assumption of viability, of a shared sovereignty between Hindu-majority and Muslim-majority groups.

The singular and invisible sovereignty exercised by the colonial state apparatus over the whole of geographical India precluded accommodations toward a divisible and fractured sovereignty. The very idea of a 'nation-state' rested on the assumed commensurability between inherent flexibility of an 'imagined community', and the inescapable fixity of territoriality. The logical solution to the impasse, then, was partition of India into two sovereign 'nation-states'. This is where migration came in: it would reconcile the communal claim of nationhood with the territorial expression of statehood in the context of the diversities and heterogeneities of India. But this was not going to be some organised and peaceful population transfer.

Colonialism's last act in India was its partition, and the way it was handled has been best characterised as 'an ignominious scuttle'. Even if partition had become an unavoidable solution to the political impasse, three avoidable decisions by the colonial authorities particularly contributed to the holocaust that followed, which, in turn, triggered mass migrations.

The first decision was to effectuate partition within 10 weeks of the announcement of the plan to partition India. This was quite obviously an insufficient amount of time to prepare the different communities of India for a major event that would change their lives forever.

The second decision was to break up and allocate the colonial apparatuses of state between the two new sovereignties even before the date of partition. This resulted in an immediate disruption, bordering on collapse of the civil administration, at a time when a breakdown of law and order should have been anticipated and effectively responded to.

The third, not only India, but the two main Muslim-majority provinces, i.e., Punjab and Bengal, were also partitioned. These factors directly led to the holocaust in northern India, particularly in Punjab, that cost more than a million lives, and triggered an unprecedented mass migration.

By March 1948, six million Muslims had migrated to Pakistan and four and a half million Hindus and Sikhs had migrated to India. In this tragic human drama one could witness those bewildered streams of people pouring over one brand-new border into another, hurting as they ran. It was extravagant, history's wrenching price: farmers, villagers, living in some other world, one day awoke to find they no longer inhabited familiar homes but that most modern thing, a Muslim or a Hindu nation. The sections of population that migrated from Muslim-minority areas to Pakistan included:

a) The political leadership and senior cadre of the Pakistan movement from north-central India;
b) Sections of the Muslim salariat from north-central India who saw better prospects of advancement in the bureaucratic structures of the new state;
c) Sections of Muslim capital owners from north-central India who saw investment opportunities in the new state free of competition from the more entrenched capital in India;
d) Many Muslims who feared social and political vulnerability in their new status as an even smaller minority in the new India; and
e) Targets and victims of post-partition communal violence.

While other factors indigenous to India facilitated partition, it primarily resulted from a combination of imperial designs of governance and modern Eurocentric notions of nationhood, statehood, and sovereignty. While orientalist projects of knowledge production, imperial designs of governance, and the Eurocentric arsenal of possible frameworks of polities furnished the necessary context of partition, partition was not some logical, inevitable, or predetermined result. It was the combination of the necessary context with indeterminate, contingent, and even accidental factors that resulted in the final outcome.

Similarly, the relationship between partition and the subsequent mass migration remains ambiguous, arbitrary, unpredictable, and autonomous of any fixed causal relationship. Even if the migration of the political leadership and the salariat was a predictable outcome of partition, numerically these constituted a very small section of all migrants. The largest number migrated as a result of communal riots and violence. This violence was predictable and avoidable, and so was the mass migration that it triggered. Ironically, this mass migration represented both the triumph and failure of the colonial project. It was a triumph because it resulted from the institutionalisation of the concept of a sovereign nation-state, a concept transplanted to India by colonialism. It was a failure because it came about due to the collapse of the structures of governance installed by colonial rule.

REFERENCES

1. M.L. Qureshi, *Survey of Economy, Resources and Prospects of South Asia,* Marga Institute, Colombo, 1981, p.61.
2. World Bank, *World Development Report 1991: The challenge of Development,* Oxford University Press, New York, June.
3. Ibid.
4. Akhteruzzaman, A.K.M., 1982, *A geographical Analysis of International Migration of Workers,* Department of Geography, University of Dhaka.
5. Ibid.
6. Ibid.
7. Ibid.

8. Ali S.A. 1981, 'Labour Migration from India', *World Bank Staff Working Paper* No. 454.
9. Ibid.
10. Azad A.K., 1989, 'The Cost and Financing of Individual Contract Migration', *Working Paper*, ILO, Bangkok.
11. Ibid.
12. Ibid.

4

Migration in South Asia

The migration which accompanied the partitioning of British India in August 1947 certainly constitutes one of the largest and quickest mass migrations seen this century.[1] As in the case of similar population movements elsewhere, this transfer of population, quite apart from the immediate short-term dislocation involved, has contributed directly towards high levels of instability in the region. One of its more unavoidable long-term legacies has been the creation of circumstances in which ethnic tension has been the hallmark of the relationship between the original population of the region and the newcomers.

Throughout the Indian subcontinent, migration has led to substantial levels of ethnic conflict, usually provoking resentment on the part of the locals against the newcomers who are seen to be upsetting the existing balance of interests in the region or state.

Nowhere in Pakistan has this kind of tension been more pronounced than in the towns and cities of the province of Sindh. Prior to 1971, the main source of ethnic tension within the country was that which resulted in the secession of East Pakistan and the creation of Bangladesh in its place. Migration had a differential impact on the country as a whole. In some parts, notably Punjab, the process of settling was fairly smooth and contributed towards the strengthening of the province in relation to the rest of the country. In other places, such as Sindh and Karachi, almost the reverse was the case, and the political unrest of more recent years is directly related to the changes which the province underwent during the late 1940s and early 1950s. The period following independence thus offers a context in which to examine the processes of integration and assimilation, and the factors which can encourage and inhibit these processes.

By focusing on West Pakistan, with particular emphasis on the southern province of Sind, the chapter seeks to provide an appreciation of why and in what ways Indian Muslim migration to Pakistan has left its impact. At least eight million Muslims crossed over into Pakistan from India in the years immediately following partition with equivalent numbers of Hindus and Sikhs moving in the opposite direction. Migration on this scale took place as a popular response to the political decisions which accompanied the ending of British power and resulted in the creation of Pakistan, the first modern state to be set up on the grounds of religion.

The Muslim League's Pakistan demand, issued as a counterweight to Congress's claims to authority at the political centre of an independent India, called for a 'homeland' for the Muslims of the subcontinent on the grounds that they constituted a distinct nation and had the right to a separate state after independence. Pakistan was, therefore, intended to protect Muslims against the perceived dangers of living in an independent Hindu-dominated India.

While a historical question mark hangs over whether or not the League leader, Muhammad Ali Jinnah, intended Pakistan to become a separate state in the way that it eventually emerged, there is no doubt that the extent of the territory which became Pakistan, fell short of his and the League's final expectations.

Deadlock in negotiations with Congress together with growing communal tension resulted in a British plan to partition India, including the provinces of the Punjab and Bengal, which, as they contained slight Muslim majorities, the League had expected to receive in full in any territorial division of the spoils. According to the 1941 census, Muslims had then comprised only 24.3 per cent of the total population of the subcontinent.[2] It was the concentration of Muslims in certain parts of India which made partition possible six years later. Out of a total of 435 districts, or other comparable divisions in India in 1941, there were 76 whose population was more than half Muslim. Had these districts been scattered throughout India, partition would have been a non-starter. But, instead, they were grouped into two clusters, one in the north-west and the other in the north-east of the country. Not a single Muslim-majority district existed apart from these two clusters, nor did either cluster completely contain a Hindu-majority district.

Consequently, the two clusters, embracing some 56 million Muslims in 1941, "formed the geographic and demographic reality that made the idea of Pakistan feasible". While the geographic concentration of Muslims was great enough to give weight eventually to the political arguments in favour of Pakistan's creation, it was not however great enough to ensure that either the new country would contain all the Muslims in India or that it would contain no non-Muslims.

The existence of 38 million Muslims outside the concentrated areas and 20 million non-Muslims within them, meant that instead of one minority problem—that of a Muslim minority living in a Hindu-majority state—there would be two, with considerable numbers of Sikhs and Hindus living in a Muslim state.[3]

One way around this problem might have been the mutual exchange of populations, but such a plan would have been virtually impossible to organise, notably because of the difficulties of matching the people exchanged so as not to upset the economy on either side of the border as well as actually inducing people to move in the first place. Such obstacles to a 'planned' migration, however, were overwhelmed by the spontaneous massive cross-migration that actually took place. Despite warning signs, such as the Hindu attacks on Muslims in Bihar in October 1946 which had led most politicians to fear that there would be some loss of life as a result of partition, few observers envisaged that the creation of Pakistan would trigger off the extremely bitter communal reactions which provided much of the impetus for migration. Thus, it turned out to be almost as much as a surprise to British officials and the respective governments of India and Pakistan as it was to the bewildered refugees themselves.

The suddenness of the political deal which ended British rule in India made all attempts at a planned exchange of population an impossible task. Within the six months of partition, hundreds of thousands of Hindus, Sikhs and Muslims had died, caught on the wrong side of the new borders. Many were killed by a combination of so-called 'natural causes', such as disease, hunger and exhaustion, but many others were victims of intense communal violence.

Millions of rupees worth of property was also destroyed and the social and economic organisation of the affected areas were seriously dislocated.[4] Both new governments were faced with large refugee populations who required immediate assistance and lengthy rehabilitation programmes at a time when both states were in the process of trying to establish themselves with limited resources at their disposal. The cross-migration inevitably became a matter of official concern to both governments because it created almost insuperable difficulties in connection with evacuation and transportation, the provision of shelter, food, means of livelihood, public hygiene and medical relief.

Migration to India en bloc of Hindus and Sikhs who had previously filled a majority of senior posts in the local administration of what became West Pakistan nearly paralysed its administrative machinery. Problems of this kind contributed to Pakistan's failure to secure accurate statistics of the refugee movement during the early chaotic months of the country's existence. It is not surprising to find that the estimates of the refugee movements vary a great deal depending on the agency which attempted to make them. The discrepancies between the Pakistani and Indian estimates were particularly great—each country attempting to claim that it had received a considerable net surplus of refugees over evacuees and each country insisting that their respective nationals had been forced to abandon the greatest amount of wealth during the evacuation. The overwhelming majority of migrants who crossed into West Pakistan, however, were poor, predominantly Punjabi, cultivators fleeing communal violence further east. By the end of 1947, nearly all Muslims from East Punjab had migrated westwards.[5]

There were also substantial numbers of migrants from Delhi and surrounding districts, as well as Muslims from the United Provinces and Bihar. Muslims living further south, in the princely states of central India such as Hyderabad, or in western India such as Bombay and Rajasthan, also made their way in large numbers to West Pakistan.

In contrast, the migration pattern in Bengal during the first two years following partition was largely a one-way movement—Hindus leaving East Bengal for the new Indian state of West Bengal—and it was not until a resurgence of communal activity in 1950 that large numbers of Muslims crossed into East Pakistan from India.[6]

The main reception centres in the immediate aftermath of partition, therefore, were in West Pakistan and in the Punjab in particular. Lahore had the largest refugee camps, while 1.5 million refugees alone occupied the four West Punjab districts of Lyallpur, Montgomery, Shahpur and Multan. The southern province of Sindh also experienced a huge influx of migrants which placed equally large strains on local resources. Karachi expanded from about 400, 000 in 1947 to over 1.3 million in 1953, placing a huge strain on the life of the city where building activity had almost totally ceased during the Second World War.[7]

In overall terms, the Muslim refugees who migrated to West Pakistan represented only about 20 per cent of the total population of the new country and yet the long-term significance of their arrival was great.[8]

Economically, socially, politically, and out of all proportion to their numbers, they proceeded to contribute to the shaping of subsequent developments in the parts of Pakistan where they settled. Nowhere was this more obvious than in the city of Karachi and its hinterland, the southern Pakistani province of Sind.

Table 4.1

Approximate number of refugees in each province of West Pakistan to 1950

Province	*No. of refugees*
Punjab	5,567,000
North-West Frontier	47,700
Sindh	889,000
Baluchistan	15,000
Karachi	956,000
Bahawalpur	351,500
Khairpur	23,900

Although not the main recipient of migrants from India in terms of total numbers, nor the scene of much communal violence prior to independence, the influence of partition proved to be far-reaching. Before partition, Sindh had been a relatively sleepy backwater of British India. Its population of under five million was overwhelmingly rural: apart from Karachi on the coast and a handful of minor cities further inland, Sindh's urban profile consisted of small trading centres and market towns.

There was very little industry and Karachi itself was first and foremost important as an entrepot centre for goods being moved to and from parts of India further north and east. The migrants who settled in Sindh were also, on balance, a more educated group than the province's original Muslim population which had lagged far behind the province's former Hindu population in terms of educational attainment and the jobs which accompanied it. The position of Muslim women also underwent subtle but significant change. The overall trend during the decade following independence was a steady movement towards greater participation by women in the public life of the province led by migrant women from more urban backgrounds.

Female educational facilities expanded, as did the participation of women in the workplace, albeit often within traditionally acceptable spheres of employment such as education and medicine. Most symbolic of this newly acquired 'freedom' was the frequent discarding of the *burqa* or veil upon arriving in Pakistan and the emphasis placed on the role which migrant women could play in helping to create a new future for themselves and their families. At the same time, many migrants brought with them a style of Islam which emphasised the scriptures and thus contrasted with Sindh's strongly Sufistic and more syncretic religious tradition.

In consequence, the years following partition saw the growing popularity among refugees of religio-political parties, when disillusionment with what both local society and the machinery of the state had to offer encouraged them to look for religious solutions to their problems. On a lighter note, other new habits began to take root in the province. The twin vices of the chewing of betelnut leaf or paan and tea-drinking accompanied the migrants to Sindh.

By the early 1950s, the authorities had become so conscious of the burden of importing *paan* leaves that attempts were made to cultivate the crop locally—but without much success. Cricket and hockey began to replace football as the dominant local sports, reflecting the interests of the migrants from India. The popularity of locally-produced Urdu films, not to mention that of films imported from India, formed part of the wider process by which Urdu, the language of north Indian Muslims, established itself in its new cultural home.

While English remained the language of the bureaucracy, Urdu rapidly became the *lingua franca* of migrant-dominated cities such as Karachi and so its dominance over provincial languages such as Sindhi was assured even early in the 1950s.[9] The kinds of changes which were set in motion in Sindh after August 1947 were not restricted to that province alone. From the point of view of agriculture, industry, urbanisation, education, social change, even religious practice, developments in the Punjab followed a similar pattern.[10]

Yet, the outcome for each province was significantly different in terms of the kind of society which was produced. Unlike Sindh, Punjab has exhibited few of the ethno-political problems from which Sindh has suffered: it has become a much more integrated society compared with the ethnic 'chaos' which has characterised Sindh. This difference, in large part, can be traced to the fact that migration had a differential impact on the provinces making up Pakistan. The capacity of different provinces to deal with and absorb their quota of refugees played an important part in determining how smoothly the process took place.

It was Punjab, not Sindh, which bore the main brunt of the initial refugee avalanche. The point has already been made that problems exist in calculating the exact number of refugees, largely because no records of the mass movements were compiled on the Pakistani side during the first two years following partition. But there can be no doubt that the number of migrants to Punjab far exceeded the total number for the rest of the country. However, Punjab was the largest province in West Pakistan and it was also economically strongest. Sindh, in contrast, was smaller and had fewer resources.

The eventual arrival there of over a million refugees represented about one in four of the population of the province compared with the national average of one in six. Punjab and Sind also differed in the pattern of refugee arrival which they experienced. In Sindh, the cycle of refugee arrival repeated itself for far longer than was the case elsewhere and effectively dragged out much more the practical problems associated with the rehabilitation process.

In 1953, migrants were still arriving in formidable numbers in Sindh while, in marked contrast, the trickle crossing from India into the Punjab had all but dried up by this time.[11] Another equally important distinction was the variety of migrants who sought to settle in Sindh.

Most of the refugees who ended up in Punjab were Punjabis themselves, nearly two-thirds at least started off as individual cultivators who could continue as such once the process of rehabilitation had got under way. The economic and cultural dislocation involved in their migration was reduced by the fact that they were still operating within an environment and an economic framework to which they were accustomed. This helped to ease their acceptance by West Punjabis despite some local resentment at what seemed to be the preferential allocation of resources to refugees.

The migrants who ended up in Sindh were far more heterogeneous. They also had much less in common with the host community than their counterparts in Punjab. This was the case whether the migrants were 'overspill' East Punjabis, forced to opt for Sindh when evacuee land was no longer available in the Punjab itself, urbanised Urdu-speakers from north India, or Muslims from western India with strong commercial connections.

Some 70 per cent of the second of these categories settled in Sind'hs towns and cities.[12] To some extent, this choice of province had been made for them when, during the initial panic to leave India, many Muslims from the United Provinces, for instance, took trains which were routed through Jodhpur to Sindh in order to restrict the number of refugees entering the Punjab and avoid the communal violence which characterised Punjab during this period. Economically and culturally, these two groups were distinct both in relation to each other and in relation to local Sindhis. Apart from anything else, they spoke different languages. So, in contrast to Punjab, very basic obstacles to communication threatened from the outset to slow down the rate of integration in Sindh.

Divisions between the muhajirs, as the largely Urdu-speaking refugees came to be known, and the so-called 'ethnic' Sindhis were reinforced by the fact that the former were predominantly urban while the latter remained overwhelmingly rural. Although large numbers of formerly rural Punjabis became workers in the expanding towns and cities of Punjab, the gap between the two worlds was less pronounced than in Sindh.

For a start, the process of rehabilitation proceeded much more quickly in Punjab. By 1954, a scheme to grant provisional permanent rights over allotments of evacuee land to migrants had been virtually completed in Punjab whereas in Sindh progress lagged far behind.[13] Under these relatively more settled conditions, agricultural production in Punjab became more commercialised than in Sindh, and in this way, the links between town and countryside were strengthened by economic forces which, while present in Sindh, did not exist there to nearly the same extent.

Even such basic factors as the relative ease of communications between the countryside and town in Punjab were reinforced by the superior network of roads and railways which linked villages into a wider framework of connections.

Much of western Punjab had been systematically developed with the construction of 'canal colonies' by the British when irrigation in the region was greatly expanded at the turn of the twentieth century. The outlook of the average Punjabi cultivator was also affected by the enduring ties which linked Punjab with the military. A tradition well-established during the British period of recruiting from the supposedly hardy peasant stock of the province and then resettling ex-soldiers on the land continued into the post-independence period.

Many rural families in Punjab had direct experience of a wider world than was the case for Sindhis, who carried on being regarded, as under the British, as unsuited to military service. The first decade following partition represented a crucial period in the forming and hardening of the perceptions of the different communities living in Sindh. On the one hand, many Sindhis began to resent the way in which other groups seemed to be benefiting at their expense. On the other hand, instead of growing closer to the host community, many refugees came to see their interests as being distinct and even special. The basis of their relationship was decidedly shaky, and it grew more unstable during the years after 1947.[14] The initial Sindhi response to the plight of the arriving migrants was welcoming.

There was a sense of shared responsibility for what was happening, in that Sindhi Muslims prided themselves on having played a crucial role in advancing the Pakistan cause, and with this came sympathy on a humanitarian level for the migrants and their accounts of experiences en route to Pakistan. But as the numbers of refugees climbed and their economic impact was felt more keenly, the welcome wore thin and was often replaced by resentment.

Sindh, like its neighbouring provinces, experienced the practical difficulties of looking after so many destitute people, and under these circumstances, competition for resources such as land and the scramble for jobs in urban areas combined to produce a gradual coolness towards the migrants on the part of certain sections of the Sindhi population.

Even before independence there had been some dissatisfaction at the presence of non-Sindhis in the province, encouraged to migrate there in increasing numbers by British policies connected in particular with the expansion of irrigation and agricultural production in Sindh. The authorities, to recoup the cost of constructing new irrigation systems, had actively assisted the arrival of Punjabi settlers, whom they regarded as more hard-working and generally more competent compared with Sindhis who tended to be seen as lazy and afraid of any kind of strenuous activity. This situation was not helped further by the fact that migrants often expected a degree of preferential treatment, regarding it as just compensation for what they had been forced to leave behind in India. The name by which they were increasingly known—muhajir—widened this gap in perceptions.

Whereas a refugee is pushed largely by circumstances, a *muhajir*, it is said, makes a positive decision to migrate, and hence might well consider it reasonable to receive respect, including material benefit, from the wider Muslim community. In reality, the majority of muhajirs were acute migrants—refugees who had seen little option, but to leave for Pakistan: however, once in their adopted homeland, it was possible for different interpretations of their flight to come into play.

Muhajirs often could not understand that Sindhis were facing the difficult problem of how to reconcile provincial identity with the reality of an increasingly centralised Pakistani state dominated by non-Sindhi interests. Hence, muhajirs perhaps expected more of Sindhis than was realistic under the circumstances. It was not long before newspapers recorded outbreaks of friction between refugees and local people, and mention of them disappeared only when editors began to cooperate with a government request not to publicise such incidents. Politicians exhorted both sides to coexist peacefully: for Sindhis to think of themselves as *Ansars*, the original inhabitants of Madina who had welcomed the Prophet Muhammad and his companions, the original muhajirs after they had left Mecca; and for muhajirs to consider the Ansars as their elder brothers and if there were any grievances against them, to forgive them as was done in the case of elders.[15]

Both sides, in their own interests as well as those of the state, were asked to think of the migrants as Sindhis for talk of Sindhi and non-Sindhi was regarded as suicidally divisive. The official government of Sindh reaction to the arrival of the migrants, however, played its own part in helping to establish suspicions among muhajirs that perhaps they were not so welcome after all. Much discussion was generated and a great deal of pressure had to be placed on the Sindh authorities before they grudgingly accepted this extra quota.

While their objections were valid to a certain extent, in that most of the non-Muslims who had migrated from Sindh were non-agriculturalists and therefore it would be difficult for the province to take more of the cultivators who made up the bulk of the Punjabi shipment, their reluctance created a negative impression in muhajir minds. This was subsequently reinforced by the government of Sind'hs response to an upsurge in migrant numbers which started during the first half of 1950 as a reaction to heightened communal tensions in India. The authorities objected to the influx, which reached the rate of 3,000-4,000 a day at its peak, on the grounds that it placed enormous strains on the province's ability to handle their arrival when the resettlement of earlier refugees had hardly got under way. Initially, they simply called on refugees to return to their homes in India. When this did not work, they withdrew facilities, in the shape of camel-trains and drinking water, for refugee reception at the border.

Crossing into Pakistan at that time of the year when temperatures could reach 120°F and which involved travelling across some 40 miles of barren sandy desert without shade, shelter or water, proved daunting. Not surprisingly, by early June 1950, this measure, together with the imposition of a permit system, dramatically reduced the number of migrants.

The combined effect of these official moves proved deeply worrying to muhajirs who felt they had good reason to fear that they might eventually be forced to go back to India against their will. All these developments in Sindh helped to reinforce the psychological as well as the physical distance separating countryside and town and Sindhi and muhajir. Most muhajirs had a set of priorities which had little in common with most ordinary Sindhis. Well into the 1950s, hundreds of thousands of refugees had not been resettled. Karachi was especially bad:

some 250,000 people were still living in 'improvised dwellings' in 1953, and over 100,000 people were in similar conditions in 1958. The worst of the so-called colonies consisted of haphazard groupings of small huts constructed from whatever material was available such as bamboo, thatch and hessian rags. Water and sewerage arrangements were usually non-existent. Small clusters of huts were also found along the walls of permanent buildings and main thoroughfares. The monsoon rains annually caused havoc, washing away homes and spoiling possessions and food supplies. The migrants' primary aim therefore was to obtain adequate housing; and government's inability or incapacity to deal effectively with the problem, generated harsh criticism.

Refugee organisations sprang up to protect muhajir interests and many were very critical of the administration. One major grievance was the 'usurping' of evacuee property by influential locals. A popular focus of migrant activity was the cooperative housing society which sought to purchase land for residential development. Many societies found their plans frustrated by bureaucratic delay, which meant that much of the 1950s was spent bickering over housing schemes.

Government schemes were even slower to produce results. The economic hardships of the first decade following partition increased economic insecurity, unemployment rose and standards of living fell. The 1950s was a period of bitterness for many muhajirs who watched the rich become richer as inflationary spirals forced down their own real incomes. For the majority of Sindhis, however, the problems of urban life were fairly remote.[16]

The main issue for them was land: either to hang on to it as in the case of landlords, or to get hold of some if they were tenant cultivators or landless agricultural workers. The 1950s as a result, saw a long-running saga of calls for and half-hearted attempts at land reform; but the strength of the landed interest in provincial politics meant that, when land reform did come, it was limited to only certain kinds of estates and did not affect the huge holdings for which Sindh was notorious.

Redistribution of land was not as significant an issue for refugees who, if they were Urdu-speaking, concentrated on their own urban concerns, while Punjabis who had settled in the countryside often saw themselves as targets of local resentment since they had been allotted land which might otherwise have been given to Sindhis. Polarisation became equally apparent on the economic front. Many of the migrants, especially those who settled in the smaller towns of the interior of Sindh, came to fill the vacuum left by departing Hindus and in the process, inherited some of the resentment which had been directed towards them by Sindhi Muslims. This was reinforced by the way in which migrant families came to dominate industrial and commercial life in the province.

By the end of the 1950s, Pakistan's leading industrial families included a substantial number who had migrated to Sindh in or soon after 1947.[17] At the other end of the economic scale, many poorer migrant families found themselves working in factories providing the labour force for this industrial growth.

An atmosphere of competition emerged in the service sector which came to be seen as the domain of the Urdu-speaking migrant. Government posts and other high-status occupations seemed to be filled with muhajirs who tended to be better qualified and consequently better placed to compete for these jobs. From some Sindhi perspectives, the migrants were becoming a new group of adversaries, replacing the old Hindu elite in the province and restricting opportunities for them once again.

There was even some talk that Hindu 'domination' had been preferable to this new situation for Sindhis. Hindus had at least spoken the same language and shared a common history—which the migrants did not. A shared religion, the reason for Pakistan's creation, did not automatically bring the two communities closer together. Although all were Muslims, differences between their styles of Islam could produce friction. Many muhajirs simply looked down on Sindhis for what the former regarded as unhealthy syncretic tendencies in Sindhi Muslim religious practices.

As Islam was so closely identified with the founding of Pakistan, religion came to be used by the new state as a means of cementing over divisions within the country; but when it was a form of Islam which reflected the traditions of northern India, its effect could be divisive in somewhere like Sindh. Islamic unity, for example, was used as an argument to persuade Sindhis to accept Karachi becoming a federal territory: thus religion was placed in direct conflict with provincial loyalties. The importance of their kind of Islam, at least symbolically, to many migrants was illustrated by the predominance of religious men among their representatives. It continued in the shape of the backing which these leaders gave to campaigns to ensure that the Constitution respected the fact that Pakistan was supposed to be a Muslim state.

The inadequacies of the state, combined with the growing belief that their interests would be best served by pursuing a political course which emphasised Islam as a means of applying pressure for change, resulted in high levels of migrant support for religio-political organisations. More generally, the two communities had political agendas which barely seemed to overlap. Sindhi politics was the preserve of large landed elites. Even urban-based Sindhi politicians normally had absentee landlord interests.

In the past, the indigenous power structure of the Sindhi countryside had tended to coalesce to prevent outsiders from disturbing the status quo; but the scale of the migrant influx was sufficiently large to threaten this state of affairs and so Sindhi politicians felt a pressing need to protect their position. Migrants, for their part, were frustrated for much of the 1950s by a lack of adequate representation, even bearing in mind the shortcomings of Pakistan's political system at the time. Their feelings of being distinct led them to consider themselves to be in a separate political category from other people in the province.

Throughout Pakistan, there were demands for separate seats for refugees in provincial assemblies; but whereas in Punjab refugees were automatically allocated seats formerly filled by non-Muslims, refugees in Sindh did not obtain them. The inclusion of a lone refugee minister in the provincial ministry was interpreted by most muhajir observers as at best a half-hearted attempt to reflect their interests or to meet their special needs. The main focus for their political activity not surprisingly became the Karachi and Hyderabad municipal corporations and parallel city political organisations. But divisions within these bodies between migrant and non-migrant persisted and were reflected in the kinds of factional divisions which emerged in these cities.

The concentration of migrants in Karachi, the seat of the federal government, reinforced the tendency of muhajirs to be identified with the central authorities. Migrants tended to support moves by the centre to extend its control over the city which led it to being separated from Sindh in July 1948. Sindhi reactions to this move were vehement and Karachi's separation acted as a potent symbol of the antagonism felt in Sindh towards the central government.

Muhajir support for the scheme was seen to be 'proof' that they did not have Sindh's 'best interests' at heart. Indeed many muhajirs approved of the transfer precisely because they wished to operate within a framework in which there was more possibility of their having a prominent political voice. Muhajir identification with the centre, despite all its shortcomings, at a time when centre-province relations were poor, did not endear them in Sindhi eyes when the centre was often interpreted as the extension of Punjabi interests.

During this crucial period in the forming and hardening of perceptions about each other, the main communities, which now made up Sindh's population, grew further apart rather than coming closer together. For a combination of reasons, they failed to identify mutual interests and construct a strong enough common identity vital to the creation of a more integrated society. This failure was in striking contrast to the situation in Punjab during the same period.

As Punjab's influence over the country as a whole increased, so 'Punjabi' and 'Pakistani' identities tended to merge to the point that most Punjabis saw no discrepancy between the two. In contrast, the Sindhi identity seemed to be totally submerged by the Pakistani one, something which the relative weakness of the province could not resist. The introduction of one unit in 1955 when the provinces of West Pakistan were merged to create parity with East Pakistan only seemed to confirm Sindhi fears that the centre was dominated first and foremost by non-Sindhi/Punjabi interests. Many Sindhis had rejected the idea of One Unit on the grounds that it was against Sindhi interests from the time that it was first broached in the late 1940s.[18]

The migrants' support for the move was interpreted as yet more proof of their design on power locally as well as a share in national power. In the same way the imposition of martial law in 1958, which effectively ended the first decade of independence, highlighted the difference in the outlook of politicised Sindhis and migrants. While the former viewed it as the extension of alien, albeit largely Punjabi, military and civil bureaucratic control over their province, many muhajirs greeted it with a large measure of relief, such was their disillusionment with the civilian authorities' ability to tackle their continuing problems.

As so many middle-class muhajirs formed an important element within the bureaucracy, they appeared to be among the direct beneficiaries of the loss of political rights in Sindh and the country as a whole. In this area as in others, muhajir interests overlapped with those of the centre while Sindhi ones did not, reinforcing still further, the hardening political divide between migrants and Sindhis themselves. By the end of the 1950s, Sind, although considerably affected by the impact of partition-related migration to the province, had yet to come to terms with the problems, both real and potential, which were the partition's legacy.

In contrast, once the military were in overt power from 1958 and the influence of Punjabis was increasing in relation to muhajir involvement in the country's bureaucracy, the Punjab was poised to take advantage of the emphasis on economic development and modernisation which became the watchwords of President Ayub Khan in the 1960s. Sindh to some extent benefited from the economic imbalance between East and West Pakistan which increased during this period but the 'gains' which it made were largely limited to the further industrialising of Karachi and had much less impact on the province as a whole.

Similarly, the completion of additional irrigation facilities provided a boost to agricultural production but it remained debatable whether or not it was the Sindhis or 'outsiders' who gained most from the changes. There was always the perception on the part of the Sindhis that the non-Sindhis were the main beneficiaries of any development which did take place. However, the Sindhi-muhajir problem does differ from the other kinds of ethnic confrontation present in Sindh for, unlike people from other parts of the country such as Pathans and Punjabis (even those originally from the Indian side of the border) who can be called upon in theory to return to their own provinces, muhajirs cannot really be expected to return to India.

Theories on the integration of involuntary migrants such as refugees have tended to stress the concept of assimilation as the yardstick by which to measure the degrees of difference between so-called 'host communities' and the migrants. Cultural assimilation was seen as the first stage when the universal values of the receiving community were incorporated into the migrant's lifestyle in order to minimise differences with their adopted society.

Social assimilation was supposed to follow when the migrant moved into a face-to-face interaction with wider society on an equal basis. Assimilation was said to have occurred when this two-stage adjustment had been successful and the migrant was accepted by and felt 'belongingness' to the receiving society. This model, however, proved to be Western-centric even in the society in which it was formulated. Social scientists working in the Israeli context of the late 1940s and early 1950s produced theories which later had to be modified in the light of the realities connected with mass immigration.

The circumstances in which Pakistan was created meant that for many migrants there was never any question of their adopting the values of their host society—in this case Sindhi society—because of their own relationship with what the concept of Pakistan was supposed to mean. They arrived there with their own ideas and generally saw themselves to be the embodiment of the new state. If anything, they expected local society to adjust to them rather than adjustment being the other way round. The major vehicle for cultural assimilation in Pakistan has been religion rather than any kind of regional identity, and it has been the Islam of the migrant, rather than local religious practice which has been dominant.

Similarly, while social assimilation could be considered important in Western societies, its significance is bound to be much less in places like Sindh where, as elsewhere in South Asia, small-scale social groupings are still accepted and powerful features of the social landscape. These shortcomings of existing theories would suggest that other ways of considering the process of integration following migration, or lack of it, are required to understand the situation which developed somewhere like in post-partition Sindh.

In particular, it is necessary to take into account the kinds of tensions generated by the failure of the new (in this case

Pakistani) state to create for itself the shared political identity so necessary for dealing with the stresses of 'nation-building' and to satisfy the expectations of all its people. Under circumstances such as these, differences which might otherwise have been more or less tolerated became potent sources of tension, and competition and resentment became the enduring hallmarks of the relationship between ethnic groups in parts of Pakistan such as Sindh which lacked meaningful political power.

As a result, sub-state nationalities have become so important that many muhajirs—originally the group most obviously connected with the Pakistani ideal as a result of their migration to the country—chose during the 1980s, to communicate their perceived needs in the language which had become the dominant means of political expression in Pakistan, that of ethnic-based politics.

Hence, there was wide-scale support which developed during this decade for the Muhajir Qaumi Mahaz (MQM) which talked of migrants forming a fifth 'nationality' within Pakistan to add to the Punjabi, Sindhi, Baluchi and Pathan. The emphasis involved in the way in which historians have tended to look at Muslim separatism, the demand for Pakistan, and the creation of the new state, has helped to produce an impression of a fairly uniform political response on part of the Muslims of the Indian subcontinent to the prospect of independence.

Concentrating in this way, above all, on the coming together of Muslims which produced its climax in the shape of the separate state of Pakistan, symbolised by the migration which accompanied partition, has effectively obscured the reality of the differences which separated Muslims themselves at the time. Partition-related migration brought these Muslims together. Where differences were slight, the process of settling proved successful.

The large-scale displacements occurred during the pre-independence period in the Indian subcontinent prompt other states and regional organisations to deploy their armed forces. Whether such action is taken with or without the consent of the country concerned, and whether it is prompted by humanitarian or strategic considerations, it inevitably has an important impact on the local balance of political and military power.

In many cases, precisely because of the link between forced displacement and the security concerns of states, forcibly displaced people are faced with mounting rejection when they attempt to seek safety elsewhere. As a result of the physical and administrative barriers erected by states, it is becoming increasingly difficult for the victims of persecution and violence to gain access to the territory of potential asylum countries. Safety during asylum is also threatened, whether as a result of armed attacks on refugee camps, the forced recruitment of young men into military forces or sexual violence inflicted upon displaced women and girls.

At different times during the last 50 years, the construction and deployment of identity of immigrant community went through three distinct phases in tune with the changes in the positioning of this community within the power relations in the new state. The three phases are as follows:

i) This immigrant group, comprising about six per cent of the country's population, enjoyed a hegemonic position, in the power-bloc and thus dominated the political, economic, and cultural spheres of the society.

ii) As it gradually lost ground to forces seeking democratic governance, redistributive economy, and robust federalism, this group embraced the right-wing politics of religious parties in order to combat its adversaries.

iii) This is the current phase; this group has turned to the politics of ethnicity, translated its immigrant status into assertions of a distinct nationality status, and sought corresponding political concessions. Symbolically, a significant part of the last phase is that this group has chosen to call itself *muhajirs* (immigrants).

The *muhajirs* belong to the Urdu-speaking Muslim minority communities of urban areas of north-central India, where they formed about 20 per cent of the population. In the pre-colonial period, the close association of the elites of these communities with the Mughal empire provided them with a privileged social and cultural status. The consolidation of colonial rule had hurt this elite the most. Following the failure of their bloody but ill-organised attempt to regain power in 1857, as colonial governance passed from the East India Company to the British government, and as Urdu and Persian gave way to English as the medium of official communication, the ruin of this erstwhile elite was complete.

Over the next 50 years, this elite reconstituted itself through adoption of modern education to facilitate its incursion into colonial administrative apparatuses, the professions, and commerce. Their search for a distinct political voice led them, in 1906, to form the Muslim League in order to protect and advance the political interests of the Mussalmans of India. Since the political centre of gravity of colonial India remained in north-central urban areas, and the primary struggle of the Muslim League was to advance the interests of the Muslim minority in this region, the leadership of the party remained firmly in the hands of this group.

This leadership remained secure even after alliances were forged with the rural landed Muslim elites of the Muslim-majority areas, on the road to partition and on to the formation of Pakistan. Many among these choose to migrate, constituting about 20 per cent of the eight million that migrated to Pakistan. The muhajirs, who constituted five per cent of the population of the new country, settled mainly in Karachi, a major port city, declared it the capital of the new state, and proceeded to take control of the politics, commerce and culture of the society. The ascendancy of this group was linked to its pre-migration status.

The control of the leadership of Muslim League quickly translated into political leadership of the new state. Higher literacy and membership in the colonial salariat guaranteed domination of the post-colonial bureaucratic apparatus. The experience of modern commerce, coupled with patronage of the new state, assured domination of finance and industry. This group adopted two stratagems to make the disproportionate power and privilege of an ethnic minority secure and sustainable: design a political order that would keep the majority of the population disenfranchised, and forge a national identity that will privilege the position of the muhajirs. Pakistan started its political life with a built-in contradiction. An underdeveloped, multiethnic, and multilingual setting had inherited a centralised and 'overdeveloped' state apparatus. This translated into an early struggle between authoritarian centralism and representative federalism.

The muhajir-dominated bureaucracy joined hands with the Punjabi-dominated military to subvert the establishment of a representative, federal parliamentary system. Through a series of extra-constitutional usurpations, palace intrigues, and finally martial law, a centralised authoritarian system of governance was secured. Conveniently, each step in this process was validated by the muhajir-dominated superior judiciary, by deploying doctrines of necessity and revolutionary legality.

The political order was to be one of 'guided democracy', with the twin agenda of 'developmentalism' and 'nation-building.' In this general context, the muhajir elite proceeded to construct an undifferentiated and unified state-nation, the Pakistani nation, of which they would be the exemplars. Urdu, the language of the muhajirs, spoken by only six per cent of the population, was to be the national language. Islam, the religion that had provided the muhajirs protection under the colonial separate electorate system, was to be the state religion. The 'one Pakistani nation', united by the bonds of Islam and Urdu, exemplified 'official nationalism', i.e., the perception of belonging to one politically defined collectivity, a national identity that is not generated from below, but which is imposed by dominant elites from above with the help of state apparatuses. Construction of this state-nation identity entailed the creation of a 'retrospective illusion', through which the state is constituted as a national community, which recognises itself in advance in the institution of the state.

The role of 'print-capitalism', as conceptualised by Anderson, came into play in this 'nation-building' exercise. The muhajirs had a free hand to build the nation in their own image because of their command of Urdu, state ownership of broadcasting, and governmental control of the press. The nation, in this context, was made into a property of the privileged group. Armed with Urdu and Islam, muhajir identity was projected as that of the 'true Pakistani'.

'Unity, faith, and discipline' was proclaimed as the 'national' creed, where 'unity' translated into denial of federalism, and 'discipline' into authoritarianism, under the ideological cover of Islamic 'faith'. 'Conjuring Pakistan' was facilitated in no small measure by narratives of historic origins and sacrifices that were deployed to bridge "the tensions inherent in Pakistan's geographical and ideological frontiers". Like Vernant's category of militant refugees, the muhajirs did not accept their status as a stigma; if there was to be integration, it had to be from the top of the social status pyramid where they stood and not from the bottom. In the process, the muhajirs posited notions of citizenship through strategic deployment of their comparative privilege. Denial of federalism became a cardinal principle of the muhajir-dominated state.

Ethnic, cultural, and linguistic diversity of the country were seen as a threat, that may fragment the territorial integrity of the state and destroy the muhajir-dominated social order. The historic division of north-western India into distinct provinces was abolished in favour of a unified administrative structure. Any assertion of regional identity based on distinct language, culture, or history was construed as a challenge to the integrity of the 'unified nation' and consequently to the security of the state.

The 'nation-building' effort to produced an undifferentiated Pakistani state-nation failed because resistance by marginalised national groups, particularly the Bengalis, increased in intensity, proving that "one man's imagined community is another man's political prison". The 'take-off' envisaged in the model of economic development pursued for over 20 years failed to materialise, and had instead contributed to a widened gulf between the rich and the poor. The lack of civil liberties alienated the intelligentsia, professionals, and urban student groups.

Pakistan's defeat in the war over Kashmir with India in 1965 seriously damaged the standing of the military and led to serious questions about its leading role in the political structures. In 1968, all these factors combined to produce a mass movement demanding the establishment of democracy, federalism, and economic redistribution. Sensing an erosion of the building blocs of their identity and privileges, the muhajirs readjusted their identity by aligning closely with right-wing religious parties, portrayed demands for provincial autonomy and economic redistribution as assaults on the 'Islamic genius' of the nation, and projected themselves as the custodian of this new Islamic identity.

The result of the 1970 elections, in which the religious parties were routed came as a rude shock to the muhajirs.[19] In the name of Islam, they supported the military in its refusal to accept the results of the election; this refusal led to civil war, and culminated in the secession of East Bengal in 1971. At this time, power was finally transferred to popularly elected representatives. The new government, responsive to its constituencies, took measures which were seen by the muhajirs as impingements on their interests.

The first was the decision to restore Sindhi as the official language of the province of Sindh. Demonstrations against the measure by the muhajirs, escalated into language riots that claimed 55 lives in the fall of 1972. Then came the revision of the regional quota system for recruitment to the federal bureaucracy, which lowered the muhajir quota from 17 per cent to 7.6 per cent.[20] In addition, the nationalisation of large industrial and financial units was directed against the country's largest industrial and financial houses, disproportionately owned and managed by Karachi-based muhajirs.

Another change was in the rules of access to higher education, particularly professional schools, aimed at expanding opportunities for marginalised groups. These policies gradually eroded muhajir domination of civil bureaucracy, public enterprises, and large-scale private enterprise. Muhajirs, in response, played a leading role in the agitation against the civilian government and welcomed the assumption of power by the military in 1977. Restoration of military rule, however, did not translate into restoration of privileges of the muhajirs.

The changing demographic profile of Karachi and the realignments in the military's base of support, continued the relative decline in muhajir share of jobs, educational opportunities, and political influence. All this combined to produce a sense of 'relative deprivation', whereby groups become disaffected from a system when the gap between society's resources and opportunities to which they feel entitled and their share in those resources increases to an intolerable level. In this general context, muhajirs responded to the continuing decline of their privileges and power by 'an overnight ethnic redefinition', whereby they posited a distinct muhajir identity. In a complete reversal of their position, maintained since the establishment of the state, they now asserted that Pakistan was in fact a multinational society, and that muhajirs constituted a distinct fifth nationality along with the Punjabis, Pathans, Sindhis, and Baloch. In a significant symbolic move, they proceeded to adopt the term muhajir to signify their new-found national status. A signifier they had shunned in earlier days as detracting from their being part of the unified Pakistani nation now became a badge of honour.

The first concrete step was the founding of the All-Pakistan Muhajir Students Organisation (APMSO) in 1979, with the main demand being the revision of quotas for admission and employment that would be more favourable to the muhajirs. In 1984, the leadership of APMSO turned the organisation into a political party named Muhajir Qaumi Mahaz [Migrant National Front] (MQM), whose primary demands remained recognition of their status as a separate nationality, and increased representation in educational institutions, government jobs, and political decision making.

The following years saw the rise of conflict and riots between muhajirs and non-muhajirs. In 1988 and 1990, the MQM contested general elections and swept them in Karachi and other muhajir-majority urban areas of Sindh. However, the numbers were not in themselves sufficient to form a government, and the MQM was forced to enter into 'coalitions of convenience' with majority parties whose base of support was in rural Sindh and Punjab.

The coalitions proved short-lived because the conflicting and competing demands of the MQM and the base constituencies of majority parties could not be reconciled. This propelled some sections of the MQM to demand constitutional concessions to allow the muhajir nationality political autonomy. Some even talked about the desirability of secession and a state of their own. In this atmosphere, conflicts between muhajirs and other ethnic groups took a violent turn. Complete breakdown of law and order in Karachi prompted the military to launch counter-insurgency operations in 1992 and again in 1995. Things had indeed come full circle. The military, the one-time ally of the muhajirs, had now become their adversary.

REFERENCES

1. B.R. Ambedkar, *Pakistan or the Partition of India,* Ed 3, Bombay, Thacker Co, 1946, pp. 325.
2. Ibid.
3. Rabindranath Tagore, 'Through Indian Eye', *Time of India,* Bombay, April 10, 1924.
4. S.P. Verma, *Problems of Democracy in India,* Delhi, S. Chand, 1946, pp. 64.
5. Ibid.
6. Sri Prakash, *Pakistan: Birth and Early Days*, Meerut, Meenakshi Prakashan, 1965, pp. 2.
7. Ibid.
8. Ibid.
9. Ibid.
10. Choudhary Rahmat Ali, *India: The Continent of Disia or the Country of Doom,* Cambridge, The Disia Continental Movement, 1945, pp. 6.
11. Moir Shakir, *Khilafat to Partition*, New Delhi, Kalamkar Prakashan, 1970, pp. 213, 119.
12. Ibid.
13. Ibid.
14. Kenneth Cragg, *Islamic Survey Vol. III,* Edinburgh University Press, 1965, pp. 25.

15. N.H. Mitra, *Indian Annual Register,* July-Dec, 1930, Vol. II: 339.
16. C.H. Philips, *The Partition of India,* Leads University Press, 1962, pp. 2.
17. Maulana A.K. Azad, *India Wins Freedom,* Bombay, Orient Longman, 1961.
18. Ch. Khaliquzzaman, *Pathways to Pakistan*, Bombay, Orient Longmans, 1961.
19. Penderel Moon, *Divide and Quit*, London, 1961, pp. 14.
20. Hans J. Morgenthau, *Military Imusions,* The New Republic (Washington D.C.), March 19, 1956.

5
Migration in Bangladesh

In Bangladesh, large-scale movement of the population has been a feature for a very long time. People have moved within rural areas, between urban centres, from one country to another, from urban areas to rural areas and from rural to urban areas. The most consistent form of movement has indeed been from rural to urban areas. This type of movement, although quite steady and significant from the 1970s, is today assuming standing proportions.[1]

In Bangladesh, migration of labour overseas has become the most burning manpower issue. The export of manpower and the resultant inflow of remittances have largely been acclaimed as the crucial factors in keeping the Bangladeshi economy afloat in recent years. Apart from the two major traditional destinations of Bangladeshi migrants, the Middle East and the UK, the following receiving countries have also recently become popular: the USA, Canada, Japan, Germany, South Korea, Singapore, Malaysia, France, Sweden, Taiwan, Brunei, Italy, Pakistan and India.

An increasing proportion of these migrants have been adopting informal, illegal or even clandestine channels of emigration; such estimates become mere conjectures, or wild guesses. However, from official estimates for the period 1977-90, the countries in the Middle East can be ranked according to their popularity as destinations as follows: Saudi Arabia (37.6 per cent), United Arab Emirates (13.78 per cent),

Oman (12.08 per cent), Kuwait (10.92 per cent), Iraq (8.11 per cent), Qatar (7.97 per cent), Libya (3.95 per cent), Bahrain (3.92 per cent) and others (1.67 per cent) (Mahmood 199 1: 10).[2] The officially quoted figure of approximately $800 million for the years 1991/2 and 1992/3 is believed to be a gross underestimation, but there is no way of ascertaining the probable range of the underestimation.

The Bureau of Manpower, Employment and Training agency of Bangladeshi government quotes the following figures on the skill composition of Bangladeshi migrants for the year 1990:

a) professionals and semi-professionals: 5.78 per cent;
b) skilled workers: 34.38 per cent
c) semi-skilled workers: 20.04 per cent
d) unskilled workers: 39.8 per cent.

Notwithstanding countrywide variations in skill categories, the above distribution seems to be convincing because the two major destinations give credence to the picture. The proportion of unskilled workers has, however, been gradually shrinking in recent years. This is accounted for by the changing demands of the receiving countries. Most of these overseas migrants come from the regions of Bangladesh, Sylhet and Chittagong. Though other regions are fast catching up, migrants from Chittagong still dominate the migration flow to the Middle East and over 90 per cent of Bangladeshi immigrants in Britain have come from Sylhet. Other destinations show no such systematic regional bias.

Patterns of comparatively recent migration flows differ from those of the two earlier ones. Recruiting agents and individual migrants now play a more crucial role, whereas earlier flows depended far more on pioneer migrants and on prospective employers in the receiving countries. The first migrants to settle in the UK were some seamen from Sylhet who, lured by the employment opportunities in labour-short

Britain, abandoned their ships in British ports immediately after the Second World War. These pioneer settlers are believed to have formed the core of Bangladeshi migrants in Britain.

The real impetus came when the British immigration, authorities introduced employment vouchers in the late 1950s and early 1960s and that, despite the gradual tightening of British immigration laws starting in 1962, the flow was able to gain momentum through the strong chain of family and kinship structures.[3] With early immigrants having obtained British citizenship, family immigration still keeps the flow going despite Britain's recent discriminatory attitude towards Bangladeshi immigrants. Besides family reunion, numerous legal manipulations and, illegal practices now flourish to circumvent the legal restrictions. False declarations about family members, forged passports or visas, and remaining illegally after temporary visits have become fairly familiar trick. Travel agencies and manpower recruiting agents proliferate throughout Bangladesh to make arrange smuggling of migrants. Bureaucratic both ends of the chain, the complicity of some airline crews and loopholes in policing mechanics keep the flow of illegal migration going.

The Bangladeshi migration to the Middle East is quite different. Beginning in the early 1960s, small numbers of people, mostly from the district of Chittagong, started to migrate to oil-rich Middle East countries and sheikhdoms like Bahrain, Kuwait, Qatar and Saudi Arabia.[4] Until the late 1960s, the number of such migrants from Bangladesh was not very significant. The 1973 oil-boom opened the floodgate to foreign workers in the oil-rich countries, but Bangladesh followed a somewhat restrictive manpower export policy till the end of 1975.[5]

In 1976, Bangladesh joined the race to secure a share of the caке of the Middle-East labour market.[6] By that time the market was almost captured by the Western countries, on the one hand, and by India, Pakistan, the Philippines, Korea,

Taiwan, Sri Lanka and other non-oil Arab countries, on the other. Nevertheless, the flow from Bangladesh increased each year from 1976 to 1982.[7] Then it tapered off, though remaining at a substantial level even today.

Migrants to the UK are increasingly likely to be seen as semi-permanent or permanently settled immigrants, whereas migrants to the Middle East are regarded as transient workers and are thus unlikely to take their families with them. Their legal status in each of the two destinations also differs and this has important ramifications for behaviour.

ECONOMIC IMPACTS

Let us focus on the impacts of overseas migration on the economy and society of Bangladesh at both the macro and micro level. The Central Bank of Bangladesh officially estimated overseas remittances to Bangladesh during the period 1977 to 1990 at $6.4 billion, which is believed to be a gross underestimation. The government's estimates for the year 1993/4 claim that annual remittances during the previous financial year exceeded $800 million. The ever increasing use of informal channels for sending remittances in cash and kind has made it impossible even to guess the range of the underestimation. But official figures suggest that, from the late 1970s onwards, the flow of remittances has been growing fast, which has made the present flow more than 35 times larger than the flow in 1977—it has moved from Tk. 866 million in 1977 to about Tk. 31 billion in 1992.

Annual remittances from the UK have stagnated in recent years, whereas from the Middle East they have been increasing fast. Other destinations are also gaining in relative importance. The *hundi* system, the main informal channel of sending remittances, has been gaining ground over formal channels and is believed to be providing a crucial source of finance for the fast growing illegal international trade in

Bangladesh. The accompanied and unaccompanied baggage of homecoming migrants continues to be a major informal channel through which overseas savings are brought into the country. The import trade has introduced a Wage Earners' Scheme (WES) in an attempt to attract foreign currency that would otherwise have been diverted into illegal channels. This scheme is also regarded as a blanket arrangement for attracting blackmarket money originating in Bangladesh for international trade.

Remittances have been providing investment funds for housing and construction, agriculture, small-scale manufacturing and transport, as well as for the economic and social infrastructure.[8] Manpower export provides some relief from acute unemployment, both rural and urban. It encourages the development of vocational and technical skills among both returned and intending migrants; it has also led to the rapid development of travel agencies, hotels, catering, transport and communication services, improved educational facilities in the rural areas, an so on.

In the absence of large-scale productive investment of overseas earnings, a substantial proportion of the funds is spent on purchasing land, jewellery, consumer durables and food, and on social and religious ceremonies. These consumption-oriented uses of the remittance money do not add significantly to the produçtive capacity of the economy. Another negative impact is related to the economic and social rehabilitation of returned migrants within the context of increasing unemployment in the country and their changed expectations and attitudes about what constitutes a suitable job and an appropriate wage or income.

Migration flow has affected some parts of Bangladesh disproportionately because of the mass migration of mainly rural labour from them. These areas are mostly located in the two pioneering regions of Sylhet and Chittagong. Land purchase has attracted the major share of migrants' home investment. The resultant buying spree has caused an accelerated concentration of landownership in the migrant households at the expense of non-migrant households of the same communities. This has accelerated the landlessness process among non-migrant households.

Both homestead land and cultivable land attract migrant attention. Both groups of migrants show more than 50 per cent gain in landownership during their migration periods. This has resulted in a hyper-inflation of land prices for both cultivable and homestead land. Cultivable land prices are three to four times higher in the study areas than in the respective control areas.

Households of migrants have made gains in landownership, but very few of their members report agriculture as their primary occupation. This may imply that real peasants are gradually being pushed out of land ownership and that a new non-cultivator, pseudo-rentier landowning class is emerging.

On migrant-owned farms, land tenancy is characterised by an unusually large proportion of sharecropping and leasehold arrangements. A relative dearth of family labour, coupled with a growing sense of rural elitism, serves as compelling reasons for this high incidence of sharecropping and leaseholding. The cultivable holdings of migrant households comprise a number of plots, large and small, attained through purchase. These plots are fragmented and geographically widely scattered. This implies that the larger migrant landholdings are formed mainly by adding plots to land owned, rather than by consolidating the size of adjoining plots. The effect on cropping intensity is mixed, but crop diversification has suffered. The adoption rate of high-yielding varieties of rice has had a boost from migration in Chittagong, but has not changed much in Sylhet. Vegetables and rabi crop cultivation have been adversely affected.

Out-migration of adult male labour has turned the study areas into labour-scarce communities, with agricultural labour being hit the hardest. The huge boost in construction, trade, commerce, services, transport and migration-related activities has been acting as a strong pull factor to draw labour out of agriculture into non-agricultural and tertiary activities. Migrant labour from other districts has poured in to fill the vacuum. Remittances have generally eased the agricultural credit situation in the sending communities and there are cases of migrant households replacing traditional moneylenders.

The agricultural marketing get improved by migration. Post-harvest operations have improved; better storage facilities have been built, roads have been improved; modern transport systems have been introduced; marketplaces have been built or improved; links with urban centres have been made easier and less costly; and banking facilities have become more generally available. Agricultural wages in the study areas are 50 per cent higher than they are in the control area.[9] The cost of crop production has gone up because of this wage-boost, whereas agricultural prices have remained comparable to national ones. Thus, in that crop production has become cost-inefficient, this has particularly harmed farms operated by non-migrant peasant households.

Consumption-pattern of migrant households has become markedly import-biased. Remittance receiving households spend relatively more on social ceremonies and religious rituals. Migrant households spend a significant amount on expensive health care services, and have grown the habit of using hired domestic help, house tutors, religious teachers, etc. As trade and commerce, new construction, purchase of land and gold, consumer durables, etc., have been the principal attractions of the migrant households, traditional cottage industries have been adversely affected by the change in consumption habit.

Though migrant households have increased their land ownership, a large proportion of their adult members, have abandoned agriculture as a profession, and have moved into trade and services. Migrant labourers from outside the localities have poured in to take up jobs as agricultural workers. Non-agricultural employment opportunities have increased in construction, transport, trade and commerce and other service activities. Unemployment among returned migrants has become fairly widespread. It has afflicted unskilled migrants the most. Returned migrants seem to prefer self-employment because of the changed perception about what constitutes suitable jobs for them.

There have been noticeable developments and improvements in the economic and social infrastructures of the migration-special communities. Such changes are evident in improved roads and marketplaces; modern shopping facilities; electrification and telecommunication facilities; banking; institutions of education; youth clubs and recreation facilities; tubewells and better sanitation facilities; pharmacies, health centres and so on.

Inflow of remittances has generated a localised hyper-inflation of prices and wages in the sending communities. Prices of consumer items like fish, meat, clothes, bread, vegetables and sweetmeat, and the cost of the services of for example, doctors, tailors laundries, barbers, photographers, travel agents and decorators are comparatively higher in these communities because of increased demand. Fares are higher for transport vehicles like rickshaws got autorickshaws. There has been a tremendous boost in the price of land for both agriculture and housing in these area. Remittances inflow has diversified the demand and supply pattern for goods and services to reflect the changed lifestyles of migrant households.

SOCIAL IMPACTS

Migration has increased the practice of late marriage among males, but has led to a reduction of age at first marriage for females. It has also increased the incidence of polygamy among the male migrants. Marriages have become very expensive because of lavish ceremonies and the widespread practice of providing a dowry. There is a sharp reduction in the infant mortality rate in migration-special areas. Migrants tend to have larger families than non-migrants. The secondary school dropout rate among males has increased dramatically, but female education seems to have got a boost.

Pseudo-religious ceremonies have increased significantly. Community feasts have become a common phenomenon in these areas. Litigations have increased dramatically. Migrants have emerged as attractive suitors for marriages. Liquor, gambling, robbery, hijacking, drug addiction and gangsterism have increased noticeably. There is a noticeable shift in the village power structure in favour of migrants or members of migrant households because of their vastly improved economic and social status and financial strength.

Though overseas migration is a major blessing for densely populated poor countries like Bangladesh because of the ever-increasing flow of remittances it brings, some of its outcomes may not augur well for the country in the long run. We should also think about the human side of the story. The sweat and toil of Bangladeshi migrants working in the Middle East have earned them the derogatory appellation of beggars in the lands of their dreams, but their hard-earned money has not yet found productive avenues for investment in their homeland. This sadly implies that in most cases the affluence temporarily achieved during the tenure of migration may not be sustained for long in the event of a permanent return.

The refugees are harassed and ruthlessly exploited by unscrupulous and corrupt customs, police and immigration officials in their own country, as well as by the notorious manpower exporting agents. They often fall victim to robbers, cheats and local ruffians. They are frequently blamed by their neighbours for their eccentricities, reckless and ostentatious consumerism, obsession for land, outlandish spending sprees and idiosyncratic excesses, but the society seems to be quite oblivious of the painful struggles and horrendous travel experiences.

Bangladesh continues to send abroad relatively unskilled, untrained and almost illiterate migrant workers, but still wastes government revenues and public savings on unproductive items like defence, internal security and civil administration. Essential nation-building activities such as providing education, training, health care, poverty alleviation and rural development continue to be neglected in the prioritisation of public investment needs. The authorities are well aware that an increasing proportion of remittances are being diverted into smuggling or facilitating the flight of capital, but public policies do not reflect any noticeable concern for that.

URBAN MIGRATION IN BANGLADESH

The quest for a livelihood, a better income, a better job seems to be juxtaposed with a deteriorating rural economy, lack of land for cultivation, lack of employment opportunities, recurring disasters and, paradoxically enough, a harsh and pitiless existence in the city for a sizeable section of the migrants. By the year 2020, the population of Bangladesh, presently standing at more than 122 million, is expected to have reached 171.4 million, yet it will still be confined within an area of 55,598 square miles, of which around four-fifths is classed as habitable.[10]

According to the Bangladesh Bureau of Statistics, population of Bangladesh increased by nine million in the decade 1951 to 1961, while in a thirteen-year period, from 1961 to 1974, it increased by 21 million. Between 1981 and 1988 it increased by 23 million. Measures were adopted to reduce the annual population growth rate front 2.7 per cent down to 2.4 per cent, and the trend in the 1990s is towards a declining rate of increase: about 2.17 per cent and 1.6 per cent in 1997.[11] Under this scenario, it seems reasonable to identify population pressure upon land as a reason for migration from the rural areas to the urban areas of Bangladesh, but there are other equally important factors to be considered.

The socio-economic indicators for Bangladesh, such as education, family planning and life expectancy are not very encouraging. The public health and family planning system reaches fewer than 30 per cent of the total population, with rural rates far lower than urban rates. The UNICEF in 1987 accounted for only 29 per cent of rural and 43 per cent of urban inhabitants having access to safe drinking water. Nearly 60 million were lacking modern health services, and 103 million people without access to adequate sanitation. Only 1.3 per cent of the rural population and 47.4 per cent of the urban population enjoy this basic facility of adequate sanitation.

The number of city-bound migrants increased fivefold between the census periods 1951-1961 and 1961-1974. Although the government of Bangladesh estimates that 27 per cent of the population will be in urban areas, the year 2000 had witnessed nearly 40 million urban inhabitants in the cities of Bangladesh, at all urban growth rate of approximately six per cent. This is in fact 28.8 per cent of the population. Theoretical statistics record that 27 per cent of the population will be in the urban areas of Bangladesh.[12]

In the last 15 years, the population in the capital city of Dhaka has more than doubled. Dhaka's importance as a destination for migrants received impetus in the early 70s following the war of 1971 and the deterioration of the social fabric of impoverished rural societies of Bangladesh. People were cognizant of the fact that Dhaka was the new capital and the abject lack of security, lack of momentum and productivity of the rural areas could not prevail in the centre.

More than one-third of the growth in large cities is accounted for by migration from rural to urban areas. The present pace of migration to Dhaka is escalating according to the United Nations Development Programmes (UNDP) Report 1997; the annual growth rate of urban population in

Bangladesh is 5.4 per cent, while the Economic and Social Commission for Asia and Pacific (ESCAP) gives a figure of 5.2 per cent annual growth rate of urban population. Dhaka alone accounts for probably 35-45 per cent of the total urban population, although some estimates are even higher. Dhaka has a growth rate of 3.96 per cent and has very low urban-living score of 32.

The problems of metropolitan Dhaka stem mainly from the fact that its growth management strategy is underdeveloped and archaic. The problems also arise from the rapid pace of urbanisation being experienced by the capital city. Dhaka had 8.5 million inhabitants, a figure projected to swell to 16 million by the year 2010, and 25 million by the year 2025. The problems of Dhaka city are compounded since the movement of people from rural areas is not uniform from all the districts of the country and neither is the profile of the migrants equal.

Undeterred migration from rural to urban areas and increasing pressure of population upon the civic amenities of large cities has resulted in air, water, noise pollution deteriorating health care and an increase in urban crimes. Heavy concentration of population within the capital cities of developing countries creates a concomitant demand for goods and services. The government administrative organisation is unable to deliver a well coordinated monitoring system for a planned environment. The problems arise in the absence of a developed, planned and guided system. At the core of the failure to implement plans is the problem of policies which tend to undermine rural prosperity.

The overall environment created and perpetuated by the policies which governments establish condition migrants. Governments establish policies of development but the impacts of such policies are debated. Although it is difficult to determine the impacts empirically, economic restructuring affects low-income communities disproportionately. Despite economic growth, about 33 per cent of the people of the region live in absolute poverty, with millions of others suffering a rapidly increasing relative poverty, which is aggravated by high levels of rural-urban migration. The role of the government in pursuing a strategy of modernisation, with its undiluted belief in emphasising industrial and technological development in the large metropoles of the Third World countries, has led to an acceleration of rural-to-urban migration.

Although labour mobility is essential for a well-functioning labour market, the current rates of rural-urban migration are excessive. The problem arises from policies that suppress the demand for agricultural labour by bringing about excessive protection for industry in relation to agriculture and capital market imperfections, and in policies that increase the costs of urbanisation by providing free or subsidised public services. The solution, therefore, is to be found in the reformulation of pricing and investment policies.

Natural population growth and low agricultural productivity are just two of the contributory factors of rural-urban migration. Migration proceeds in response to urban-rural differences in expected rather than actual earnings. The fundamental premise is that migrants as decision makers consider the various labour market opportunities available to them as between, say, the rural and the urban sectors, and choose the one which maximises their expected gains from migration. Expected gains are measured by the differences in real incomes between rural and urban job opportunities and the probability of a new migrant obtaining an urban job.

Migrants to the city of Dhaka comprise old and young males and females, mostly unskilled and uneducated. Many of the migrants are living in very poor housing and some do not own even a roof to shelter them from the elements. Despite the evidence of misery in the cities, people continue to pour in. Spurring them on would be some sort of expectation: an expectation not yet defined and rather obscure. One profile of that expectation has been projected as a desire to earn a higher income in cities.

The migrant to the city is unlikely to get a job immediately because, in developing countries, unemployment and underemployment are generally chronic; the migrants' actual probability of getting a higher-paying job in the urban sector rather than in the rural sector will influence the permanent income calculation, and thus the likelihood of moving. The migrant is responding to the opportunity for employment although the unemployment indicators may all be very high in the urban area. Evidently it is the possibility of employment or the expectation of employment that directly affects the likelihood of moving rather than the wage differentials.

High urban unemployment does not appear to deter migration and it is borne out that expectations about employment and income differentials in urban areas are not the only factors which encourage rural-urban population flows. Expectation about social and cultural amenities, housing, social services and quality of life in the urban areas seem to play a role in motivating the rural-urban flow. Also inter-regional inequality or sharp opportunity differentials between two areas enhance the likelihood of movement from the low to the high opportunity area.

For Third World countries, migration has become an intractable problem. After decades of planning, the situation of migrants to the city is unrelieved. Both in the rural areas and the urban areas the poor are suffering severe hardships. There is a need to understand why the poor continue to migrate to the city despite the apparent squalor in the cities. Development targets remained unachieved in the decades of the 1950s and the 1960s, when many of the present-day LDCs pursued a strategy of development, which envisaged raising GNP through large-scale, capital-intensive, urban-centred, entrepreneurial, import substituting industrialisation. This strategy proved incapable of bringing about improvement in the socio-economic condition of the rural masses in these countries.

The growth centre policy pursued by Bangladesh has made little headway in diverting migration away from the large cities. This is primarily because the policy has concentrated upon towns of smaller size than those having populations of between 25,000 and 200,000. The problems are that in smaller towns, the economic base is insufficiently developed and does not exert the same attractive influence as do the largest centres, with their production-facilitating institutions, such as banks, administrative offices and transport facilities, where the hopes for any form of livelihood seem brighter.

Measures of alleviation of overcrowding, poverty, injustice, mass exploitation and environmental degradation in Bangladesh were sometimes bordering on strategies of controlling the rural migrants to the urban areas. Although there is a greater understanding among social scientists of the nature of migration and its role as a force generating change, policy makers continue to conceive migratory movements in a simplistic and confined manner.

In the last three decades, many studies have confirmed that migration was selective of the young, the educated and the skilled. Concomitantly, only the old, the infirm, females and children were left in the rural areas. As a result of this, agriculture was being neglected. It was also not clear whether the remittances were reinvested in the land, whether new technology was being adopted to increase productivity, and the resources were not in fact being squandered in conspicuous consumption.

In urban areas, it was the migrants who were identified as representing a transfer of labour, creating an imbalance, and aggravating urban squalor. Thus migration from rural areas was identified as the cause of the malady and remedies adopted accordingly. Migration had to be curtailed because it was degrading the city and depleting the rural countryside of its resources, while some claimed the reverse.

In fact, the urban areas were getting serviced cheaply and also that rural areas were benefiting from migration. However, the previous negative view of the opportunities of migrants in their place of destination, problems in adjusting to all urban environment and culture, etc., has been altered in the light of new evidence. Migrants have been able to increase their welfare as a result of migration, in spite of adjustment difficulties and urban unemployment. A positive effect of the resource and information inflow due to migration is enhancing land productivity at the rural end.

In Dhaka, few of the migrants are really prospering in the city, but some continue to have a harsh existence while some also return. Of those who remain in the city, the majority lead marginal lives in slums and squatter settlements, and the minority on pavements. For the former, their temporary structures are congested and unsanitary, lacking adequate supplies of electricity, running water, paved roads and means of garbage disposal.

Migration rates in excess of growth of urban job opportunities are not only possible but also rational and probable in the face of expected large positive urban-rural income differentials. The points of relevance are the two italicised phrases, known to the potential migrants and expected large positive urban-rural income differentials. Many studies have found that migrants have taken high risks and based their migration decisions upon information which is imperfect. Unrealistic aspirations and poor information on urban unemployment are important factors which could be overcome by efforts to disseminate information on urban labour markets in rural schools and villages.

That many migrants have been successful is not being refuted, nor the fact that migrants possess some expectations. Simultaneously, there are also migrants who are living marginal lives in the city and who will continue to survive in the city rather than go back to the village. However, whatever their motivations, some anticipated level of returns from migration which we will call expectations must have existed. Migrants to the streets of Dhaka were found to be cognisant of better life-chances in the urban areas, given the context of unemployment, exploitation and natural calamities in the rural areas.

The urban good life fails to touch a majority of the poorer migrants. There are migrant populations for whom the returns from migration are minimal. The most important reason for suspecting that there is a paradoxical situation among migrants is the evidence so frequently encountered—the poverty prevalent amongst squatter settlement dwellers and pavement dwellers of the city. They move from marginal farmer to marginal urban dweller, seeking out a subsistence in deplorable conditions. There are economically motivated migrants endowed with attributes of information, education or skills, young in age or able-bodied. Their choice to migrate is based upon their ability to succeed in the urban environment. In addition to these migrants, there are the distress migrants who are largely affected by external factors. These migrants move because their environmental and structural situation suggests that it is the only survival strategy. Whether attempting to avoid risk in the yearly crop or just underemployed, it is not a distinct choice of higher income but the immediate need for ready cash through any form of employment which impels them from the land. These migrants might initially join the ranks of the unemployed in the city for a short period.

The scope of defining the migrant population is narrowed by the primary criteria of the economic expectation—high expectations concomitant with higher income levels of the discerning, educated or skilled migrant. Lower levels of expectations exist and could be imagined if the reasons for migration could be broadened to include social, physical, and political reasons as well. Migrants could be motivated by economic reasons but not necessarily only rural-urban income differentials. Once committed to the urban way of life, convinced of benefits in the long term, having little to return to, they then opt for the poverty of the city farther than the poverty of the village.

International migration for employment and inflow of remittances from the nationals working abroad have been major catalysts in the growth and development of various activities in Bangladesh during the past decades. Intrigued by job situation at home and allured by high income and better living conditions abroad more than a million Bangladeshis have so far migrated abroad on employment dispersed across different parts of the world. Overseas remittances, the most tangible aspect of international migration for employment are now the most important sources of disposable income for thousands of migrant households and one of the most important sources of foreign exchange for the country.

The process of migration of Bangladeshis has long been in operation. During the 1940s there were already Bangladeshis, people from the geographical area now called Bangladesh, who migrated and settled in the port cities of London. After the Second World War, a large number of Bangladeshis migrated to the UK on employment.

The mass exodus of people for overseas employment, however, took place during the mid-70s during which time the Middle East emerged as the major destination of migration for employment. With an initial stock of about 6,000 nationals working in the region until 1976, gross migration to the region rose to 816,877 as of December 1990. Compared to the annual flow of about 5,559 in 1976, the level of flow of migration to the region was as high as 101,563 in 1990. Of the 13 Middle Eastern countries importing manpower from Bangladesh only eight of them account for almost the whole of migration to the region. These are Bahrain, Iraq, Kuwait, Libya, Oman, Qatar, and the UAE.

During 1977-1990, of the total gross migration of 811,318 to the whole of the Middle East, more than 98 per cent went to these eight countries. Among the individual countries the kingdom of Saudi Arabia stands up as the most important importer of labour from Bangladesh, accounting for about 38 per cent of the total migration to the region so far. This is followed by the UAE 14 per cent, and Oman 12 per cent. The migrants comprise mostly unskilled and semi-skilled workers and the relative share of those who could be classified as professionals and semi-professionals. The latter accounted for hardly six per cent of the migrants going to the Middle East during the period 1977-1990.

Table 5.1
Migration of Bangladeshis to the Middle East

Year / period	*No.of migrants*	*Yearly average*
upto 1976	5,559	5,559
1977-80	92,191	23,048
1981-84	2,32,600	58,150
1985-88	2,86,817	71,704
1989	98,147	98,147
1990	101,563	101,563
1977-90	8,16,877	57,951

Bangladeshis living in UK have been estimated at 136,000 as of 1982. This is based on an estimation of the initial stock of Bangladesh's population of 70,000 by the 1971 Population Census of Great Britain. Added to this has been a natural increase of about 29,000 over the base population. Between 1973 and 1982 a total of 32,000 Bangladeshis were allowed to enter into the UK and remain there. Although new entrance into UK has now been almost stopped, it is, however, still being allowed to the dependents and spouses of those who have already settled in that country. Assuming that new entrants have maintained the same pace during the 1980s as before as dependents are still migrating to the UK, the number of Bangladeshis currently living in UK would be near about the mark of 200,000.

Occupational distribution of Bangladeshis in UK could be grouped under three broad categories: (i) skilled, semi-skilled and unskilled, (ii) semi-professionals, and (iii) professionals. Added to these are also different types of self-employment, and miscellaneous other occupations. Alongside migrating to UK, a large number of Bangladeshis have also been migrating to the major Western European countries such as West Germany, Sweden and Norway. Then there are the United States of America and Canada where, it is believed, there is a large contingent of Bangladeshi nationals. In the East, Japan has lately emerged as an important destination of Bangladeshi workers.

Table 5.2

Number of Bangladeshi immigrants in the UK

Year	*Population at beginning of the period*	*Natural Increase*	*New Entrants*	*Total*
1971	70,000	1,820	—	71,820
1972	71,820	1,867	—	73,687
1973	73,687	1,916	1,689	77,292
1974	77,292	2,010	763	8,90,065
1975	80, 065	2,082	2,978	85,125
1976	85,125	2,213	3,680	91,018
1977	91,018	2,366	2,980	96,364
1978	96,364	2,505	4,040	1,02,909
1979	1,02,909	2,676	3,690	1,09,275
1980	1,09,275	2,841	5,000	1,17,116
1981	1,17,116	3,045	5,620	1,25,781
1982	1,25,781	3,270	7,620	1,35,871

Beginning from the early 1980s, taking the advantage of visa at the port of entry, and in the guise of tourists and business, many young Bangladeshis entered into Japan and took up jobs. Given job prospects and high remunerations on the one hand, and lack of serious restrictions on the part of the employers to appoint foreign workers, on the other hand, the number of those migrating to Japan increased significantly until visa requirement was introduced in March 1989.

The overall trend of migration from Bangladesh would seem to be quite positive. This is reflected in the current level of migration to the Middle East, and an increasing presence of nationals in other parts of the world. The latent enterprising qualities of migrants are responsible for the discovery of newer places of migration and innovation of ways and means to migrate to these places even though not always on legal basis.

The most important factors behind migration is economic motives. Overseas remittances are the major sources of disposable income for thousands of migrant households, and of foreign exchange for the country. Bangladesh earned a total of Taka 178 billion as remittances from nationals working aboard during the period 1977 to 1990. This is equivalent to US $6.4 billion. The level of remittances received by Bangladesh as early as in 1977 was Taka 866 million, equivalent to US $56 million. This grew to Taka 16 billion, US $637 million, in 1983. In 1990 overseas remittances reached the level of Taka 27 billion which was equivalent to US $774 million.

Middle East and Western Europe are the two major sources of remittances to Bangladesh. The relative share of these two regions of the total remittances went through significant changes over time. The Western countries would account for more than three-fourths of the remittances flowing into Bangladesh as early as in 1977. As of 1997-99, overseas remittances were equivalent to about 56 per cent of the export receipts: one quarter of the import payment and 46 per cent of the current account deficits. They were equivalent to five per cent of the gross domestic product. Remittances received during 1987-88 were 3.5 times higher than the Annual Development Programme (ADP) allocation for industrial development in that year, nine times higher than the allocation for agriculture.

The official statistics cover only that portion of the savings of nationals working abroad coming into the country through the institutional channels—cash remittances through banks and post offices. Excluded from these flows are remittances flowing into the country through the unofficial channels either in cash form or in the forms of goods and services. Accordingly there are leakages in the flow of remittances giving an underestimation of their actual level.

Table 5.3

Importance of overseas remittances

Macro parameters	*(Remittances as percentage of)* Year 1980-81	1984-85	1987-88
GDP	3.16	3.31	4.76
GDS	136.11	67.64	83.81
Export earnings	53.96	43.94	55.75
Import payments	16.62	16.88	25.06
Balance of trade deficit	23.02	27.42	45.51
Tax revenue	110.43	482.84	273.52
Non-tax revenue	110.43	482.84	273.52
Total current revenue	26.25	15.86	22.55

Developmental potentials of international migration could be seen from the need and scope for use of remittances for various productive purposes. This refers to the use of remittances for purposes having the prospects to generate income and/or employment. The success out of migration should be reflected in the capacity of a migrant to enhance his living standard, actual or potential, during the post-migration period as compared to previously. This will presuppose, first, generation of some surplus out of overseas employment—over and above the costs of migration and, secondly, acquisition of assets having the prospects of yielding a return in the future.

The development potentials of overseas remittances can be seen in terms of their contribution to the resource base of the country and their potentials for the growth and development of different sectors. Bangladesh has been earning in recent years on an average Taka 2,500 crores per year as remittances from the nationals working abroad. If even half of these could be saved and invested, the corresponding level of investment would come to Taka 1,250 crores per year.[13] The need for productive use of remittances could be seen further from the adverse consequences of the non-productive use of the same.

Unscrupulous consumption out of overseas remittances has been alleged to be responsible for an inflationary pressure in the localities where there is concentration of migrant household. This adversely effects the purchasing power of the non-migrant families, and the distribution of income as between migrant and non-migrant families. The most important non-consumption of remittances are construction and development of houses, purchases of land, machinery and transport equipment wedding and festivals and education of children. Construction and development of houses account for 19 per cent of the remittances received by the migrant households. The second most important use of remittances both in absolute and relative terms is the purchase of land.

A very small proportion of the remittances received by migrant households are used for purposes which can truly be labelled as productive. Purchase of land is seen by most of the migrant households as accumulation of assets with more of social value—a status symbol rather than to boost agricultural production. Based on the experiences of the returned migrants from Iraq and Kuwait following the Middle East crisis, most of these families can hardly depend on their accumulated assets out of remittances to supplement their income in case of an emergency.

Since most of the migrants spend a significant proportion of their overseas savings to purchase agricultural land, there is much scope for using overseas remittances for improving irrigation facilities, use of modern technologies, and mechanisation of agricultural activities such as ploughing, spraying, threshing, etc.

Small scale rural industries could include rice mills, flour mills, grinding spices, bread and biscuit factories, poultry farms, ice-cream making, and rural transport equipments such as rickshaw, carts, boat, etc.

In rural service industries one could think of three major areas for investment. These are services required in relation to agricultural activities, construction and development of houses and social activities.

The first category of services include renting of agricultural equipments such as irrigation pumps, power tillers, threshers, weeders, sprayers, etc. The second category of services include contractors and planners for the construction of houses in rural areas. The third category of services include catering for social occasions such as marriage, festivals, receptions commonly known as decorating services.

Beyond running road and river transport networks there are also ample scope for establishing workshops, garages, shipyards, assembling and manufacturing of transport vehicles. Investment in industry could provide the greatest opportunity for utilising a significant proportion of overseas remittances.

Use of remittances for productive purposes would depend on three sets of issues, viz.,

i) socio-economic background of a household,

ii) geographical location of a household, and

iii) existing government policies as pertaining to savings and investment.

The first set of issues affecting the alternative use of remittances refer to household characteristics which influence accumulation out of remittances and prudent use of the accumulation made out of remittances. The second set of factors relate to the locational characteristics of a household. Most important among these is the availability of infrastructural facilities such as good communication, electricity, banking and financial institutions, and marketplace.

Accordingly, migrant households living in towns and cities would have a greater prospect of using their remittances for various productive purpose as compared to their rural counterparts. All these will need to be complemented by appropriate public policies geared to productive use of remittances. Appreciation of the society of the need to mobilise the resources generated by overseas remittances for various productive purposes and measures taken in this direction should underline productive use of the same.

Policies taken by the government having some hearing with international migration, and inflow and use of remittances may be divided into five major groups as depending on the objective of such policies. These are policies geared to:

i) legal basis for overseas employment;
ii) institutional development;
iii) market development;
iv) workers' protection and welfare measures; and
v) maximisation of remittances.

The existing government policies emphasise on enhancing the flow of nationals abroad on employment, and channelising their earnings through the official or institutional channels. The question of productive use of remittances has received very little attention of the policy makers. The very few policies geared to channelising overseas remittances into productive ventures such as the wage earners development bond, investment from remittances free from government restrictions, etc., have very little popularity among the migrants and the respective families.

The core of any planning exercise should be in maximising the benefits from remittances. Three types of policies would be appropriate here:

i) those designed to motivate the individual migrants or the respective families to use their remittances for productive purposes by themselves;
ii) direct use of remittances by the government; and
iii) mobilisation of the surpluses generated by remittances for various productive purposes.

The migrants should be made aware of the need and the alternative avenues for investment available in the country through mass media and financial institutions. Counselling facilities by financial and specialised organisations about alternative investment opportunities, and problems and solutions in the way of investment in different sectors and areas should be made available. Provisions of basic infrastructures such as electricity, gas, road communication, marketplaces, financial instructions, etc., in areas where there is a concentration of migrant household would greatly encourage the migrants to invest remittances for various productive purposes.[14]

Training could be provided to those who would like to make productive investments, in areas such as project appraisal, maintenance of accounts, identification of investment opportunities, by specialised agencies both in the public and the private sector.

The government could take up investment projects on its own and later sell them to a group of migrants.[15] The ownership of such establishments could be jointly between the government and the representative of the migrants. Popularisation of the various means of portfolio investment, available in the country such as defence savings certificate, investment Corporation of Bangladesh certificate, with an extension of the services of the organisations involved therein in the areas where there is a concentration of migrant households is necessary. Establishment of a specialised financial institution should be aimed at recycling overseas remittances to prospective investors within the country.

Despite the development potentials of overseas remittances to generate income and employment in the country, policy interest in this regard has been quite low. This underlines the inability of those who are in the helm of decision making in the country to duly appreciate the latent potentials of overseas remittances. A greater utilisation of overseas remittances for productive purpose would presuppose awareness building among the migrant households about the need, creation of politico-economic environment encouraging investment outlays, and adoption of appropriate policy commensurate with the socio-economic background of the migrants.

REFERENCES

1. *Board of Investment, Guide to Investment in Bangladesh*, Prime Minister's Office, Dhaka, March 1998, pp. 53-54.
2. Ibid.
3. *Outlook*, New Delhi, June 19, 1996.
4. Government of Bangladesh, *The Fifth Five Year Plan,* 1997-2002.
5. Ibid.
6. *Hindustan Times*, New Delhi, July 3, 2000.
7. *Outlook,* New Delhi, December 9, 1997.
8. *The Economic Times,* New Delhi, December 9, 1997.

9. *Regional Studies, Rohingya Refugees in Bangladesh: Their Impact on Regional Stability,* November, 1993.
10. Ibid.
11. *The Political Economy of Bangladesh—Perspective and Trends, Regional Studies,* January, 1995.
12. Ibid.
13. Ibid.
14. SAARC, *Sub-regionalism and Bangladesh, Regional Studies,* September 1997.
15. Ibid.

6

Migration in Sri Lanka

From the mid-19th century, Sri Lanka faced a steady stream of immigrants, mainly from South India linked to the British economic activity that prevailed at the time. In the 1830's British enterprises developed coffee plantations in the hill country of then Ceylon. Later towards the end of the 19th century rubber plantations were also opened in the midlands and the low country areas of the country.

All this hectic economic activity necessitated an extensive and cheap labour force which Sri Lanka could not provide at that time. The most practical alternative was to obtain this requirement from nearby South India, which had a surfeit of cheap unskilled labour, ideally suited for the Sri Lankan plantations. Several factors subscribed to this unprecedented migration. The principal advantage was proximity. Travel facilities were unrestricted, at least until Sri Lanka gained independence in 1948 and difficulties arose over the preponderance of South Indian Tamils in the majority of the estates.

Almost the entire South Indian labour force was Hindu by religion and were part of the joint family system which prevails in several parts of India. These workers left behind part of their families in South India and they were often obliged to send regular remittances to their dependents back home and invariably a substantial part of their savings were repatriated. They even undertook journeys to visit their with and kin periodically. The short journey involved also suited the British plantation managers as in the event of any depression in the industry some of the estate workers could be asked to return.

Conversely, in the event of any economic distress in South India due to drought, crop failure or famine the scale of South Indian immigration would substantially increase. Therefore, what emerged at the very inception of South Indian immigrations was that the Indian estate workers lived a life of isolation in separate estate communities, cut off from all contacts with the surrounding Sinhala villages and never participating in their political and social life.[1]

After their independence, both countries decided to reform the Constitution. The first controversy arose during this reform which was based on the recommendations of the Donoughmore Commission which had proposed that a semi-responsible form of government based on adult franchise be introduced in Sri Lanka and that all existing forms of separate communal representation be abolished. Sinhala leaders had difficulties with the franchise question as it was feared that the introduction of universal adult franchise would lead to the unrestricted enfranchisement of Indian residents in Sri Lanka. The second critical development was the depression in the early 1930's which seriously affected the plantations and created problems of severe unemployment.[2] Sinhala leaders were firmly convinced that this was mainly due to the practice of free immigration from South India and throughout the 1930's began to exert sustained pressure in the State Council, as the Sri Lankan parliament was then known, for the curtailment of estate labour immigration.

When independence was achieved by both countries, the stage was set for a major confrontation between the two countries over this contentious issue often involving the Prime Ministers themselves. It is interesting to take note of the series of meetings that took place between the two countries during this period to try to ease this problem. The first was the Indo-Ceylon Relations Exploratory Conference in November 1940 followed by the Indo-Ceylon Conference in September

1941.[3] Then followed an important meeting at the Prime Ministerial level between Pandit Nehru and Prime Minister Senanayake in 1947.[4] This was mainly concerned with two questions. Firstly, who among the 80,000 Indian residents in Sri Lanka should be considered eligible for Sri Lankan citizenship and, secondly, how they should be admitted to such citizenship and what criteria should be adopted. The Ceylon Citizenship Act provided for two types of citizenship, by descent and by registration. The provisions relating to citizenship by descent applied mainly to indigenous Sri Lankans and very few Indian residents could claim citizenship by registration with its rigid residence prerequisites.

On the other hand, the Indian and Pakistani Residents Act of 1949 laid down somewhat less restrictive conditions for the grant of citizenship to the Indian community. Basically an applicant for registration under this Act had to possess the special residential qualification of continued residence in Sri Lanka before 1 January 1946, of seven years for married persons, 10 years for others, occasional absence from the Island for less than one year not being deemed a break in the continuity of residence. In addition he was required to possess an assured income of a reasonable amount and prove that no disability rendered it impossible for him to comply with the laws of Sri Lanka. If married, his wife and dependent children should have been resident with him in Sri Lanka during the qualifying period of residence required by the Act. India's reaction to the Act was very adverse and Pandit Nehru in his correspondence with Prime Minister D. S. Senanayake in 1948 found the Citizenship Act unacceptable. In fact, the process of registration and investigation of applications became so slow and tedious that even by 1962 only 134,188 Indians had been granted citizenship under this Act.[5]

It was only in the 1950's that the aspect of 'statelessness' crept to this problem. From the very outset Sri Lanka's assumption, as enuniciated at the highest levels, was that those Indians who had failed to qualify for Sri Lankan citizenship were unquestionably Indian nationals and the Indian government would regard them as such. The Government of India was clearly unwilling to accept this position. Although India had not passed a specific citizenship law until 1955 the Indian Constitution had made provision for acquisition of Indian nationality by overseas Indians under Article 5 of the Indian Constitution which stated categorically that only a person born in India, or one of whose parents was born in India or a person who had been ordinarily resident in India for over five years prior to the inauguration of the Indian Constitution would be regarded as an Indian citizen. Under Article 8, persons of Indian origin ordinarily resident outside India would be regarded as Indian citizens only if they were registered as such after application to the Diplomatic Representative of India in the country where such persons resided.[6]

In Sri Lanka, apart from the question of unemployment, there were increasing demands, mainly by the members of the Kandan community that the Indian workers were depriving them of their legitimate livelihood in the plantations. This was also frequently taken up in parliament. On the Indian side was the situation that the Indian estate workers mainly hailed from South India and if repatriated would eventually have to be resettled there. This was a problem which the centre in New Delhi could not unilaterally decide on without consulting the southern states, and centre-state relations in India have always been bedevilled by such problems. Another cogent reason, which in fact Pandit Nehru explained to Prime Minister S.W.R.D. Bandarnaike, was that there were over 12 million Indians overseas in countries such as Malaya, Myanmar and South Africa and if India accepted the principle of repatriation as advocated by Sri Lanka the same concession would have to be extended to the Indian nationals in these countries.

The first realistic appraisal towards these problems took place at the high level meeting on the Indo-Ceylon Agreement relating to persons of Indian origin in Ceylon. For the first time at this meeting, illicit immigration between the two countries was taken up by the two Prime Ministers as part of this question. The Sri Lankan government continued to maintain that only two categories of Indian residents in Sri Lanka would emerge as a result of the Agreement, nationals of Sri Lanka and nationals of India. The Indian government envisaged a third category of 'stateless persons' in addition to these two whose status would have to be further reviewed by the two governments.

After further debate and disagreement between the two governments the Prime Minister of India, Lal Bahadur Shastri and the Sri Lankan Prime Minister, Sirimavo Bandaranaike, inspired by a mutual desire to explore every possibility of reaching an equitable compromise on this vexatious question of persons of Indian origin in Sri Lanka finally held a historic meeting in New Delhi in October 1964. The agreement concluded on October 30, 1964 between the Governments of India and Sri Lanka provided that India would agree to accept, within a period of 15 years, as repatriates, 525,000 persons of Indian origin living in Sri Lanka with their natural increase, and that Sri Lanka would agree to grant citizenship to 300,000 persons with their natural increase.[7] This agreement also provides for a further supplementary agreement to grant citizenship of one or the other country to the balance of 150,000 stateless persons of Indian origin.

The agreement aimed at enabling all stateless persons of Indian origin in Sri Lanka to become citizens of one country or the other. The period of repatriation was phased over a 17 year period so that, on the one hand, Sri Lanka would not be faced with a large exodus of plantation labour if the timeframe was shorter and, on the other hand, India would not be faced with the problem of rehabilitating a large number of repatriates within a short period. Despite the sincere and intensive effort on the part of both governments to fulfil the terms of the agreement there was ultimately an excess in the number of applicants for Sri Lankan citizenship and a shortfall in the number who applied for Indian citizenship.

Therefore, in the final count, 94,000 persons were reckoned to be in this category, who would have to be deemed stateless. In a spirit of accommodation and in a desire to strengthen bilateral relations Sri Lanka generously accepted this additional commitment of 94,000 persons which meant that Sri Lanka's eventual intake was 469,000 persons.[8] On the other hand, India gave an undertaking that they would grant Indian citizenship to all of the 506,000 persons who have applied for citizenship and repatriate them to India. This process is yet underway.

Until the beginning of the 19th century, stateless persons of South Indian origin did not encounter too many problems.[9] Mostly illiterate, they led a life of comparative isolation in their rather frugal estate quarters, with the estates also providing minimum facilities for children's schooling, health care and other needs. However, they were content as their basic need of repatriating a part of their saving back to the rest of their families in South India and even periodic visits to their kith and kin were freely permitted. In later years, with increasing resistance and even some hostility to their continuing presence in the plantations by mainly the Kandyan Sinhala community which was status, undoubtedly made their lives less comfortable.

This was the time when there was progressive 'Ceylonisation' not only of employment but also of trade and industry. This was officially described as a process "to ensure a higher percentage of participation by the nationals of the country in trade, commerce and industrial activities, as regards management, labour and finance". However, this did not materially affect the South Indian community which more or less confined itself to the plantation sector. However, by the 1960's and 1970's, when the Indo/Ceylon Agreements of 1964 and 1974 had more or less settled the 'Stateless' problem, the situation of the Indians in Sri Lanka, particularly of those who had since been conferred Sri Lankan citizenship, was completely normalised and they were treated not differently to those Sri Lankans who had acquired citizenship by descent.[10]

The Ceylon Indian Congress (CIC) was founded way back in 1939 to protect the interests of the Indian estate workers in Sri Lanka. Incidentally, Pandit Nehru visited Sri Lanka in 1939 as a special emissary of the Indian National Congress, and he was considered as one of the founders of the CIC. Perhaps due to the circumstances of its origin the CIC long retained marked signs of Indian influence. The successful settlement of what might have been a continuing stateless problem between Sri Lanka and India was indeed a triumph for statesmanship at the highest level.

After so many decades of difficult and often acrimonious debate over this question, an agreement was finally reached between the two governments at the highest level in a spirit of compromise that was indeed a good example of how the self-interests of two countries, large and small, were made secondary to the larger interest of maintaining and strengthening good relations between two neighbours who had, up to that time, not known any other political problem in the long history of their cordial relationship.

In Sri Lanka, there is a total absence of provisions with regard to refugee protection. The laws governing immigration and emigration are silent on this subject. Neither the Controller of the Immigration and Emigration nor any other official possesses guidelines or authority to determine refugee status, to provide protection to asylum applicants and refugees or to enforce the principle of non-refoulement. Only the Extradition Law No:8 of 1977 marginally provides for this latter aspect by prohibiting the extradition of persons who may be persecuted on the basis of race, religion, nationality or political opinion.

As a member of the UN, Sri Lanka is obliged to respect the protections guaranteed by the Universal Declaration of Human Rights (1948). However, Article 14 of the Universal Declaration merely recognises the right of individuals to seek and to enjoy in other countries asylum from persecution. It does not delineate the obligation on the part of states to provide protection to refugees. The Convention against torture (1984) which was ratified by Sri Lanka in 1994 provides for the non-refoulement of persons to a country where the person would be in danger of being subjected to torture (Art 3). Although the parliament of Sri Lanka adopted a legislation to enforce the Convention, it does not contain provisions to enforce Article 3. In the absence of a legal framework of refugee protection, there appears to be an informal and *ad hoc* understanding between the Controller and the UNHCR to provide provisional protection to asylum seekers and those stranded.

The UNHCR as been informally permitted to take care of such persons exclusively at its expense and to make efforts towards their repatriation from Sri Lanka.[11] However, those who seek asylum cannot regularise their stay in Sri Lanka unless they can fulfil other legal recognised conditions for doing so. In the absence of grounds enabling them to do so, their stay in Sri Lanka, although protected by UNHCR, is technically illegal.

Under the Immigrants and Emigrants Ordinance of 1948 (Cap. 2458 as amended) an alien (other than those aliens who are exempted by the law), aside from possessing a valid passport, has to either obtain a visa or an endorsement by an authorised officer at the port of entry (Articles 10,13 &14). Where an airliner is obliged under ICA/IATA rules to take back passengers who are not admitted into the country, then such persons will be sent back, usually to the port of origin, without affording them an interview with the UNHCR at the airport. If, on other hand, an airline is not obliged to take those who are not admitted to Sri Lanka, the controller permits the UNHCR to interview persons so stranded if they request protection. If not, for this informal understanding between the Controller and the UNHCR, all those who are not admitted into the country and who are not accepted back by the airlines will be subjected to detention by the immigration authorities.

The UNHCR gets to know about persons needing protection from the airport immigration authorities, the detention centres at the request of the persons seeking protection or embassy staff and UNHCR officials who discover such persons at detention centres when checking the cases of others. The UNHCR states that the cooperation extended by the Controller in this regard is excellent. When the UNHCR takes over the persons seeking protection, UNHCR certificates are issued. They in effect operate as visas.

All the needs of those under its protection have to be borne by the UNHCR. If for some reason a person receiving protection has a visa, and it has to be extended under prevailing laws, UNHCR has to obtain that extension as well, utilising its resources. The UNHCR office in Colombo is able in some instances to make arrangements to resettle persons in its care in third countries through the embassies of those countries in Colombo. Examples are Canada, Australia and Switzerland. Aside from that process, the UNHCR submits cases to other countries through the resettlement unit of the division of International Protection at UNHCR headquarters. However, the available number of settlement places tends to be few given the worldwide need. Those who are facing threats to physical safety are medically at risk, are facing the danger of refoulement, or are members of vulnerable groups who receive priority in resettlement.

When compared with other countries in the subcontinent such as India and Pakistan, the number seeking protection in Sri Lanka is very small. Yet, the need for a legal refuge protection regime is palpable from a human rights and humanitarian perspective. If not for UNHCR intervention those who seek asylum or are stranded in Sri Lanka will be an unknown group of humanity left to wither in detention facing an extremely uncertain future. The irony is that India and Pakistan have received and continue to provide protection to thousands of asylum seekers, albeit without having legal provisions or process in place to determine refugee status and to provide for protection.

In Sri Lanka, what is essential is the creation of a social and political environment, through policies and educational activities, which is sympathetic to and respects the needs of refugees. The high intensity military for the retaking of the Jaffna Peninsula meant that the logistical systems that had been temporarily in place during the period of dual control for the transport and distribution of food and other supplies were initially disrupted. However, by June 1996 the government succeeded in effecting control over the entire Peninsula and security—transport, health, education and food distribution systems are improving in operation.[12]

The implications of changes in the political and economic environment is that the government's obligation of providing relief and rehabilitation to the displaced has become easier and more practicable to fulfil. Although precise information on numbers and the condition of the displaced in the Peninsula is difficult to come by on account of the prevailing tight censorship on news and movement of media personnel in the north, it can be presumed that as normalcy is restored the condition of the displaced will continue to improve. The work of UNHCR along with the ICRS, MSF and other international NGOs working in the northern province has been considerably disrupted as a result of the conflict in recent months and their services to the displaced have consequently been affected. UNHCRs activities in the fields, particularly after the liberation of Jaffna city by the military in February 1996, have been from Killinochchi but here too there have been restrictions on account of the delays in obtaining permission from the government, for high frequency radio transmitting facilities.

Security considerations of the government have taken precedence over considerations of providing facilities to UNHCR and other external agencies which would have had the effect of relieving, to some extent, urgent needs of the displaced. Along with this has come an increase including the UNHCR which has proved restraining in terms of the expansion of the role of UNHCR and other agencies. While this may be deemed a natural corollary to the sensitivity that can accompany a long, fluctuating and not wholly successful military campaign against the LTTE, the widespread attitude of not trusting external agencies could have deleterious effects on the ability of these agencies to continue the support they have been providing in protection and relief services to the internally displaced today and in the future.

In the period 1984 to 1991, one of the major issues was that of the possible spillover of the internally displaced to South India as refugees. Such movement in large numbers has potentially destabilising effects on the bilateral relations between India and Sri Lanka. It has been the cause of friction in the past and can bring a new dimension to interstate relations in the future. According to official reports there apparently still remain in camps in South India about 50,000 refugees from Sri Lanka who went out with the outbreak of hostilities in June 1990. These are those who are not included in the repatriation which was conducted with some monitoring by UNHCR in the years 1992-94.

In these years the outflow was minimal owing to possibly three reasons; firstly the fact that UNHCR, a neutral party, was present in a practical way in overseeing the return and resettlement of returning refugees, in the overview of conditions at welfare centres and had initiated, in 'Uncleared area' the concept of the Open Relief Centres (ORCs); secondly, the fact that the Jaffna Peninsula which was under the virtual control of the LTTE, constituted, at least for the Tamil internally displaced, a place of relative security; and thirdly, the fact that the then Tamil Nadu Government was strongly discouraging the entry of more Sri Lankan refugees.

Undoubtedly these emerging issues have also several implications for UNHCR's own role both as regards its protection of returning refugees when they are eventually repatriated and for those who remain internally displaced. Government officials are confident that the movement of refugees across the Palk Straits will subside since food convoys have begun reaching the large groups of displaced civilians now scattered in various parts of the LTTE-controlled Vanni. The strict controls imposed by the South Indian authorities on the intake of refugees may also deter their flight.

REFERENCES

1. *Regional Studies*, 'The Agony of Sri Lanka', December, 1987.
2. *Regional Studies*, 'Polls and Politics in Sri Lanka', January-February, 1984.
3. *Regional Studies*, 'The Tamil Factor: Genesis and Prospects of the Indian State in Sri Lanka', November-December, 1982.
4. *The Island*, May 27, 'Alleviating Lanka's Poverty', 1992.
5. *The Island*, February 27, 'Land, Landlessness and Poverty in Sri Lanka', 1989.
6. *Regional Studies*, 'Indo-Sri Lanka Relations, Retrospect, Problems and Prospects', April, 1986.
7. *Regional Studies*, 'Peace Process in Sri Lanka: Problems and Prospects', November-December, 1996.
8. Ibid.
9. *The Island*, May 22, 'Growth of NGO Sector in Sri Lanka Due to Open Economy and Ethnic Problems', 1991.
10. Ibid.
11. Central Bank of Sri Lanka, *Annual Report*, Colombo, 1998.
12. Perera, KKYW, 'Energy Issues and Alternatives', *Economic Review*, People's Bank, August 1996, p.7.

7

Migration into the Nepal Tarai

The problem of national integration vis-a-vis the Tarai has arisen because people from one cultural background have migrated into a region over which people of another cultural background have established political control. An impression is being created by certain quarters that a substantial section of the Tarai population consists of immigrants from India. But it is far from reality. Dor Bahadur Bista maintains that the majority of the Tarai people are indigenous.[1] R.D. Aajad states that the Tarai people are part and parcel of the Tarai land and they did not come from outside[2]. Shankar Lal Kedia presents a glorious picture of the Tarai community ever since the ancient times[3]. In fact, these people have always been there on this land, though it is a different question that sometimes they were under the rule of their own rulers, sometimes under the Mughal emperors, sometimes under the British East India Company; and now under the Nepalese rulers.

The fact that the Tarai people had their own identity is evidenced by the facts that they sometimes resisted against the British East India Company and sometimes against the Gorkha rulers.

The early history of the Tarai is a record of the ebb and flow of people. Kingdoms successively arose and disintegrated. People have been migrating into the tarai since the first Aryan tribesmen pushed eastward from the confluence of the Ganges and Jamuna Rivers around 900 B.C. During the period 900 to

500 B.C., the Aryans penetrated into what is now northern Uttar Pradesh and Bihar, and the powerful kingdom of Videha was established in northern Bihar and the eastern tarai. The capital of Videha was called Mithila, and it may have been located at the site of modern Janakpur in Dhanusha district of the eastern tarai. Janakpur, the centre of extensive ruins, is named after king Janak of Videha, who married his daughter Sita to the great king-god Rama of the Hindu epic, the *Ramayana*.

A line of less powerful rulers, the kings of Sakya, had their capital at Kapilavastu in the mid-western Tarai. The Buddha was born in about 563 B.C. to a Sakya king at Lumbini, near Kapilavastu. Ruins of the capital have been excavated by a team of Nepalese and Japanese archaeologists. In the tarai exist many other ruins which, when identified, will shed more light on the long and complex history of the region.

It appears that nearly all the settlers in early Tarai history were of Aryan or pre-Aryan indigenous stock. The ancient and medieval history of the region is a cyclical one in which men and forest have dominated in turns. From time to time, people from more settled parts of the Gangetic plain pushed back the forest, cleared the land, and established settlements that grew into kingdoms. When the kingdoms withered away because of natural calamities or war, the forest reclaimed the land.

Information about settlement in modern times comes from three sources—records of British East India Company officials, records of Nepalese government officials, and oral histories of the tarai villagers themselves. The British records, particularly the reports of Colonel William Kirkpatrick and Francis Hamilton, provide the earliest information. Kirkpatrick crossed the tarai at the head of an expedition to Kathmandu in 1793 and described the settlement pattern in what is now Bara and Parsa districts. He observed that the land was cleared and settled from the border north for about four miles and then partly cleared for another four or five miles. From these, dense and uninterrupted forest extended north to the Siwalik[4]. Hamilton found that a majority of the inhabitants of the eastern tarai were plains tribals, Tharus throughout and Rajbanshis, Mechis, and Gangais in the far eastern Tarai[5]. He reported that they practised slash-and burn cultivation, shifting their location every three or four years when the land lost its fertility. Although the land fell into disuse, it was not reclaimed by the forest because of continual grazing by herds of cows and buffaloes driven north from India during the dry season of Ahirs and other caste Hindus.

The Nepali-speaking Sen kings of Palpa and Makwanpur gained control of the mid-western tarai in the fifteenth or sixteenth century and extended their control to the eastern Tarai around the mid-seventeenth century. They looked upon the dense, malarial tarai forests as a defence against invasion from India and, therefore, did not encourage settlement. Instead, they drew tarai revenue from logging, the trapping and selling of elephants, and taxing the seasonal posturing of cattle. The Shah kings wrested the eastern tarai from the Sen kings in the 1770s and permitted some settlement[6].

Still it was not until the 1860s that those who controlled the tarai[7] felt that the region had lost its utility as a defence perimeter and that diplomacy was a more effective defence against increased British intervention. For its military assistance to the British during the Indian Mutiny 1857-58, Nepal received the title to the far-western tarai territory that the British had taken away from Nepal during the Anglo-Nepali war of 1814-16. Jung Bahadur Rana, the founder of the line of hereditary Rana Prime Ministers, immediately began to encourage settlement in the far-western tarai and in other parts of the tarai as well. For example, he promised to grant the status of free men to all Nepali slaves who would settle there[8]. Details of the new government policy are included in government documents of the period[9].

The policy of settling the tarai was not solely the result of more stable and friendly relations between the Nepalis and the British following the mutiny. It was also due to population pressure and the expansion of the economy throughout the subcontinent, accompanied by rising prices and a need for increased revenue to finance the government and to purchase goods in India for the nobility. Revenue could be increased most readily by expanding logging operations and agricultural activity in the tarai. Since logging and clearing land for farming went hand in hand, settlers moved in large numbers to forested areas, encouraged by promises of land ownership and low tax rates.

Generally speaking, the oldest continually inhabited villages in the tarai are those established near a religious site such as Sita's birthplace at Janakpur or near a fort of some long-forgotten king. Still other villages grew up around customs posts, public stations, or rest stations along trade routes between the plains and the hills. Early settlements were also cut out of the forest along riverbeds which, during the dry season, furnished broad, flat roads for travel through the dense jungle plains. Hindus and Muslims were settled within the last eight to 10 generations ago.

The treaty of peace and friendship concluded between Nepal and India is 1950 also provided the Indian nationals the right of ownership of property and the right to participate in trade and commerce. Article VII of this treaty states, "The Governments of India and Nepal agree to grant, on a reciprocal basis, to the nationals of one country in the territories of the other the same privileges in the matter of residence, ownership of property, participation in trade and commerce, movement and other privileges of a similar nature[10]. In order to make the provision of Article VII of the Treaty of Peace and Friendship null and void, the Panchayat Government imposed strict 'citizenship' laws. Accordingly, no Indian national could buy land or enter into any economic or commercial activity in Nepal[11]. Having imposed the citizenship rule strictly, it became easier for the Panchayat Government to restrict the prospective flow of Indian migrants in Nepal.

In Nepal, it was mainly from the 1950s that the migration of population started from the hills to the tarai. Factors like population pressure, scarcity of arable land, limited food production, underemployment/unemployment and indebtedness in the hills were some of the push factors responsible for the migration of the population to the tarai. On the other hand, apart from the eradication of malaria, planned resettlement, government incentives and prospect of employment opportunities were some of the pull factors that encouraged migration to the tarai.

Efforts were also made to encourage the migration of population from the hills to the tarai at the institutional level. The Rapti Valley Development Plan (RVDP) in the year 1954 was the first such resettlement project introduced in the Rapti Valley in Chitwan district of the tarai. At the time when RVDP was introduced there were 36,000 indigenous Tharus in the valley. But within a few years in 1967, the population of the valley grew tenfold[12]. The success of RVDP led HMG/N to increase the number of resettlement projects significantly.

In 1964, the Nepal Resettlement Company (NRC) was established to execute the planned resettlement. Accordingly, many resettlement projects were set up in different parts of the taral. The Department of Resettlement of HMG/N distributed land and foodgrains to the migrants in the resettlement areas. Land was made available to these people free of cost in the beginning and at a nominal price in the later stage. Additionally, education, health and other facilities were also provided.

Those who could not be given land by NRC and the Department of Resettlement of HMG/N, cleared the forest illegally and settled there as squatters. At the time when 77,700 hectares of forest land in the tarai was distributed among migrants, additional 237,600 hectares of forest land was encroached upon illegally[13]. Thus, the informal encroachment of forest was nearly thrice the formal clearance of the forest. Subsequently, between 1973 and 1979 the Department of

Resettlement distributed 34,771 hectares of land among the migrants.

At present, six resettlement projects are being run: Jhapa Resettlement Project, Sarlahi Resettlement Project, Nawalparasi Resettlement Project, Taratal Resettlement Project, Kailali Resettlement Project and Kathmandu Resettlement Project. All these resettlement projects were established by clearing the dense forest land. Apart from the hill migrants, the refugees from Burma, Assam and other places were also made to settle there; on the other hand, the landless people in the tarai were rarely given any land in such resettlement projects.

A committee was also formed under the Chairmanship of late Prime Minister the Tank Prasad Acharya, to recommend the names of the political victims with the view to providing them land in the tarai. Accordingly, many politicians and hill elites in the same of 'political victims' were allotted land in Nawalparasi, Sarlahi and other districts by clearing the forest land.

Above all, HMG/N set up Ban Sudridhikaran Aayojana (Forest Strengthening Project) at a political level in various districts of the tarai under the chairmanship of a member of National Panchayat. The members of this project were given powers and privileges to find out barren and unclaimed land with the purpose of distributing it among the squatters. Until 1990, the project received thousands of applications from the so-called squatters every year and accordingly the land was distributed among them almost free of cost. In the name of squatters, only those cunning applicants who had access to Kathmandu's power circles were given land.

Many unscrupulous elements in the name of squatters encroached and destroyed the forest and declared such land as barren or unclaimed. This had a demonstration effect. Encroachment of the forest land developed as a profession. After establishing claim over the forest land at one place, the encroachers sold it and moved to another district for the same job. This process continued unabated.

At places the land along the banks of the rivers was treated as an unclaimed land. Even the public places of the native villagers were declared as unclaimed land. Such native communities as Rajbanshis/Tharus who tilled land for generations without bothering to register it with the government were evicted from the ownership of land and property. This also created a problem of pasture land and environment.

Following the introduction of the Land Reforms Act 1964 in the country, land above the fixed ceiling was acquired by HMG/N. But the local landless tarai people were denied of their share in this land.

In fact, protecting forest land was hardly anyone's business. During the National Referendum in 1980 alone, the forest wood amounting to Rs. one billion was destroyed[14].

In the early 1980s, HMG/N constituted a committee under the chairmanship of Harka Bahadur Gurung to study the internal and international migration of population in Nepal. This committee failed to recommend measures to control migration and reduce the magnitude of environmental degradation. Instead, it recommended to destroy the remaining forest south and east-west highway and convert it into an agricultural land. It also suggested to encourage further migration of population there. It was equally faulty on the part of this committee to recommend that multi-entry permit/single-entry permit system and passport system should be introduced for the tarai community so as to restrict their movement between Nepal and India[16]. The tarai intellectuals strongly opposed such ideas and consequently they could not be implemented[17].

Migration of the population has created imbalances in the tarai. As a result, many of the native people are forced to migrate outside in search of jobs during certain seasons. There are also people who migrate and settle in India permanently.

Until the 1970s, there had been a seasonal migration of population from the adjoining regions of Bengal, Bihar and Uttar Pradesh states of India to the tarai. The Indian labourers helped to cultivate and harvest agricultural crops. But the labourers from across the border stopped coming to Nepal because of the new development opportunities in several parts of India, particularly in Punjab and Haryana states. Now this process is reversed. It is the tarai labourers from almost all the districts of the tarai who now go to the different parts of India including Punjab and Haryana states in certain seasons for employment mainly in the agricultural sector. The wages earned by the tarai labourers in India is higher than what they could usually get in Nepal.

Not all settlement is unplanned nor do government officials make public statements about their interest in Nepalisation of the tarai through resettlement of hill people there. Such statements would a confirm the government's discomfort about the predominance of plains people in the region, would invite the Indian government to express similar attitudes toward the large number of Nepalis living in India and would add another serious irritant to the always sensitive relations between the two countries. The only publicly stated evidence that some people in Kathmandu endorse resettlement for political purposes appears occasionally in Kathmandu newspaper columns suggesting that Gurkha soldiers retired from the British, Indian and Nepalese armies be settled along the border as a paramilitary force to prevent smuggling detrimental to Nepal and to prevent raids by bandit gangs from India[18]. The Gurkhas, being hill people, are assumed to be more loyal to the government than others who might settle along the border.

One Nepalese newspaper, noted for its public support of plains people, has charged that the main object of the government's policy to settle ex-servicemen and other hill people in the tarai during the past 10 years has been to change the cultural composition of the population so that the plains people will find themselves in a minority. The paper warned that this would encourage 'communal tension' and suggested that the government avoid this by providing landless plains people of the tarai with an opportunity to resettle on forest land[19].

The Resettlement Department is responsible for migration and destruction of forest in the tarai. A government publication shows that 90 per cent of the resettlements have been developed by the Resettlement Department in the tarai alone, which used to be thick forest land. By 1927, a little less than half of the tarai land was covered with forest. But by 1977 the percentage of forest land reduced to a fifth of its total area[20]. Between 1977 and 1992, i.e., during 15 years, there is hardly any thick forest left anywhere except in the national parks. It has been accepted in a government publication that the migration of population from the hills to the tarai encouraged deforestation and encroachment on state lands in the tarai and for the short run at least, has taxed the economic and social service sector[21].

The migration of population from the hills to the tarai has raised regional, ethnic, and political issues. Tensions prevail between local tarai people and migrants, though on a limited scale now. There have also been occasions when the tarai people protested against the migration and also the state policies which support this trend. One of the government publications states, "The protest against the 'Gurung Report' by a substantial section of the eastern tarai population was, principally, a protest against the in-migration of the pahadis and the state policies which encourage such in migration".[22]

A long-term plan should be envisaged to discourage further migration of population from the hills to the tarai. Whenever possible the tarai squatter and landless people should also be accommodated in the existing resettlements. This is not only justified on the moral ground but also on the ground of maintaining national unity.

REFERENCES

1. Bista, Dor Bahadur,. *Fatalism and Development: Nepal's Struggle for Modernisation,* Orient Longman Limited, Hyderabad. 1991, p.49.
2. Aajad, R.D., *Tarai Jal Rahi Hai* (Hindi), 1992, Kathmandu.

3. Kedia, Shankar Lal, *Madhesiya Samaj aur Uski Utpatti* (Hindi), Nepal Tarai Vidyarthi Bhasa Sanskriti Samanwya Samiti, Kathmandu, 1991, pp.1-23.

4. Kirkpatrick William, *An Account of the Kingdom of Nepal*, London, 1981, pp. 12-16.

5. Hamilton Francis, *An Account of the Kingdom of Nepal* Edinburgh, 1819, pp. 156-164.

6. *Ibid*, pp. 64, 131-132.

7. By this time the Rana Prime Minister of Kathmandu: the Shah Kings still reigned but the Ranas had gained control over them and exercised their power.

8. Nepali, Chittaranjan "Nepal Ma Kariya Mochan Ko Itihas", *Nepali XX* July-September, 1964. pp. 10-11.

9. Nepal, Department of Land Revenue, *Administrative Regulations for Tarai Districts*, 1810, 5 Volumes, Trans. by Regmi Research Project, 1967.

10. *Treaty of Peace and Friendship*, Kathmandu, July 31, 1950,

11. Baral, Lok Raj, *Regional Migrations, Ethnicity and Security: The South Asian Case*, Sterling Publishers Private Limited, New Delhi, 1990, p.3.

12. Moran, Keray, *Partnership for Development, 40 Years of American Assistance*. USAID, 1991, p.17.

13. HMG/N, National Commission on Population, *Inter Regional Migration in Nepal: Problems and Prospects*, Kathmandu. 1984, pp.83.

14. Pant, Shastra Dutta, *Vyabasthit Vasti Ra Gaun Vikas* (Nepali), South Asian Research Centre, Kathmandu, 1992.

15. National Commission on Population, *Nepal ma Antarik Tatha Antarrastriga Basai-Sarai*. (Nepali), Kathmandu, 1989, pp.498-99.

16. *Ibid.*, pp.482.

17. Jha, Hari Bansh. "Gurung Report: A Pandora's Box", *Media Nepal*, Vol. I, No. 1. Kathmandu. 204 1, pp.25-32.

18. *Gorakhapatra*, Apr. 26, 28, 1998.

19. *Dainik Nepal*, Mar 3, July 5, 1972.

20. HMG/N, No. 13, p.84

21. HMG/N, National Commission on Population, *Population and Development in Nepal,* Kathmandu, 1988, p.107.

22. *Ibid.*

8

Urbanisation and Migration

Today's developed countries were characterised by considerably smaller populations than currently developing nations when the former embarked on the urbanisation transition, that is, when their urban places began accommodating more than half of their population. Between 1990 and 2005, the urban places of the developing world are expected to gain over one billion inhabitants, a figure at least 10 times larger than the estimated 100 million involved in the urban transition that took place in Europe and North America between 1815 and 1915.[1]

The population growth rates of developed countries were much lower than those being experienced today by developing countries. Thus, between 1776 and 1871, the population of developed countries grew at approximately one half the rate of that of developing countries today.[2] There were some structural blockages in employment and city growth related to the rates of economic growth; the urban transition in developed countries generally involved the growth of cities populated mostly by wage-earners, engaged in factory and service occupations.

The population of urban places can increase for four reasons: the balance of births and deaths is positive, leading to natural increase; there is migration from rural to urban places within the country; there is international migration to the urban areas of a country; and there is territorial expansion of urban places as their boundaries are redefined or as rural areas become urbanised. In Asia, net rural-urban migration and reclassification still account for over half of urban growth. Natural increase is a major component of urban population growth in certain regions. Indeed, the urban populations of developing countries tend to be heavily concentrated in the younger ages and particularly in the main reproductive ages.

The concentration of recent migrants in the young adult ages is a well-known fact. The high levels of natural increase prevalent in both urban and rural areas not only fuel the growth of the former, but also lead to rural-urban migration by increasing the population in rural areas that are hard to keep on absorbing large numbers of agricultural workers.

With regard to the influence of net rural-urban migration on the growth of cities, it is difficult to obtain acceptable estimates of rural-urban migration, be it for Europe during the nineteenth century or currently for developing countries. Indirect evidence suggests that net rural-urban migration has been an important component of urban growth in developing countries since 1950.[3]

In addition, because migrants tend to be concentrated in the child-bearing ages, their impact on natural increase is also significant. The impact of internal migration on urban growth has varied from one country to another. Another problem in assessing the dynamics of urbanisation is related to changes in the territorial configuration of urban places. In some cases, the failure of data gatherers to take into account changes in the boundaries of urban places may result in the underestimation of the urban population and consequently in the overestimation of the rural population.

Recently, there have been several attempts to conceptualise and document the phenomenon of city expansion, particularly when it involves growing linkages between previously independent urban places. Indeed, rapid urbanisation in both developed and developing countries has been associated with the concentration of the urban population in a small number of urban centres within each country. Such concentration has given rise to mega-cities, that is, cities with at least eight million inhabitants. As large urban agglomerations, including mega-cities, grow, they show a tendency to spread outwards, often beyond the boundaries of their so-called metropolitan areas to form what we shall hereinafter call extended metropolitan regions.

In the post-colonial period, developing countries have been playing catch-up, but their rapid urban population growth has generally outpaced the development of urban infrastructure and the expansion of industry. The result has often been deficit financing, as developing countries have tried to provide modern services to a growing population. In developed countries, the manufacturing and industrial sectors have traditionally provided employment for a major share of the urban population.

Since 1945, however, more and more jobs are being generated by the service and financial sectors. In fact, since the 1973 economic crisis, a growing number of jobs in the industrial and manufacturing sectors have been transferred from developed to developing countries as foreign direct investment in the latter has grown.[4] In developed countries, such changes have brought about a shift of population away from older industrial areas to those where the service and financial sectors are expanding.

In the developing world, the industrial base has always been small in comparison with the service sector, which was more thoroughly developed by the colonial powers. The Newly Industrialising Economies (NIEs) have moved faster than other Asian countries on the road to economic development and by now their growth process relies heavily on industries intensive in the use of human capital and technology.

The countries of Southern Asia have been more inward-oriented and have protected their industry to a greater degree, thus favouring, particularly in India and Pakistan, the emergence of heavy industry and other capital-intensive industries. During the 1980s, countries in the subregion began to foster the expansion of labour-intensive industries oriented towards both local and international markets. India in particular has begun to develop a high technology sector. Although the reforms adopted have injected considerable dynamism to their economies, they have also complicated economic management. Relaxing central controls before macroeconomic tools are fully in place has given rise to imbalances and created strong inflationary pressures.

Among the highly urbanised countries, agriculture has made a relatively small contribution to Gross Domestic Product (GDP) since the 1960s and is currently at minimal levels. Manufacturing and industry were both important in the 1960s for most of the ASEAN four countries and Asian NIEs and their contribution to GDP increased significantly in the cases of the Republic of Korea and Singapore. In the rest of the highly urbanised countries, the joint contribution of manufacturing and industry to GDP remained virtually unchanged between 1960 and 1990 or declined slightly.

Among the countries with intermediate levels of urbanisation, the contribution of agriculture has generally declined dramatically between 1960 and 1990, and that of manufacturing and industry has tended to increase. The main exceptions are the Philippines, where the share of agriculture in GDP declined only slightly, and Fiji where the contribution of manufacturing failed to increase. Among the rest of the countries in South Asia and China, the patterns of structural change are even more variable. Only in China, India and Sri Lanka do manufacturing and industry account for relatively high proportions of GDP, but only India has experienced a significant drop in the share of agriculture. In Bangladesh, Myanmar and Nepal agriculture still accounts for the major share of GDP, and only Bangladesh has experienced some increase in the share of manufacturing and industry.[5]

In most of these countries, the service sector continues to make a sizeable contribution to GDP and it helps accommodate the excess labour force in urban areas. The changes observed in terms of the labour force are similar. In the highly urbanised countries there has been a major reduction of the proportion of the population working in agriculture and, in most cases, a rise of that working in the service sector.

Countries with intermediate levels of urbanisation display even more variability in the patterns of change of their labour force. Again, all of them have experienced reductions in the proportion of workers in agriculture. Yet there is only a weak tendency towards the growth of the proportion of the labour force in industry or manufacturing, and greater consistency in the increasing trend displayed by the service sector. When these changes are juxtaposed with those regarding the components of GDP, it becomes clear that the growing contribution that manufacturing is making to GDP in a number of the countries in this group has not been matched by a proportionate increase in the share of the labour force devoted to manufacturing and industry. The growing labour force has had to be accommodated by agriculture or by the service sector.

South Asian countries continue to have sizeable proportions of their labour force in agriculture and in the service sector. In socialist economies, changes in the structure of employment are more difficult to ascertain, but it is clear that the majority of the labour force remains in the agricultural sector.

The persistence of large populations engaged in agricultural production in most of the Asia-Pacific region increases the potential for large flows of rural-urban migration. However, one may cast some doubt on the accuracy of the statistics available. Information on labour force participation is often weak or misleading because—particularly in developing countries—individuals often have more than one job. In rural areas in particular, it is increasingly common for persons to be engaged in both farm and non-farm employment.

Survey data indicate that between 20 and 30 per cent of all rural workers in Asia may also have some type of non-agricultural employment that constitutes a major source of income and there are reasons to believe that proportion may be increasing.[6] In South Asian countries and particularly in the coastal regions of China, non-farm income in rural areas is also rising and it has important implications for the urbanisation process, especially because a major part of non-farm employment is being generated by the heavily populated regions surrounding the largest urban centres of the Asia-Pacific region. Non-farm employment permits, not only improvement in household income, but also investment in agricultural diversification and in small industry. The symbiosis between urban centres and the rural communities located near them creates growth areas that are attractive to both indigenous and foreign capital. If the government provides public infrastructure, such as electricity and transportation, the process of consolidation and expansion of those areas is enhanced. The per capita income shows a strong relation with the level of urbanisation.

The changing structure of the urban labour force is one of the most important facets of the urbanisation process. Research on the urban labour force has been dominated by models that divide it in two components: an informal sector made up of largely self-employed persons or small-scale entrepreneurs that covers virtually every type of urban activity, from manufacturing to services; and a formal sector consisting of salaried workers employed by legally chartered enterprises or by the public sector. The informal sector is usually characterised as having low productivity and producing low incomes. Since 1970, there have been major policy debates concerning the problem of labour force absorption and the capacity of governments and the private sector to generate sufficient productive employment for the rapidly growing urban populations of developing countries. One policy position has considered the informal sector a holding sector for the surplus labour force that can provide unskilled workers with some employment opportunities. Another position has been focused on increasing employment in the formal sector by fostering rapid industrialisation, particularly of the export-oriented kind. This strategy has been successful in the NIEs and in certain ASEAN countries.

However, estimates of labour force growth in the Asia-Pacific region indicate that, during the 1980s, the urban labour force was growing only one per cent faster than the total labour force of the region. During the 1990s, the difference between the two rates of growth will increase to about 1.5 per cent, and by the first decade of the twenty-first century, the urban labour force will grow almost three times as fast as the total labour force.[7]

There are many differences between the urbanisation experience of developed and developing countries, a number of global processes seem to be leading to a greater homogenisation of urbanisation around the world. Two types of processes can be distinguished: the transactional revolution; and the impact of globalisation on national space. The transactional revolution involves fundamental changes in the means of communication, exchange and interaction between and within countries. The transactions of interest involve people, commodities, capital and information.

Commuting is a form of geographical transaction involving people; the shipping of automotive parts from Thailand to Montreal is a form of commodity transaction; the transfer of funds from New York to Jakarta is a capital transaction; and Cable News Network (CNN) transmissions to all parts of the world represent informational transactions. A major recent development is that the constraints of time and distance are no longer important for the transmission of information and capital through space. However, the flows of people and commodities, though they are becoming more efficient, are still subject to a number of constraints, including those related to time and distance.

The transactional revolution is strengthening the processes leading to the greater centralisation of the urban system, to the extent that urban development is increasingly concentrated in a few urban regions within a country. Centralisation stems from the importance of transaction nodes whose existence permits the minimisation of transaction costs. Therefore, the new extended metropolitan regions are characterised by the inclusion of international container ports, international airports, industrial estates and free export zones, as well as international hotels close to multinodal offices, and retailing complexes scattered throughout urban space.

The transactional revolution leads to a form of urbanisation that at the level of individual regions, can create discontinuous patterns of land use which are generally most marked in the urban periphery where agriculture, industry, leisure activities and residential developments are juxtaposed. In the peripheral areas of the extended metropolitan regions there are often major environmental and administrative problems as well as conflicts regarding land use.

Despite these difficulties, it is the emerging extended metropolitan regions in the developing world that evince the most rapid economic growth. The causes for their dynamism therefore deserve to be better understood so that policies to enhance it may be developed.

The transactional revolution is also affecting the global and regional mode of operation. At the global level, the emergence of the new international division of labour has involved the relocation of industrial activity to developing countries where labour costs are low. Such relocation has been made possible by improvements in transport and communication, as well as in production technologies. The major international investors have identified production niches in various locations. The industries created are producing goods both for export and for local consumption, especially if the local population is generating enough surplus capital to buy those products.

The decentralisation of production at the global level has been made possible by new forms of organisation and marketing. During the 1980s, order-cycle times in developed countries were reduced by 400 per cent and the use of just-in-time production and delivery systems expanded. Clearly, better logistic management depends on improvements in telecommunications and information systems.

To become part of the global market and maintain competitiveness, developing countries have to provide access to those systems. Another facet of accelerating globalisation is the emergence of global cities serving as major nodal points in the movement of capital, people and commodities. Developing countries are currently competing to develop a niche in the global market. Virtually no major city today lacks a world trade centre or first-class convention facilities. Joining the global market entails important changes in cities, in terms not only of the built environment but also of establishing and expanding telecommunication networks, improving airports, and expanding the road system, especially in areas linked to the global market.

The move towards globalisation implies that national boundaries will become less important as barriers to the movement of goods and people. From the economic perspective, it is indeed advantageous to development to increase cross-border economic activity. The relative proportion of nuclear or extended families depends on a great variety of macro and micro factors, for instance, in rural areas, they include local forms of agricultural production, land availability and inheritance, kinship patterns and demographic variables such as life expectancy.

In most societies there is or has been an increase in the proportion of nuclear families and a fall in the average size of households, which has accompanied an increasingly monetised economy and increasing proportions of the labour force working in non-agricultural activities and living in urban areas. Another important change, recorded in many countries in the North, is a rapid increase in the proportion of single person households. In much of Europe, over a quarter of all households are one-person households; in the USA, over a fifth of all households are one-person households. These and other changes in the size and composition of households have important and often underrated influences on urban changes and housing markets. They bring major changes in the number of households which need accommodation; a rapid growth in the number of households can mean that housing demand rises, even as the overall population of a city falls. However, the scale and nature of changes in household size and structure appear too varied from society to society or within a society over time to permit much detailed generalisation.

International comparisons are also hampered by the differences in definition or interpretation of 'household' between countries and the fact that there is no recent data on households in many countries. In addition, the assumption that economic changes always promote a change from a predominance of extended families to a predominance of nuclear families has been challenged both by historical studies which show that household composition has long been highly variable in rural areas and by contemporary studies which find extended households common in urban areas.

There is also evidence of a rising proportion of extended families in many urban areas, largely as a response by households to falling real incomes. Thus, while there is little doubt that household composition usually undergoes some change in the course of urban development, these changes take different forms at different times and in different places and they can by no means be generalised. There are large variations between regions and nations in the proportion of women-headed households and in the extent to which this proportion is changing. For instance, only an estimated 13 per cent of households in Asia and the Pacific are women-headed compared to 19.1 per cent in Africa and 18.2 in Latin America.[8] The proportion of women-headed households can rise to more than a third of all households.

The urbanisation process is itself frequently shaped by gender roles and relations, for instance, through the scale and nature of female migration into urban areas and the influence on the urban labour market arising from constraints placed on women's right to work outside the home by households and societies and by the extent of the demand for female labour. The degree and nature of gender selective movement to urban areas is often a major influence on both the frequency and the spatial distribution of women-headed households within countries. In the towns and cities of East and South-east Asia, Latin America and the Caribbean, rural out-migration is female selective, urban sex ratios usually show more women than men and levels of female household headship are higher in urban areas.

For instance, women-headed households are likely to be free of patriarchy at the domestic level, while other benefits may be greater self-esteem, more personal freedom, higher degrees of flexibility in terms of taking paid work, enhanced control over finances, and a reduction or absence of physical and/or emotional abuse. Women-headed households are not always over-represented among the lowest income groups. In addition, when women decide to set up their own houses, it may be a positive and empowering step, especially if in doing so, they are able to further their personal interests and the well-being of their dependants.

The expenditure patterns of female-headed households are more biased towards nutrition and education than those of male-headed households, with less spent on items that contribute little or nothing to the households basic needs. However, while female-headed households may be better off than they had previously been when male-headed, in most societies, they are still disadvantaged by the widespread discrimination against women and against single parent households.

Women-headed households face greater difficulties than male-headed households because of the discrimination women face in, for instance, labour markets and in access to credit, housing and basic services. And single parent households, most of which are female headed, also face the difficulties of one adult having to combine income-earning with household management and child rearing.

The last few decades have brought a world that is far more urbanised, and with a much higher proportion living in large cities and metropolitan areas. Soon after the year 2010, there will be more urban dwellers than rural dwellers worldwide. There are also tens of millions of 'rural-dwellers' who may live in settlements designated by censuses as 'rural' but who derive their livelihood from work in urban areas or who work in industries or service enterprises located in 'greenfield sites'.

Population growth rates for most major cities in both the North and the South were slower during the 1980s, compared to the 1970s and 1960s.[9] And for many of the world's largest cities, including many in the South, more people moved out of the city than in during the last inter-census period. For instance, the steady increase in the level of urbanisation worldwide since 1950 reflects the fact that the size of the world's economy has grown many times since then. It has also changed from one dominated by relatively closed national economies or trading blocs to one where most countries have more open economies and where production and the services it needs are increasingly integrated internationally.

The period since 1950 has brought not only enormous changes in the scale and nature of economic activity but also in the size and nature of households, in the scale and distribution of incomes within and between nations, and in the scale and nature of government. All, inevitably, influence settlements patterns. Perhaps the most fundamental influences on the world's settlement system in recent decades have come from the unprecedented changes in economic and political conditions.

Countries with the most rapidly growing economies since 1950 were generally those with the most rapid increase in their level of urbanisation while the world's largest cities are heavily concentrated in the world's largest economies. The more recent economic, social and political changes in east and central Europe and the former Soviet Union and in South Africa are also fundamentally changing settlement patterns, although these changes are too recent to have been captured by available census data. Over 20 nations with one million or more inhabitants in 1990 had populations that had more than tripled since 1950—most of them in Eastern Africa, Western Asia and Central America.[10]

Rapid population growth does not, of itself, increase the level of urbanisation. In most nations in the South it is the most important factor in increasing urban populations. Even in regions with much less dramatic population growth and political change such as Western Europe and North America, there have been major demographic changes, for instance, in age structures and household sizes and types, and as described, these have contributed to major changes in settlement patterns. The average size of the world's largest cities may have changed enormously but their location has changed much less. For instance, in most of the worlds regions, their is perhaps a surprising continuity in the list of this largest cities and metropolitan areas; more than two-thirds of the world's 'million-cities' in 1990 were already important cities 200 years ago while around a quarter have been important cities for at least 500 years.[11]

Studies of various regions of India have also found that most of the urban centres, even down to small administrative centres and market towns, have long histories. In most countries, settlement patterns have changed much less than the degree of economic, social and demographic change might imply. One reason is that existing cities represent a considerable concentration of human and physical capital, and it is difficult for new cities to arise that can compete with the old ones.

Another is that in most instances, cities adapt to changing circumstances. There are two reasons for caution. The first is the extent to which this transition could be hastened or delayed by changes in definitions. It would only take China, India or a few of the other most populous nations to change their definition of urban centres for there to be a significant increase or decrease in the proportion of the world's population living in urban centres. The proportion of the world population currently living in urban centres is best considered not 'as a precise percentage but as being between 40 and 55 per cent, depending on the criteria used to define what is an 'urban centre'. The second reason for caution arises from the confusion between the terms 'urban centre' and 'city'. Many people have commented that more than half the world's population will soon be living in cities, but this is incorrect since a significant proportion of the world's urban population lives in small market towns and administrative centres.

The current population of most of the worlds largest urban areas including London, Los Angeles, Shanghai, Beijing, Jakarta, Dhaka and Mumbai can vary by many million inhabitants in any year, depending on which boundaries are used to define their populations. The boundaries of the metropolitan area may be extended further to include urban centres or other settlements from which a considerable proportion of the economically active population commutes to work in the metropolitan area or whose work is tied into the economy of the metropolis. Comparing the size, population growth rate or density of the central city population of one city with the size, population growth rate or density of another city but for its metropolitan area or 'extended metropolitan region' will produce dramatic contrasts but this is not comparing like with like.

Most of the 'million-cities' with the highest population growth rates during the 1980s were not among the world's largest cities. But population growth rates can be misleading in that the larger the city population at the beginning of a period, the larger the increment in population has to be to produce a high population growth rate. Mumbai had a population that had an annual increase of more than 400,000 during the 1980s, and a large part of this is the result of much-mended boundaries being used in the 1990 census compared to the 1980 census.[12]

The population of most of the world's largest urban agglomerations actually grew quite slowly during the 1980's. Three urban agglomerations had populations that grew by more than 300,000 a year between 1980 and 1990—Tokyo, Jakarta and Lagos—although this may overstate the scale of population growth in Lagos. Again, some caution is needed in interpreting these figures, as the population growth rate or the annual average increment in population will depend on which city or metropolitan boundary is chosen. Most of the others that grew to become among the largest cities in the region were also cities with long histories. Most were the major cities either in the most populous countries or in the most successful economics, for instance, Kyoto in Japan, Seoul and Pusan in South Korea, Karachi and Lahore in Pakistan, Delhi, Mumbai and Bangalore in India, Jakarta and Surabaya in Indonesia and many of China's major cities.

Europe was the first of the world's regions to begin a rapid and sustained increase in its population, as birth rates came to regularly exceed death rates but also the first region to undergo a rapid decrease in birth rates to the point where the total population is hardly growing or even declining in many European countries. The problem of urban boundaries is evident here. For instance, the number of 'million-cities' in Europe is considerably increased—and the share of the total population they concentrate considerably increased—if urban populations are defined by functional regions rather than by city cores.

For many of the world's largest cities, part of the slow-down in their population growth is explained by a rapid growth in production and population just outside their boundaries, and with much of this production intimately connected to enterprises still within its boundaries. All major cities or metropolitan centres experience a decentralisation of population and of production, as they grow. This generally begins with suburban housing being developed at ever greater distances from the city centre and then a widening commuting field and an increasing concentration of enterprises in suburban locations or in belts around the metropolitan area.

In most major cities, there has been a declining proportion of the population living in the central city and the outward sprawl of the urban agglomeration, especially along major roads and highways. This has probably gone furthest in the United States where population densities in outer suburbs are generally much lower than in Europe and where many enterprises have also developed close to major highways outside the central areas.

Decentralisation of urban population within core regions can also be seen in the rapid growth of smaller cities that are close to the major cities or metropolitan areas as these attract both industrial and service enterprises that previously would tend to concentrate in major cities.

The increasing share of the world's economy controlled by multinationals has led to certain cities becoming what are often termed 'global' or 'world' cities, as they are the key command and control points of the world economy. Some are unambiguously world cities as they are the 'commanding nodes' of the global system—London, New York and Tokyo. New York and London are not only leading financial markets but also leading producers and exporters in accounting, advertising, management consulting, international legal services and other business services. Tokyo, developing as an important centre for the international trade in services, such as construction and engineering services, has developed beyond, its initially restricted role of exporting only the services required by its larger international trading houses.

Several of the world's largest cities do not owe their size and economic base to their role within global production but to being national capitals in more populous nations with a high concentration of political power there, for instance, Delhi and Cairo. It is interesting to note that the former national capitals of the most populous nation in Africa (Lagos in Nigeria) and Latin America (Rio de Janeiro in Brazil) are among the 30 largest cities in the world and both owe much of their size and economic importance to the period when they were political capitals. Calcutta too grew to be much the largest city in India as the former capital; Delhi, to where the national capital was moved early in the twentieth century, has grown much faster than Calcutta in recent decades and may soon have a larger population than Calcutta.

There has been relatively little recent research on the scale and nature of internal migration flows. There is much more work on the scale and nature of international migration flows, even though there is far more internal population movement than international population movement. The much increased volume of research on international migration is no doubt linked to political worries of governments in wealthy countries, for instance, for countries close to areas of conflict or potential conflict that might create large flows of refugees and other emigrants and for wealthy countries that are close to low-income countries and with borders over which it is difficult to control population movements.

There is very little idea of the scale and nature of internal migration flows, except that they are almost always diverse, complex, constantly changing and include rural to urban, urban to rural, urban to urban and rural to rural flows. Urban to urban migration flows outnumber rural to urban flows. In virtually all nations, there are also large urban to rural migration flows, even in countries which are urbanising; the fact that the nation is urbanising merely reflects the fact that rural to urban migration flows outnumber migration flows in the opposite direction.

There is also considerable diversity between nations and regions in the migrants themselves, for instance, in terms of age, level of education, the extent to which the move is considered permanent or temporary and the extent to which this move is part of a complex and diverse household survival strategy. Various studies have shown how female migration is of much greater volume and complexity than was previously believed and also how the migration of women differs in many ways from that of men in its form, composition, causes and consequences. There is also great diversity in the scale and nature of migration.

There are around 30,000 urban centres in the South and each has its own unique pattern of in-migration and out-migration that constantly changes, reflecting changes in that centre's economic base, labour market and age structure. Each detailed study of migrants in urban settings and of conditions in areas of out-migration reveals a long list of factors which influence migration, including those relating to individuals or household structures and gender-relations within households; local, social, economic and cultural factors; regional and national social and economic change; and international factors.

There are also large populations of foreigners within the wealthier countries in Africa and Latin America, most of them being from lower-income countries close by. There is great diversity in the types of international migrants and the forms that their movements take contract labourers, students, professionals and skilled workers, immigrants joining their families through family reunification, people who retire to a foreign country, asylum seekers and refugees. There has also been a considerable growth in international migration flows of highly qualified or skilled labour migrants, that include the professional and managerial staff transferred within the international labour markets of transnational corporations.

There is also great diversity in the scale of emigration out of and immigration into each nation, and also in who moves. A distinction can be drawn between countries where there is far more immigration than emigration—generally the wealthiest countries that also have relatively open policies to immigrants, and countries with high levels of emigration. There are also the exceptional cases of certain oil-exporting Middle East countries that have foreign workers making up more than half their workforce.

An increasing number of countries from which there were large emigration flows have changed to become major centres for immigrants. There are also many countries with large emigrant and immigrant flows, for instance, with large emigration movements of skilled and professional emigrants and with unskilled immigrants coming in from lower income countries. Many of the main migration flows have well-established historical roots. A considerable part of them is also a consequence of an increasingly globalised economy.

Urbanisation and rapid population growth in large cities have often been considered problematic because governments and international agencies fail to ensure that infrastructure and service provision keeps up with the growth in population. Also governments often fail to enforce pollution control and other regulations needed to protect the quality of life in urban areas.

Rising levels of urbanisation are strongly associated with growing and diversifying economies, and most of the nations in the South whose economic performance over the last two decades is so envied by other nations are also the nations with the most rapid increase in their levels of urbanisation. The nature of this relationship between the scale of the economy and the scale of the urban population is also illustrated by the fact that most of the world's largest cities are in the world's largest economies. The world's five largest economies on that date had between them half of the world's 10 million plus inhabitant urban agglomerations and a third of its 'million-cities'. Some argue that, whilst increases in the level of urbanisation may be high, they are not abnormal when compared to other countries at a similar stage of their development.

Urban growth has been detrimental to economic growth and the term 'over-urbanisation' has been used to describe countries where the level of urbanisation relative to national income is considered to be high in comparison to reference countries.

Growth or stability may be compromised by high levels of government investment in urban infrastructure and services. One basis for the 'over-urbanisation' thesis is that specific urbanisation levels in the South have been achieved at lower levels of per capita income than those associated with similar levels of urbanisation in the North. Increases in the level of urbanisation in the South have been achieved without economic growth industrialisation and increases in agricultural productivity.

In developed countries many rural areas are urbanised, as manufacturing and service enterprises can locate on 'greenfield' sites with many of the service and infrastructure benefits of urban locations but none of the congestion; and city workers, can live in rural areas and travel each day to work. Levels of urbanisation for each country are likely to reflect not only the level of per capita GDP and the nature of the economy but also a number of other factors including definitions used for urban areas, the nature of agriculture, physical factors such as the size and topography of the country, political factors including the relative degree of security in rural locations, and cultural preferences for types of lifestyles.

Almost all the governments have favoured urban rather than rural areas within their investment strategies and pricing policies. This has encouraged the migration of people from rural to urban areas and therefore an increase in the level of urbanisation, although within the Indian context public sector policies do not seem to have had a significant impact on the level of urbanisation. These influences on the level of urbanisation suggest that countries may have very country-specific components to the relations between levels of urbanisation and economic variables, although the underlying nature of such relations may be broadly similar.

Countries with high levels of urbanisation show little increases in recent decades, despite the fact that incomes have continued to rise. Urbanisation levels will stabilise at different levels in different countries, although the different levels may simply reflect different definitions used for urban centres. In the wealthiest countries, an increasing proportion of the rural population are either urban workers or work in manufacturing and service enterprises located in greenfield sites.

REFERENCES

1. World Bank, *World Development Report*, 1995.
2. *Census of India, 1991*, Series, Paper 2 of 1992.
3. *Economic Survey,* 1996-97, Government of India, Ministry of Finance, New Delhi.

4. Ibid.
5. *SAARC SCAN*, November, 1996.
6. Ibid.
7. Ibid.
8. *Economic Times*, May 19, 1997.
9. *Economic and Political Weekly, Vol. XXXII*, No. 19, May 10-16, 1997.
10. 'Direction of Trade Statistics', *Yearbook,* IMF, 1996.
11. 'International Trade Statistics' *Yearbook,* United Nations, 1995.
12. Ibid.

9

Human Development in South Asia

In the South Asian region, challenges of human development has continued for several decades against large-scale natural disasters, expanding nuclear capabilities and global economic slow-down. Consequences of these events have raised fears of this region slipping into even greater poverty, with worsening nutritional, health, and educational outcomes. These human development issues must be at the core of regional developmental programmes and policies.

Accounting for nearly half of the total world population living in poverty, over 500 million people in South Asia suffer from severe deprivation, with little or no access to adequate nutrition, health, housing, water, sanitation, education, and employment.[1] Illustrative of the state of the region's poor is their lack of access to basic facilities.[2]

Among the developing countries, South Asia's share of human deprivation is almost twice its share in the population. In South Asia, a staggering 45 per cent of the population lives below the income required to meet minimum daily needs, compared to 24 per cent in the rest of the developing world.[3] Similarly, the illiteracy rate in South Asia is two and a half times the rate in the rest of the developing world; the proportion of malnourished children under five is almost three times as high; and access to health facilities one and a half times as low. To achieve sustainable human development, progress in human capabilities and opportunities needs to be substantial.

What is critical for human progress is to address poverty of opportunity, and not just poverty of income. Poverty of income is often the result, poverty of opportunity is often the cause. To capture the multiple dimensions of poverty, the Human Poverty Index (HPI), developed by United Nations Development Programme (UNDP), uses indicators for measuring basic dimensions of deprivation: a shorter lifespan, illiteracy, and lack of access to safe water, health, and nutrition.[4]

There is an alarming increase in absolute poverty in some South Asian countries over the last decade. Despite continued efforts of governments, civil society organisations, and international agencies, poverty persists in South Asia. The region has the largest number of people living in poverty. According to World Bank $1 a day estimates, out of 1.3 billion poor people in the world, 515 million live in South Asia, even though the region accounts for only 23 per cent of the global population.[5]

Through the mid-1970s and the 1980s, South Asia saw a remarkable reduction in poverty. But the last decade witnessed either a reversal of this trend or a slow-down in poverty reduction in all countries, other than India. Poverty rates have gone up in Bangladesh, Pakistan, Nepal, and in urban sectors of Sri Lanka. Even though they have declined sharply in India, the proportion of South Asia's population earning less than one dollar a day has remained stagnant at 43 per cent.[6]

The *Bangladesh Household Expenditure Survey* data shows that by 1991, poverty incidence both in rural as well as in urban areas, had risen compared to 1985. Though poverty rates have since improved, they were still higher in 1995 than those a decade earlier. The absolute number of poor rose by 1.2 per cent annually during this period faster than any historically observed rate.[7] The depth and severity of poverty also increased, demonstrating the worsening condition of the poor.

In Sri Lanka, though national poverty estimates showed an improvement, urban poverty estimates indicated a worsening condition. Lastly, Nepal's case also showed resembling evidence. In fact, Nepal fared even worse than the other cases cited, as poverty rates increased from 36 per cent to 49 per cent between 1977 and 1992.

Table 9.1
Rural and urban poverty in India and Bangladesh

		Head Count Index		
	Period	*National*	*Rural*	*Urban*
	1970/71	52.9	54.8	45.0
India	1977/78	48.4	50.6	40.5
	1987/88	38.0	39.2	36.2
	1993/94	35.0	36.7	30.5
	1973/74	70.5	71.3	63.2
	1981/82	63.5	65.3	48.4
Bangladesh	1985/86	43.9	45.9	30.8
	1988/89	47.8	49.7	35.9
	1991/92	49.7	52.9	33.6
	1995/96	47.0	51.1	26.3

Poverty rates continued to decline in India, contrary to these regional trends. Since 1970, poverty has declined by almost 18 percentage points. During the 1990s, other than the year reforms of 1991, the steady decline in poverty has been maintained. Even so, India has been unable to reduce the absolute number of the poor remaining between 294 and 315 million from 1970 to 1994—leaving India with the largest backlog of poor people in the world.

In India, five states—Bihar, Orissa, West Bengal, Assam, and Maharashtra—account for 56 per cent of rural poverty while containing only one-third of the total rural population. In Bangladesh in 1991, the Divisions of Rajshahi, Barisal, and Dhaka had the highest incidence of rural poverty, whereas urban poverty in Chittagong and Dhaka was less than 15 per cent. However, there is some success stories as well. For instance, Kerala's decline in poverty, despite its slow economic growth rate, is noteworthy—it declined from 48 per cent in 1984 to 29 per cent in 1994. Kerala's rate of lowering poverty was four times that of Bihar and three times that of Rajasthan. Its success is explained by a firm commitment by the state and civil society to expand infrastructure, to promote education, and to further health services. To formulate effective poverty alleviation programmes, it is important to collect disaggregated data on poverty.

In India, where the gap between poverty of opportunities and income poverty is the least in South Asia, poverty has declined from 53 per cent in 1970 to 35 per cent in 1994.[8] Poverty alleviation is a part of the national policy agenda in India. These policies have been bolstered by the favourable economic conditions of the early nineties. Research suggests that economic growth has been an overwhelming engine of poverty reduction in India.

Since 1994, India's growth rate has been higher than in any previous phase in its history. In the face of this rapid economic growth, the headcount index of poverty was expected to decline by a further six percentage points by 1997. To spread the benefits of higher growth more evenly, Indian policy makers have concentrated on rural areas, providing food security to the poor through the Public Distribution System (PDS)—which supplied 18.4 million tonnes of foodgrains in 1990-92. Other initiatives include self-employment and wage employment programmes concentrated in rural areas, such as the Integrated Rural Development Programme and Jawahar Rozgar Yojana.

Meanwhile, in Pakistan, the rising poverty level during the 1990s is partly a by-product of the slow-down of the economy, and partly due to successive governments' inability to translate the economic growth of the 1980s into a better life for the poor. Governments have played a marginal role in transferring income to the needy. Currently, only 0.22 per cent of Gross Domestic Product (GDP) is transferred to the poor as

Zakat, less than three per cent is spent on education; and a meagre one per cent on health services. There are, however, positive initiatives underway: encouraging examples are the recently initiated 2010 Vision that aims at ambitious advances in human development; the Social Action Programme's increasing allocation to social sectors, from 1.96 per cent of GDP in 1992 to a projected 2.7 per cent in 1998; and the Poverty Alleviation Fund.[9]

Bangladesh has taken considerable measures to address poverty through building a larger human capital base. The total allocation to social sector development in 1998-99 was 18 per cent of the total government expenditures. Complementing this is the wide network of non-governmental organisations (NGOs). The provision of micro-credit by Grameen Bank, other NGOs, and government organisations benefited almost 8.8 million people in 1998.[10]

In the case of Sri Lanka, despite low growth, significant advances have been made in improving income distribution and general living standards. The incidence of poverty in Sri Lanka is lower than that in other South Asian countries. This has been achieved by a strong commitment to the social sectors. This was possible through political will to target policies effectively. Undoubtedly, Sri Lanka would have made even more impressive progress on the poverty front had it not suffered from civil unrest.

The most glaring levels of poverty of opportunity in South Asia are found among women and girl children. This is reflected in the gap between male and female literacy rates of 26 per cent points: female adult literacy rate is a dismal 36 per cent as compared to 62 per cent for males. Of the 50 million out-of-school children, 28 million are girls. This gap can be traced to discrimination against girls and women, which begins at home, and extends to the preferential treatment of boys in the provision of food, nutrition, health care, and education at the community and national levels.

In its most extreme form, discrimination turns into direct violence against women: ranging from infanticide to child abuse and from rape to dowry death. The fact that there are only 93 women for every 100 men in South Asia, against the global norm of 106 women for every 100 men, reflects their low status. Multiple forms of discrimination raced by women severely limit their opportunities for leading productive lives. Women's share in private sector employment in South Asia is about 30 per cent and their wage rate is approximately three-fourths the male rate. They comprise about three per cent of managers and administrators, hold about five per cent of government posts and about six per cent of the cabinet positions.

Natural disasters such as floods, earthquakes, cyclones, landslides, etc., also have affected the well-being of many South Asians. Besides the loss of human lives, such disasters have caused extensive damage to livestock, housing, roads and infrastructure, standing crops, and therefore, the livelihood of the people. These translate into colossal economic and social costs that reach far beyond the immediate havoc they cause. They decrease growth prospects, increase unemployment, and play havoc with the lives of the poor and the vulnerable.

Floods in Bangladesh have highlighted their impact on human development. The flood of 1998 inundated two-thirds of the country. Thirty-three million people were marooned, of which 18 million needed emergency food and health services. The prolonged flood caused unemployment, leaving daily wage workers and disadvantaged groups with no income support and no food. The food shortage and assistance required for their subsistence was estimated at 14,000 metric tonnes over a six-week period. The flood also brought associated concerns of health and disease, as diarrhoea and hepatitis spread through contaminated water usage.

Such natural catastrophes in South Asian countries have undermined efforts to alleviate poverty and human deprivation. In Nepal, for example, periodic landslides and floods have remained a threat to people. Each year, over 350 people fell victim to natural disasters. Similarly, in India floods and cyclones cause immense human distress. Every year, more than 1,400 human lives are lost, over 7.5 million hectares of land is affected, and almost Rs 10 billion worth of damage is done. But nature is not always to blame some disasters are man-made. For example, Nepal is experiencing deforestation at an annual rate of two per cent.[11] Besides altering the ecosystem, such developments increase the risk of landslides through soil erosion. This further increases the rubble that is carried down by rain and river water to riverbeds in the plains, thereby decreasing the river depth and increasing risk of floods.

Climatic change and rising sea levels are also partly man-made. It is thus important to address the causes behind these unfolding environmental problems in order to limit the human costs of disasters. Effective post-disaster measures are necessary to limit the impact of such catastrophes. To provide income support of the affected poor, micro-credit programmes have to be initiated. Citizen and NGO initiative can help in this respect. At the same time, state and international agencies can be active in rebuilding infrastructure initiating rehabilitation programming. In order to minimise the costs of these catastrophes, South Asian governments need to chalk out both response plans, as well as preventive strategies. Pre-disaster preparedness requires forecasting and warning systems to be in place. Timely delivery of information is vital. Governments and media should ensure expeditious action and raise awareness in risk-prone areas.

The evidence indicates that in South Asia, equitable patterns of growth are essential for sustainable poverty reduction. This requires a two-pronged approach consisting of broad-based economic growth and improved access to social services. Thus, policies supporting economic stability, as well as embedded safety nets are necessary to reduce poverty and protect the poor. Since it is always social expenditures that are cut back under unforeseen circumstances and adjustment, there should be both flexibility and rigidity in the allocation of budgets: flexibility to extend greater support to the poorest sections while rigidity in terms of fixing minimum support to social sectors and development even during recessions.

For tackling poverty in rural and urban areas of South Asia, separate strategies are required. This is since the factors augmenting poverty are vastly different in these areas. Rural poverty requires more immediate attention, as four out of five poor people live in rural areas. Elimination of urban bias in public expenditures and redirection of resources to rural development and agricultural support programmes are essential to address rural poverty. Strategies to reduce poverty must be situation specific, directly addressing the realities on the ground. These should concentrate on building local capacities, improving asset distribution and providing micro-credit.

Since the region has variable experiences in poverty reduction, it is important for policy makers to draw upon success stories from within their own countries as well as from their neighbours. Experience shows that effective poverty redressal requires the active involvement of local governments. Local governments must prioritise poverty alleviation in order to serve people's needs and respond to their immediate concerns. This can increase participation, making development more people-centred. Kerala presents one positive example of community and state participation in the implementation of effective poverty alleviation programmes.

Despite considerable progress in some countries in expanding basic human capabilities, the absolute number of poor in South Asia has continued to increase. It is evident that the challenge of poverty alleviation in South Asia has only just begun. The immediate task facing policy makers is to address basic human concerns in times of regional military escalation and global economic crisis.

The South Asian region is found to be one of the most militarised regions in the world. Yet the governments continue to redirect scarce resources toward building new weapons of mass destruction. Such non-productive investments, in the name of national security, are taking a high toll on human security while people's lives, the means as well as the ends of all development concerns, are left unheeded. An alarming development for South Asia is the open nuclearisation of an already vulnerable and volatile region.

India's three nuclear tests, one on 11 May 1998 and two on May 13 in Pokhran, heralded a new age of nuclear politics for South Asia and a seismic shift in the region's relations with the outside world. Pakistan's six nuclear counterblasts in Chaghai, Baluchistan on 28 and 30 May in the same year. further shattered the global nuclear nonproliferation framework under the Nuclear non-Proliferation Treaty (NPI), sharpening tensions between the two South Asian rivals. India and Pakistan's overt nuclear capabilities have undermined the 'security in ambiguity' surrounding the subcontinent's nuclear deterrence.

Military expenditures, already high in the region, are projected to increase considerably with the advent of full-scale nuclear programmes. The implications for promoting human security and human development in South Asia are disturbing. Following India's announcement, Pakistan immediately responded by increasing its defence expenditure by an additional 8.5 per cent in nominal terms to $3.3 billion dollars for the fiscal year 1998-99. The rising defence burdens in India and Pakistan continue to impose prohibitive social and economic costs on their people.

Embroiled in an internecine 15 year conflict with Tamil separatists leaving over 50,000 dead, the Sri Lankan government's defence spending has also expanded to alarming levels in recent years, crowding out investments in people. While the government of Bangladesh concluded its long-standing conflict with guerrilla forces in the Chittagong Hill Tracts through a peace accord, it too has witnessed a considerable growth in its military spending, today claiming nearly 18 per cent of the budget.

Table 9.2
Military expenditure in South Asia as a percentage of GDP

Countries	*Year*		
	1985	*1994*	*1997*
India	2.6	3.6	3.1
Pakistan	5.2	7.0	5.3
Bangladesh	1.3	1.5	1.8
Sri Lanka	2.7	4.7	5.1
Nepal	0.8	1.1	0.9

South Asian countries maintain substantial paramilitary forces whose funding falls outside regular defence budgets. For instance, India's combined allocations for its paramilitary forces, numbering in excess of one million soldiers, amounted to $773 million in 1998-99 within the budget of the Ministry of Home Affairs. Numbering nearly a quarter of a million, Pakistan's paramilitary forces were reported to cost the country $200 million for the fiscal year 1998-99.

Furthermore, India and Pakistan have supplied weapons valued at millions of dollars to rebel groups in neighbouring countries over the past several decades.[12] The transfer of hi-tech military hardware from abroad has been plagued by corruption and overspending. Besides the losses to corruption, the social costs of expensive arms transfers from abroad are immense. If the immense costs of conventional weapons and large land armies are not already enough, new estimates for maintaining full-scale nuclear arsenals including command and control with nuclear safeguards, training, and delivery systems are expected to run India and Pakistan each, at a bare minimum of, $750 million per annum.[13]

Over a 10-year period, a projected $15 billion may be spent by the two adversaries on the production and maintenance of these instruments of war. This is enough to educate, properly nourish, and provide health care to almost 37.5 million neglected children in South Asia. The price for an effective command and control structure alone costs millions of dollars, and ballistic missile testing, resumed in April 1999, holds a price tag of several hundred million dollars.[14]

Non-transparency of military budgets, especially regarding defence-specific nuclear spending, hinders complete accuracy by researchers. Further, published defence expenditures are regularly estimated to be underreported by 20-30 per cent. Many items related to nuclear programme spending are, for example, camouflaged under various budgetary heads, and the details of the prices paid for nuclear equipment are often missing, making precise analysis nearly impossible. Nevertheless, it is fair to acknowledge the defence policy choices that result in staggering social trade-offs.

Since 1945 the United States spent just under five and a half trillion dollars to maintain its nuclear capability. The Soviet Union's overall military rivalry with the West significantly crippled the Soviet economy by the late 1980s. Iraq too has reportedly spent $5-$10 billion in its efforts to produce nuclear weapons—an enormous sum for a poor country devastated by two decades of conflict.[15] Pakistan and India can only incur the costs of nuclear build-up by further depriving their people of the essential means for a dignified livelihood.

These costs only refer to direct nuclear weapons programme related expenditures. Other economic losses should also be calculated in any attempt to determine the aggregate financial consequences of India and Pakistan's decision to go nuclear. These losses range from the sanctions imposed by Japan, the United States and Canada, to the loss of Foreign Direct Investment (FDI) that immediately occurred after the nuclear tests. For Pakistan, FDI fell 46 per cent (from $286 million to $155 million) from July to November 1998, and private foreign investment dropped (from $471 million to $156 million) in the same period.[16]

The recent nuclear tests have cost Pakistan $10 billion in economic terms—pushing the country's development back by two and a half years. A slow-down in foreign guest worker remittances flowing through the country's banks in 1998 has also affected the country's balance-of-payments position and overall resource gap. Combine these losses with the estimated costs of the subcontinent's nuclear build-up in 1998, and the realisation is bound to be shocking.

The alarming developments in India and Pakistan's nuclear and ballistic missile programmes have further threatened to undermine the region's stability. Rather than improving each country's national military security, full nuclearisation and new missile tests have upset the ability of conventional forces to provide adequate territorial defence, and have eroded the relatively safer non-weaponised nuclear deterrent in the subcontinent.

A nuclear sword perilously hangs over the more than one billion people of South Asia. Given the considerable repercussions for human security from a nuclear stand-off in South Asia, a delicate balance must be sought between an investment in arms and an investment in people. Such a balance can only come about through a concerted effort to build confidence and devise a new framework for peaceful coexistence in the region. The three wars fought between India and Pakistan, coupled with constant low-intensity conflict along the Line of Control (LoC) and Siachen glacier, have left a legacy of deep mistrust. To surpass the nuclear dangers of the present, an integrated strategy for peace and human security must be evolved.

India and Pakistan must desist from any further testing and avoid hair-trigger situations by refraining from deploying and arming tactical missiles with nuclear warheads and forming sound nuclear doctrines. Military training exercises should be banned near border areas. Besides border patrols, soldiers and military hardware should not be stationed within a reasonable distance of the border between Pakistan and India, including the LoC. Renewed dialogue should be staged between Pakistan and India to settle the core Kashmir conflict and other outstanding disputes. High level negotiations must be pursued with even greater vigour and deeper commitment to resolve issues.

Regional security arrangements, along the lines of Association of South Asian Nations (ASEAN) should be encouraged by formally incorporating political and security issues into the South Asian Association for Regional Co-operation (SAARC) agenda. Each South Asian country could then resolve to peacefully settle regional and internal conflicts through the good offices and mediation services provided by the secretary-general of the SAARC, as well as through SAARC member-countries. Innovative measures-building trust, confidence, and security should be adopted to buttress, rather than replace, conflict resolution processes in South Asia. In this regard, all South Asian countries should mutually decide to reduce their existing levels of military spending by an agreed fixed percentage a year in real terms and to earmark the potential savings to accelerate the pace of their economic growth and human development.

Further, as India and Pakistan consider tough decisions concerning the Comprehensive Test Ban Treaty (CTBT), Fissile Material Control Treaty (FMCT), and Nuclear non-Proliferation Treaty (NPT), they have many useful lessons to draw on, including Brazil and Argentina's nuclear weapons free-zone and South Africa's recent decision to denuclearise after years of investing in nuclear weapons. Nuclear disarmament and a decrease in total military spending are impossible unless the security of nations and people can be guaranteed. This requires cognisance of South Asia's relations with China, the Middle East, and the rest of the world. Regrettably, the five nuclear powers continue to evade their obligation under article IV of the NPT to work for complete disarmament under strict and effective international control. Inspired by the growing number of South Asian people-to-people non-formal dialogues, a renewed global peace movement have become a need of the time.

Use of nuclear weapons, with their potential for the mass annihilation of innocent civilians and environment, will become a distant possibility when a concerned and knowledgeable global civil society demands from governments the complete abolition of these armaments and the establishment of a new global regulatory framework. Perhaps with such a strategy in place, the nuclear race will not only be abated, but the insanity of arms races in poor countries will also be controlled, enabling governments to concentrate on the urgent task of improving people's lives.

Peace can never be achieved through nuclear or conventional force superiority. Building large nuclear arsenals is not so much a threat to other countries as it is to the human security of the people of the nuclear state. The collapse of the Soviet Union bears testament: despite having enough nuclear weapons to destroy the world, the Soviet government could not feed its people or provide them with productive jobs and decent social services. Conversely, Costa Rica chooses not to maintain a military, while spending one-third of its national income on education, nutrition, and health. Costa Rica today is the only prosperous democracy in troubled Central America.

South Asia has been slow to adopt broad-based liberalisation policies taking place in the western world, and can learn a great deal from such experiences. Liberalising trade and allowing greater capital mobility can promote growth in developing countries, through increased technology and knowledge transfers. The reality is that the world's industries and financial systems are today inextricably intertwined. Just as no one anticipated how swiftly the recent local panic in Thailand would bring down the entire East Asian region, no one could really understand how the collapse of the world's biggest growth zone would ripple through the West.

Today, South Asia confronts more and more daunting economic and human development challenges. The global economic slow-down has already retarded South Asia's growth. Slackening of the export market has pulled growth down to 4.6 per cent in 1998 and is expected to remain below five per cent till the year 2020.[17] This will hinder South Asia's efforts to reduce poverty and raise the living standards. Further, social expenditures are often the first to be cut to achieve fiscal discipline during economic recessions and adjustment. The twin effects of an economic slow-down and fiscal adjustment exacerbate the burden on the poor. Thus human development in South Asia, in the aftermath of the East Asian crisis, may receive a further setback.

The implications of globalisation for South Asia are critical. Policy makers in South Asia need to effectively manage liberalisation and structural adjustment policies. South Asia continues to repress financial sectors and protect goods markets. Lower vulnerability to international capital flows is simply an accidental by-product of this reluctance to liberalise. But, the correct lesson to draw from this experience is not to forgo the many advantages of openness. Rather, trade liberalisation must be combined more effectively with controls on short-term capital movements. Indeed, curbs on free capital mobility have also been proposed by some advocates of free trade.

Until recently, most South Asian countries have been encouraging import substitution policies and have been slow to adopt trade liberalisation strategies. If liberalisation is properly sequenced and hot flows carefully managed globalisation is beneficial to all. Comparative lessons from Russia and the People's Republic of China (PRC) are helpful. When Russia moved from a centrally-planned to a market-oriented economy, it quickly dismantled both its legal and political administrative machinery and authority to carry out the market reforms were thus lacking. The result was economic chaos runaway unemployment effects galloping inflation, and currency collapse. The PRC is busy developing a solid civil service system and a strong banking and financial framework.

From such experiences, South Asian policy makers should realise that building markets and institutions of governance takes time. Without regional cooperation and mutually beneficial competition, South Asia cannot expect to meet the challenges of the next millennium. There is much to be gained from technical cooperation within the region.

HUMAN GOVERNANCE

Humane governance is a powerful concept which, if implemented, can help enrich the life of the common people and lay the basis for fairer and more just societies in which human, political, and economic rights of all people are protected and their freedom of choice expanded. It is a norm appropriate to all countries, not just to South Asia. It remains an ideal even in mature democracies of the developed countries. But the need for humane governance is most acute in the poor populous democracies of South Asia.

Humane governance requires effective participation of people in state, civil society and, private sector activities that are conducive to human development. It further enjoins the state, civil society, and the private sector to help build capacities which will meet the basic needs of all people, particularly women, children, and the poor. Humane governance will also ensure that human development is sustainable.

The concept of governance, in its present day form, was born out of the frustration with the effectiveness of foreign aid. It has received great impetus in the wake of the collapse of communism in the transitional economies of Eastern Europe and the former Soviet Union. These transitional economies, their people and their governments, found themselves ill-prepared to deal with the emerging market economy without regulatory institutions, habits of contract fulfilment, without agencies to facilitate transactions, and with no adequate insurance mechanism or safety nets for the poor. Thus, the issues of good governance, with which developing countries have been struggling, came into force in the transitional economies as well.

In recent years, the concept of governance has been evolving from then arrow definition used by the World Bank as the manner in which power is exercised in the management of a country's economic and social resources to the broader definition adopted by the Commission on Global Governance as the sum of the many ways individuals and institutions, public and private, manage their common affairs. However, often good governance is defined in a descriptive instrumental way without a clear end purpose.

Good governance in the South Asian context has to go well beyond good politics or even the creation of a decent society. It must enable the state, the civil society, and the private sector to further broad-based economic growth and social development as a means to greater human development and increased human welfare. The governance debate of the late twentieth century must be expanded to capture the growing realisation that people are moving to the centrestage in dialogues on political and economic change.

The role of formal and informal institutions in South Asia is evolving from a neo-colonial past but the progress is extremely uneven, and not always positive. In some countries, there is increasing apprehension that progress towards democracy has not brought about an advance towards a rule-based society. Formal institutions have been in decline and informal rules, connections, and processes have gained ground overtime and are impeding good governance. Good governance should be judged by success in advancing human development in the broadest sense. The state, or its immediate realisation, the government, the market, or the society ultimately can have only one purpose—to enhance the well-being of the people who are members of the society, citizens of the state, or participants in the market.

The upsurge of democratic demands in civil societies across the world has clarified the fundamental principles of humane governance. Governance must be seen by people as participatory and in their own interest ownership. It must be conducive to building of a society in which none feel humiliated-'decency'; and should be embodied in structures which are transparent and accountable to the owners, i.e., the people, 'accountability'. Ownership, decency, and accountability are the bedrock principles underlying humane governance. While good governance must reduce transaction, costs and enforce contracts, humane governance must be based on both real and perceived ownership, decency, and accountability for and by all citizens.

People's active participation is the guiding force behind the concept of humane governance. Humane governance is conceptualised in three interlocking dimensions: good political governance, good economic governance, and good civic governance.

Political Governance

Good political governance emphasises the rule of law, accountability, and transparency. It seeks to achieve these goals through a constitutional framework that is not easily amendable, free and fair multi-party elections, and a clear separation of powers among the executive, judiciary, and the legislative branches of the government. The new political economy has defined the ideal polity in terms of constitutions which are not easily amendable by legislature, even democratically elected ones. It views the state as captured by special interest groups, lobbyists, and politicians eager to follow short-sighted policies that will ensure re-election. The electorate is represented by average voter whose preferences are for minimising taxation, maximising private gain, and the exploitation of free-riding opportunities.

This school of thought has little trust in the voters' benevolence and even less faith in the politicians' honesty. It also considers civil servants as given to inflating their budgets and expanding their empires rather than serving the people. Voters vote, and that is the sum total of their political activity. Politicians as legislators seek to pursue policies that maximise their chance of re-election, while special interest lobbies exploit rent seeking opportunities by cultivating the legislators and the executive.

According to the new political economy, good political governance, includes: a regular, free, and fair elections, with multi-party democracy; an impartial judiciary protected by a separation of powers; and a constitution not easily amendable by any of the branches of government. As the experience of South Asia indicates, the basics of good political governance are not enough to ensure effective delivery of public goods and services, a stable law and order situation, and prompt and affordable justice.

The problems of lawlessness in South Asia have grown in recent years, and the provision of speedy and inexpensive justice remains a distant dreams. Furthermore, corruption, both in the public and private spheres, is widespread and entrenched, precluding the channelling of development resources to the intended beneficiaries. High population growth rates and constrained fiscal resources have compounded the problems of political governance.

Yet, notwithstanding these trends, the chief sources of poor political governance are the over-centralisation of state powers, the limited transparency and accountability of elected representatives and bureaucrats and a deficiency in the means to articulate the needs and aspirations of the people. To achieve humane governance in such a setting, the policies for good political governance should include:

i) Decentralisation and deconcentration of power to afford people ample opportunities to participate in making decisions that affect their life.

ii) Accountability and transparency of elected representatives and public officials;

iii) Full access of all citizens to justice that is prompt and affordable;

iv) Elimination of all forms of discrimination against women and minorities; and

v) Maintenance of peace and social cohesion within and between the states.

By the careful execution, decentralisation can serve as one of the chief instruments of people's participation for advancing humane governance. By decentralising power from the national capitals to regions, towns and village, people's access to decision-making and efficiency in the delivery of public service can increase. Many industrial countries delegate 25 per cent or more of total government spending to the local level. But the governments of South Asia remain much more centralised, delegating less than 10 per cent of the budgetary spending and giving local governments few opportunities to raise funds through taxation or borrowing.

By giving local people a chance to choose, for example, ready access to basic education and health care rather than the construction of distant colleges or hospitals, decentralisation generates political pressure necessary to focus governments' attention on human development priorities. Decentralisation can take several forms, such as horizontal decentralisation, where power is dispersed among institutions at the same level, and vertical decentralisation, which is far more important as certain legislative, financial and administrative powers are shifted downwards to lower tiers of authority. With the huge corpus of NGOs working in South Asian countries, some observers maintain that a new kind of decentralisation by default is underway.

However, decentralisation is not a panacea for resolving South Asia's perennial crisis of governance and underdevelopment. When practised successfully, it has the potential of contributing to a more people-centred framework of governance by decreasing the distance between citizens and the state, enabling governments to be more responsive to local needs and to make better use of scarce resources for basic human priorities.

Responsiveness and accountability of elected representatives to people's needs and concerns are crucial elements of the political dimension of humane governance. The concept of humane governance is not starry-eyed about the state or the politician. It would like legislators to be more accountable to the voters and more responsive to their needs. That is the politician's job; elections are but the means to get the opportunity to do the job. But the voters are also meant to be actively participating in shaping, if not making, the decisions that affect their lives. Participation in political activities on an ongoing basis is a valuable function. It relates to basic human rights such as freedom of speech, freedom of association, and freedom of belief, which have been fought for and won in some parts of the world but are still to be won universally.

Economic Governance

Good economic governance emphasises the role of the state not only in securing macro-economic stability, guaranteeing property rights, removing market distortions, and eliminating rent-seeking opportunities, but is also concerned with investment in people and basic infrastructure, protection of natural environment, and a progressive and equitable fiscal system to promote economic growth with social justice.

The basic problem concerning good economic governance is the appropriate role of the state in relation to the market. The neo-classical economists believed that Adam Smith's invisible hand would allocate scarce economic resources optimally. Specifically, the neo-classical economists were concerned that the state will create rent-seeking opportunities by increasing distortions and deviations from the norm of competitive behaviour; and will jeopardise wealth and wealth-enhancing activities by threats of expropriation or unpredictable taxation. These ideas encouraged the notion of a minimalist state—a state in which the volume of state activity in the economy is to be minimised and, where the state concerns itself with ensuring macro-economic stability with the help of an independent central bank; and guaranteeing property rights and respect for legal frameworks and the rule of law.

In the post-war world after 1945, there was an almost explosive growth in the role of the state in all countries. In the OECD countries (Organisation of Economic Co-operation and Development) the total government expenditure as a proportion of GDP had grown to nearly 50 per cent by 1995 compared to about 20 per cent and 10 per cent in 1937 and 1913, respectively.[18] In developing countries, the central government expenditure increased from around 15 to 30 per cent of GDP over the period 1960-85.[19]

In recent decades, as a result of several global events, a serious rethinking took place on the role of the state. The collapse of command and control economies in the former Soviet Union and Central and Eastern Europe, the fiscal crisis of the welfare state in most of the established industrial countries, widespread failure of the state in directly productive activities in developing countries, and continuing neglect of critical human development issues in many parts of the world have led to a serious search for a definition of good economic governance, which will blend economic growth with social justice. It is now realised that the state's activities should match its capability. There is greater recognition that governments should concentrate on core public functions which will create an enabling environment for civil society and the private sector to function efficiently and equitably.

There is a broad consensus in South Asia that a liberal economic framework in which critical prices reflect their scarcity values and in which the private sector is afforded maximum opportunities to operate freely, is in the best interest of long-term development, provided markets can be regulated in the best interests of the less privileged. However, there is more to good economic governance than only competitive markets. Human security is ensured not so much by armament expenditures, important though they may be for territorial security, but by human development related expenditures, which will lead to the development of cohesive, well-informed, and, hopefully, more tolerant societies.

Good economic governance must seek to make the market a fairer place by insisting on elimination of discrimination not only against women but also against the disabled, the elderly, and the children. To achieve humane governance, the conventional elements of good economic governance would need to be supplemented by

i) sufficient budgetary allocations to social priority areas, such as basic education, primary health care, safe drinking water, adequate nutrition, family planning services, and micro-credit schemes for the poor;
ii) a progressive taxation system; efficient and well-targeted subsidies for thc poor; and
iii) equitable access to credit and land.

Effective economic and political governance also requires strong institutions. Institutions are rules, both formal and informal, that bring predictability and stability in modern economic exchange. For competitive capitalism, these rules need to be conducive to production and the creation of wealth.

In modern market economies, legal and regulatory structures assist in providing incentives for saving and investment by protecting property rights, enforcing contracts, and determining the efficiency of government policies. Accessible courts, effective bankruptcy laws, sound securities and competition regimes, and strong anti-corruption policies are essential for greasing the wheels of a market economy. They are required for encouraging new innovations, absorbing investments, and easing economic transitions.

Absence of contract enforcement and property rights comes down harder on the poor, since they often lack secure property and have limited, if any, political connection.

Traditionally, women have limited access to property rights, particularly land. But this deprivation is intensified when the few who own some property cannot exercise control over it. The poor cannot find a fair place in the market without regulatory institutions to protect them. In contrast, the rich can survive without such regulatory structures, since they are powerful enough to protect their own property rights and get their business contracts enforced.

Without clear, fair and predictable rules, economic activity not only breeds inefficiencies but also reinforces existing inequalities in the society. It is inefficient because it hinders the accumulation of wealth and, therefore, retards growth; it is inequitable because it tolerates a marketplace that discriminates against the poor, particularly women. As a result, when institutional inefficiencies are reduced, economic growth increases and the degree, severity, and incidence of poverty diminishes.

Civic Governance

The realisation of the importance of civil society in good governance is relatively recent and owes a great deal to the efforts and successes of non-governmental (NGOs) and grass-roots self-help organisations. The broader civil society groups, including households, media, professional groups, and business are increasingly seen as vital in securing the fundamental human, political, and economic rights. These rights are implicit in good economic and political governance but are rarely available to those excluded from the formal structures of power. These are women, the poor, and ethnic and religious minorities. The informal structures of the civil society are important not only in supporting formal processes and keeping the rulers accountable but also for increasing the capacity of the people to fend for themselves through creating trust and cementing community relations.

Civic governance has been ignored till recently by economists and political scientists. This is the civil society broadly defined as all voluntary and private sector activities. This is the sphere where individuals and households operate most of the time. They may form companies and NGOs or they may create informal associations of households within the community, savings and credit organisations, voluntary fire-fighting services, and child-care groups. This is where the principle of self-organisation comes into play.

The freedom to organise is a basic human right, and often, many such activities are in defence of human rights. Trade unions are part of civil society, as are business associations and religious groups. Much of this is self-governance, but it requires a framework of human rights to flourish. In the former Soviet Union and the countries of Eastern Europe, for instance, it was civil society that was conspicuously absent and has flourished since 1989. This is the dimension of self-help and self-development that is vital to human development at the household and community levels in South Asia and elsewhere.

At the core of civic governance is the determination and self-initiative of people to improve their capacity to govern their lives, by creating informal structures and processes to address their basic concerns. For those who are excluded from the formal structures of power—women, the poor, and minorities whether ethnic, religious, or racial—these governance alternatives enable people to fend for themselves and to reduce their dependence on the centralised state. At another level, good civic governance involves civil society's role in protecting basic human rights, particularly the rights of the disadvantaged members of society.

Fundamental human rights are enshrined in the constitutions of the South Asian countries. Without powerful voices from civil society defending these rights and freedoms, however, the majority of people may not be able to exercise their constitutional rights. An independent media, which is an integral part of civil society, has an important role to play in protecting people's rights and holding rulers accountable.

Good civic governance includes good citizenship, good corporate and employer behaviour, good neighbourly activity, and the effective self-policing of rights violations. By channelling social and cultural resources from the bottom up and stressing both the rights and responsibilities of citizens in relation to the state, good civic governance supports formal political and economic processes. The forces promoting good civic governance complement and encourage the evolution toward good political and good economic governance.

The three dimensions of humane governance are inextricably linked and complementary to one another. Bound together by the principles of ownership, decency, and accountability, good political, economic, and civic governance are equally integrated to form a governance framework that is both dynamic and progressive. The nature of institutions and decentralisation, for instance, are key governance issues that cut across these three major dimensions of humane governance. Institutions are needed to lessen the transaction costs of political, economic, and social activities. Actively involved citizens demand the decentralisation and diffusion of power. In short, a holistic approach toward humane governance entails an engaged citizenry working for a responsive, efficient government, a market that creates jobs and generates income, and a civil society that encourages informed debate, socially responsible businesses, and non-profit, community-building associations.

Humane governance is not merely a means to human development. It expands the idea of human development by adding significant dimensions, which are best captured in the notion of human freedom. If human development were simply measured by the three variables which go into the Human Development Index (literacy, life expectancy, and per capita income), high Human Development Index (HDI) results could be achieved despite a lack of freedom. By contrast, free democratic societies may fail to achieve high HDI values.

In 1989, however, the world witnessed a historic human revolution that established democratic government as an unchallenged norm almost throughout the world. Thus, the question shifted from a rivalry between ideologies to one of variations of the democratic order. It was then that the issues of good governance came to the fore. Democracy, while necessary and desirable, can be insufficient in the face of declining living standards. Democracy must deliver what people want, such as economic betterment and the means to exercise one's freedom to choose. This is possible only when humane governance delivers human development. While it is a means to human development, humane governance is also a vital complement to human development by guaranteeing that it is achieved in a free, effective, and equitable manner.

The pathways to humane governance are many and varied. The juxtaposition of the state, market, and civil society, in accordance with the needs and desires of the people, is at the heart of humane governance. Managing and sustaining this process will be unique in each society and subject to change. The achieving humane governance in South Asia are complex and varied. Reversing the region's present course, however, is not a hopeless endeavour. Certain principles of action that maximise people's initiative and identify conditions favourable to change can bring about the desired institutional and policy changes. At the same time, it is important that the governance innovations proposed are also politically acceptable, financially and administratively feasible, and developed over time through a consultative process involving all stakeholders.

Humane governance recognises that human institutions are imperfect and often driven by the self-interest of those in charge. Nevertheless, the search must continue for a participatory, responsive, and accountable polity embedded in a competitive, non-discriminatory yet equitable economy. This, in turn, requires that people's money is plowed back to serve their basic needs which will expand the opportunities open to them, and where people have the ability and the freedom to self-organise.

Human Governance Index

It is to be expected that a country with high economic, political, and civic governance would also have high human development. It is possible to examine this connection by arriving at a measure of humane governance, however crude, and exploring its correlation with the Human Development Index. Thus, we make an attempt here to construct a Humane Governance Index (HGI). The HGI is a composite index of indicators measuring economic, political, and civic governance. The three composite indices were compiled using currently available indicators.

Economic governance is assessed by measures of fiscal policy (budget deficit), monetary policy (inflation rate), trade policy (current account deficit), social priority spending (public expenditure on both health and education), and liberalisation of the economy.

Political governance is assessed by measures of various political perception indicators including corruption, quality of bureaucracy, accountability, law and order, ethnic tension, etc.

Civic governance is assessed by measures of freedom of expression (relating to the right of the governed to express their views on government policies and actions), non-discrimination (relating to mistreatment on the grounds of race, ethnicity, gender, religion, etc.), political participation (relating to free and fair multi-party elections), and rule of law.

Table 9.3
Human Governance Index (HGI)

Country/Region	*Economic*	*Political*	*Civic*	*HGI value*
India	0.599	0.591	0.540	0.577
Pakistan	0.565	0.469	0.472	0.502
Sri Lanka	0.647	0.303	0.445	0.465
Bangladesh	0.494	0.441	0.451	0.462
South Asia	0.590	0.560	0.520	0.560

Humane governance can only be achieved through a combination of all three dimensions of economic, political, and civic governance. One dimension does not come before another. They must occur in unison for the concept of humane governance to be realised. Hence, a simple mean of the economic, political, and civic governance indices was taken to form the HGI.

A higher number of HGI indicates higher levels of humane governance and vice versa. The HGI is a very preliminary, and admittedly crude, attempt to provide a quantitative measure of what is a complex, multi-faceted concept of humane governance. Neither the absolute numbers nor the ranking should be taken as anything other than tentative and exploratory. To make an accurate quantitative measurement of humane governance, much more work needs to be done by many more people before it can become acceptable as a tool of analysis.

From an inefficient deployment of resources and crippling debt burdens to social divisions drawn on ethnic and sectarian fines, arbitrary law enforcement and failed political leadership, few regions shoulder governance challenges with the scope and intensity of those found in the South Asian region. The perverse incentive structure in Bangladesh's eroding civil service, the refusal of Pakistani citizens to pay income tax or monthly utility bills, and the internecine conflict ravaging North-East Sri Lanka are deviations from humane governance behaviour that are merely symptoms of a much deeper, system-wide social and political disease.

In studying this highly complex problem, efforts must be made to avoid convenient generalisations, the predicament afflicting the South Asian countries today cannot be attributed to the failure of any particular institution or group of institutions. Humane governance, by discussing policy attention on the betterment of human lives, also provides a blue-print for reform that places people at its centrestage. By viewing politics as a central part of economic systems and civil society apparatus, the humane governance framework, unlike the new political economy and neo-classical economics, envisions a constructive role for politics in empowering people.

Governance Reform Efforts

The historical fragility of multi-ethnic states in the twentieth century underscores the high stakes involved in achieving viable democratic institutions. If states are to survive today, they will have to establish new relationships with their people. South Asian countries maintain considerable institutional and human resources that can be mobilised to advance humane governance in all its dimensions. Governance reform efforts in South Asia are few and far between. This despite the growing clarity on the nature of the region's problems and what needs to be done to overcome them.

When deciding policy priorities and approaches to reform, efforts must be made to avoid convenient generalisations. The policy predicaments afflicting South Asian countries today cannot be attributed to the failure of any particular government or any particular institution, but rather to long-term structural and process deficiencies. In accord with humane governance principles of ownership, decency, and accountability, all proposals for policy and institutional changes are aimed at accelerating national levels of human development.

To develop policies and institutions that work to the benefit of its people, South Asia will need to make a sustained effort along three broad policy areas. These are:

i) Redirecting the priorities of the state.
ii) Revitalising state institutions, and
iii) Building new alliances with civil society.

The effectiveness of the proposed reforms will rest on the three basic virtues of transparency, accountability, and decentralisation that cut across all dimensions of governance.

Redirection of state priorities

South Asia must advance the core human development concerns. To re-focus the states' efforts towards human development four key actions are required. They are:

i) Liberal investments in basic human needs of the poor,
ii) Provision of social safety nets that reach the poor,
iii) Distribution of key productive assets through land and credit reforms, and
iv) A major impetus to increase economic growth through an increased role for the private sector, more open economies, and an equitable fiscal policy that taxes the rich and spends on the poor.

Governments must prioritise the needs of the poor to overcome mass human deprivation. In South Asia, there are an estimated 515 million people living in poverty; 395 million adults are unable to read and write; 276 million people lack access to basic health facilities; 278 million people have no access to safe drinking water; and another 879 million people live without proper sanitation facilities.[20] The region stands at a lower rung of human development, having invested so little in the education and health of its people. The central task of the states is to address the basic needs of the people, especially the poor, women, children, and the disadvantaged.

Governments need to work towards a new social compact and this requires both political attention and financial resources. Political leaders must realise that there can be no real development without a strong base of healthy and educated population. Similarly, there can be no real sovereignty and no real freedom without freedom from hunger, illiteracy, malnutrition, and overpopulation. Once governments realise the need for collective action to end this deprivation, lack of resources ceases to be a hurdle. A realistic human development programme should be designed and implemented, to provide basic social services of education, health, nutrition, clean drinking water, and family planning services to people.

The minimal aim of South Asian states should be to protect those who have been by-passed by the markets, crushed underneath the burden of adjustment, and shunned by informal community networks. This requires social safety nets that are not only efficient in their reach but also adequate in their coverage.

Though almost half of all South Asians are faced with acute income deprivation, most countries still allocate too little for too many. In Pakistan, for instance, even if all the money set aside for income transfers to the poor were to reach them, it would mean a transfer of less than one cent per poor person per day. By contrast many poor developing, and transition economies transfer between five and 10 per cent of their national incomes to the poor through the ambit of various social safety nets.

South Asia needs to spend more on social safety nets and to channel these resources where they are urgently needed. The region has a long history of social safety net programmes. Many programmes have been relatively successful: Jawahar Rozgar Yojana (JRY), Maharashtra Employment Guarantee Scheme (MEGS), and Food For Education Programme (FFEP) in Bangladesh.[21] But the region still needs to devise programmes that are efficient and well targeted and could open up the opportunities of social mobility for the poor.

In many parts of South Asia, the distribution of productive assets is radically skewed. An effective land reforms package is the best answer to such a skewed distribution of land. Land reforms can be justified on economic, social, and political grounds. Empirical evidence shows that land reforms are generally associated with raising economic efficiency by increasing output per acre. An egalitarian distribution of land is also essential for breaking the strong feudal hold over politics. Inequitable distribution of land bestows inordinate political and economic power on a few, whereas the great number of land less people lack both social standing and political rights. Land reforms must be implemented with the active involvement of peasant organisations.

Provision of micro-credit will help to empower the poor. Access to credit should be treated as a fundamental human right. The experience of the Grameen Bank in Bangladesh has demonstrated that the poor are good savers and investors, and they are eminently creditworthy.[22] The banking system should take a chance on the future potential of the people, not on their past wealth. Much of the credit needs of the poor can be met by recovering defaulted loans from powerful businessmen and influential politicians.

In South Asian countries, a new economic system based on a new balance between public and private sectors, fair taxation, pro-poor expenditures, an innovative strategy to engineer industrial and agricultural breakthroughs, an export-led growth system, rapid privatisation of public assets, and a new framework of high growth and better distribution should be designed to improve the current financial crisis.

A major component of this new framework for efficient and equitable growth is the forging of a development partnership with the private sector. Governments need to provide legal and regulatory frameworks that ensure private sector growth and prevent the creation of monopolies. Another component of sustainable growth should be a vibrant and labour intensive export sector. South Asia must take its chances on global markets and discover its real economic potential that remains dormant due to decades of protectionist policies. Liberalisation of trade can create substantial dividends for South Asia, equal to nearly five per cent of GDP. Another key challenge for promoting economic growth is to address the prevailing fiscal crisis in most South Asian countries.

The most promising way to deal with the mismanagement of resources in South Asia is to prioritise the existing expenditures. The challenge is to make public spending more pro-poor and to transfer it from non-productive to the productive sectors, from consumption to investment, from defence to social development, and from projects to small workable initiatives. In this regard, the governments can take the following steps:

i) *Reduction of non-merit subsidies*: A large part of subsidies have little or no impact on poverty reduction. There is a compelling case for reducing these non-merit subsidies by recovering user charges, which are sometimes as low as 10 per cent in some countries like India. At the same time, there is a need for increasing the performance of essential subsidies. Whenever there is a powerful case for subsidies, they should be performance-oriented, timebound, efficiently targeted, and subject to periodic review.

ii) *Reduction of defence expenditures:* Military spending has claims to significant resources in national budgets. There is an urgent need to design a new budgetary paradigm in the short-run, where the legitimate claims of both defence and development can be met.

iii) *Privatisation of loss-making corporations*: Though most South Asian governments have embarked on their separate privatisation programmes, the implementation of such disinvestment reforms leave a lot to be desired. The process has been very slow: the proceeds stand at a mere two per cent of South Asia's cumulative GDP. Moreover, a weak regulatory framework, allegations of corruption, and problems with absorbing laid-off workers have emerged as key irritants. There is an urgent need to ensure that privatisation is carried out in an honest, transparent, and credible way.

iv) *Enactivation of fiscal responsibility acts*: There is a need to check the profligate behaviour of governments whose economic strategies are based on a short-term horizon. Imposing a legislative limit on public debt is emerging as a key reform option. National parliaments must make governments responsible for their spending decisions. A workable strategy can be designed, where a consensus is developed on whether the ceiling should be placed on the total volume of debt or debt as a proportion of GDP.

v) *Presenation of severity gestures*: There are many visible gestures to institute honest behaviour. Unnecessary perks for high officials can be eliminated, expenditures on foreign delegations and trips can be reduced, the provision for free medical treatment in foreign countries can be abolished, the power to allot expensive plots and permits at throw away prices can be taken away, and less resources could be spent on constructing and furnishing palatial buildings. The budgetary savings from such measures may be small, but they are essential for cementing a culture of financial responsibility.

vi) *Reformation of tax systems*: Tax systems must rely more on direct taxes and less on indirect taxes. The foundations of a new tax culture can be easily laid if tax discipline is enforced at all levels and if the ruling class sets an example by paying its own taxes scrupulously and transparently. There is a need to formalise the informal sector and to limit the growth of black economy by weeding out perverse incentives and by introducing proper surveillance on the borders. Introducing greater transparency in the discharge of tax concessions is also central to reform of the tax system. South Asia needs to set up economically sensible tax systems that could lead to higher incentives for tax compliance and greater opportunities for production. An efficient tax administration, including widespread documentation and computerisation, is also critical for revenue reform. Both revenue and expenditure reforms remain ineffective without effective compliance by provinces and states.

Revitalisation of State Institutions

The affirmation of broad-based democracy, complemented by reforms in the production and distribution mechanisms of society is designed to eradicate the most desperate forms of human deprivation, such as hunger, illiteracy, and insecurity. It is these desperate conditions which foster linkages based on patronage and stand in the way of a responsive political system.

The real challenge is to create an environment where people are able and free to earn a living, to five in security, to access their human rights, and, indeed, to participate in the decisions that shape their destiny. Transparency in all public actions, accountability of elected representatives, adherence to rule of law, and devolution of power into the hands of ordinary people will provide just such a state. In the two federal states of India and Pakistan, diverse segments can be brought into the political mainstream by undertaking fundamental restructuring of the balance of authority between the centre and the states.

An effective way to nurture a pro-people political system is to guard against the personalisation and concentration of power. This involves separating power among state institutions—the parliament, the executive, and the judiciary, to serve as checks and balances. For any process to work, the rules must be observed transparently, neutrally, and universally.

Reformation of parliamentary system: Parliaments ought to be representative of the population, open to public scrutiny, free of corrupt practices, and assume ultimate supremacy over state affairs. Programme for strengthening the sovereignty of people must include nine core strategies:

i) Ensuring the supremacy of the legislature over the executive, both legally and practically, as the chief source of legitimate democratic authority;

ii) Prohibiting the practice of private money buying public power through party funding for elections. All accounts of parties must be audited and open to public;

iii) Developing a stable party system without prejudice to individual party member's freedom of action;

iv) Improving the quality of voter rolls and facilitating voter-friendly registration;

v) Stopping the practice of enacting legislation from outside parliament through presidential ordinances;

vi) Initiating legal controls to monitor expenses and misuse of the state's financial or institutional resources;

vii) Increasing the effectiveness, efficiency, and powers of parliamentary committees that serve as watchdogs over the executive;

viii) Improving the quality of legislation by making use of the legislative support mechanism within and outside the parliamentary secretariat; and

ix) Guaranteeing a minimum level of women's representation in parliament.

Reformation of civil service: In South Asia, no country can succeed without a responsible, accountable and honest civil service.

In India, 45 years after independence, only one commission on administrative reforms was appointed. The recommendations of the Fifth Pay Commission in India were aimed at cutting down the size of the bureaucracy and increasing salaries. The committee of secretaries in charge of implementation agreed to the wage hike but stalled on the proposed down sizing.

In Pakistan, the only notable reform was the introduction of lateral entry into the civil service implemented in 1973. Ostensibly, it was a measure designed to enhance the professional quality of the cadre; in truth, it was to become a powerful means of political influence.

In Bangladesh, since 1972, a total of 211 cases had been reported by the Accountant General through the Public Accounts Committee, questioning the authority and breach of rules. Of those, only 33 have been concluded.

In accordance with the recommendations of the Administrative Reform Committee (ARC) formed in 1986 in Sri Lanka, the bureaucracy was to be down sized by about 20 per cent. However, instead of reducing the cadre strength, the reforms initiated in 1989 saw the size of the management group increase by 4.28 per cent, the executive group by 56.17 per cent and middle level and minor groups by 6.42 per cent by 1992.

In the case of Bhutan, after the reforms to retrench the public sector started in 1987, public sector employment fell by 2,500. However by 1991, another 3,400 employees had been inducted into the public sector, mostly through contractual employment.

Besides improving efficiency, decreasing corruption and giving long-term direction, reforms should aim to enhance the civil service's capacity to effectively provide basic public services at an affordable cost. Specific reform options include eight priority areas:

i) Articulating precisely the roles of civil servants and their relationship with politicians, as well as channels of recourse to guard against the violation of those roles;
ii) Right-sizing the civil service to eliminate redundancies, enhance understaffed departments, and thus enhance efficiency;
iii) Improving performance through public management and specialised skills training, as well as detailed performance appraisals;
iv) Limiting the discretionary powers and privileges of civil service managers;
v) Ensuring a pay scale that is commensurate with the employee's capabilities, meets his or her general needs, and is reasonably competitive with comparable private sector work;
vi) Conducting recruitment and promotions in a manner that underscores merit in addition to national diversity;

vii) Prohibiting politically motivated civil servant transfers and dismissals, especially for applying the law honestly or exercising the legal authority vested in a post; and

viii) Redressing the gender imbalance through affirmative action reflected in laws, civil institutions, and policies.

Reformation of judiciary: South Asia's judiciary systems continue to enjoy public confidence. In a number of jurisdictions, the courts have earned respect for their proactive role in the enforcement of human rights, particularly the rights of the disadvantaged. Conversely, confidence in the subordinate judiciary has eroded. These courts are generally perceived as being manned by an insufficient number of inadequately trained and ill-paid judges. This results in long delays, huge backlog of cases, and a generally poor quality of judgments. In a number of jurisdictions, persistent allegations of corruption are registered. Corrupt practices contribute to inequities for women, the poor, and minorities, creating a general feeling of injustice in many parts of the region.

The judicial system of the region suffers from several long-term structural deficiencies. Besides the lack of material resources for both the functioning of the judiciary and the defence of poor citizens, the judiciary's shortcomings also result from political interference by state institutions intent on limiting the judiciary's mandate, autonomy, and overall effectiveness. Consequently, a fundamental reform issue is to strengthen the judiciary's independence and implement the constitutional provision for the separation of the judiciary from the executive. The allocation of new resources for improving the judiciary must also be preceded by an enhancement in the Supreme Court's powers to discharge its judicial and constitutional responsibilities for ensuring the efficiency and integrity of the entire judiciary, including the subordinate judiciary and magistracy.

The judicial system in South Asia can take progressive strides towards promoting justice and humane governance by adopting the following seven-point agenda:

i) Increasing the number and emoluments of judges;

ii) Adopting an objective recruitment criteria for judges that gives due weight to educational qualifications, professional experience, sensitivity to human rights,

iii) Reputation for integrity, and gender balance;

iv) Providing the judiciary with adequate financial resources to effectively discharge judicial and administrative functions;

v) Increasing the number of courts;

vi) Offering alternative forms of dispute settlement, such as civil arbitration and counselling, to reduce the backlog in the case load of lower courts. Oversight of this mechanism should be entrusted to an appropriate agency under the Supreme Court, rather than the ministry of local government;

iv) Launching national campaigns for legal education reform and for informing citizens about their rights under the law; and

iiv) Providing legal aid to the poor and socially disadvantaged to promote greater access to justice.

Restrcturing of security programmes: Contrary to the world wide post-cold war trend towards military demobilisation, South Asian countries have increased the size of their armed forces and have come to rely on the defence sector as a major source of overall employment. Any strategy to reduce the burden of military personnel expenditures must include the need to create alternative employment opportunities for the subcontinent's vast land armies. Education is one field that may benefit from utilising the skills of demobilised soldiers.

While formulating a realistic financial strategy for educating South Asia's 65 million out-of-school children, the main focus should be the reallocation of existing budgets. A gradual process of defence sector down sizing could facilitate the release of scarce resources necessary to enable surplus military personnel to be trained to contribute to educational development in South Asia's most deprived areas. Any region-wide steps to redeploy some soldiers to the education sector will require political vision, an improvement in external and internal threat perceptions, and a general understanding of the positive economic and, in particular, a human impact of military conversion.

Reforms should be developed on a more cost-effective system of national security, more transparency in defence spending and arms procurement, and a complete check over all non-essential expenditures. In the long-run, detente between India and Pakistan can release substantial resources for investment in the social sectors. In order to rationalise military spending and to promote human security, reforms should be geared towards four core areas:

i) Increasing the transparency of military budget decision-making and civil-military relations through active parliamentary oversight and statutory auditing, including coverage of foreign arms procurement;

ii) Improving efficiency in the management of defence resources, including public defence industries and military businesses;

iii) Expanding the developmental role of the armed forces as a transitional strategy towards demobilisation and reintegration; and

iv) Spurring debate on both the need for affordable defence programmes and possible trade-off between military spending and human development.

South Asian states already possess many institutions and laws. Governance can be improved by increasing the effectiveness and ensuring the independence of existing institutions, without creating new ones. In the longrun, the success of any reformation programme will depend upon the creation of a civic culture geared toward public accountability of legislators, organisation of constituency level opinion groups, the spread of legal awareness, and a belief in the ultimate authority of the society over the state. People should be made aware of both their rights and duties.

Vitalising state-society alliances

Civil Society Organisations (CSOs) can serve as important intermediaries between citizens and the state. They have already taken a lead in reaching the poor. Similarly, the private sector can play a vital role in generating incomes, providing employment opportunities, and fulfilling social responsibilities. However, such a progressive climate of cooperation can only develop if South Asian states provide a proper set of incentives within a well-defined regulatory framework. A code of conduct for the civil society organisations, as well as the private sector, needs to be developed in order to enhance their positive role in promoting humane governance.

The proposals for reform of civil society organisations could include:

i) Establishment of special financing facilities to promote government-CSO partnerships to improve the livelihoods of poor communities;

ii) Protecting of the rights of CSOs, while deterring them from falsifying their accounts and exploiting donors;

iii) Advise CSOs on the establishment of decentralised evaluation mechanisms; and

iv) Invite CSO leaders to advise governments and donor agencies in their area of expertise.

Today, the business community is acknowledged as the chief player in providing jobs and generating income within a country. While the private sector must be afforded adequate incentives to expand and fuel economic growth, its market power and political influence necessitates regulations, cooperative frameworks and guidelines in accordance with the imperatives of humane governance.

A new framework should be evolved for government-business cooperation to increase incentives for private sector innovation, transparency, and accountability. A healthy expansion of South Asia's private sector requires greater trust and cooperation between the government and the business community. Formulating a policy that addresses the concerns of the public and private sectors can best be achieved through mutual consultation. A forum, similar to the deliberation councils of East Asia, is needed to bring the government and business community closer together. Reform proposals floated in the forum would need to be approved by representatives of each sector before becoming a policy.

Voluntary guidelines for corporate social responsibility, prepared collectively or individually by businesses, could encourage the private sector to take civic action on issues ranging from business ethics and environmental responsibility to social development. For its part, governments could offer tax rebates on capital gains to those corporations that invest a certain percentage of their profits in social responsibility programmes. Another integral part of corporate social responsibility is the proper treatment of firm employees and a healthy environment for their work. This involves labour's right to freedom of association and collective bargaining, and the elimination of all forms of forced labour, child labour, and discrimination in respect of employment and occupation.

Most governance failures in South Asia are failures of implementation. Over-ambitious targets are set which delay the process of implementation. In most cases, implementation is essentially a question of balancing conflicting interests of those who are supposed to implement reforms and those who benefit from reforms. Many South Asians, particularly those in leadership positions, are already aware of the nature of their governance problems and how to overcome them. Reformers will need to ensure that their ideas are politically acceptable and financially and administratively feasible.

The reformation strategy needs to be based on the following factors:

i) Reformers must openly deliberate the context, characteristics, and implications of reforms. People, being the principal agents of change, must be included in all stages to encourage a sense of ownership.

ii) The next step is to inform and mobilise progressive forces from different constituencies nationwide, including advocacy organisations and think tanks, the press, business and workers' association, and from within the government.

iii) The implementation of reforms will almost certainly generate opposition among those who extract rents from a system rife with inefficiencies, corruption and injustice. While implementing long-term changes, positive results should be publicised as soon as they emerge to weaken the formation of opposing forces and encourage lobbies for change. Moreover, rulers must be made to use the services that are available to common people, so that they develop a stake in improving them.

iv) Skilfully sequencing the implementation of reforms will be the key variable in determining whether they succeed or fail. Complex reforms should not be rushed for implementation unless some political support has been mobilised. It is difficult to decentralise authority to the district level unless political stability is assured, a strong constituency for change is mobilised, and some visible successes are achieved in the initial reforms.

v) Credible performance criteria would strengthen the reform process. Independent evaluators should regularly monitor and assess the impact of reforms.

A collective action by five important sets of actors such as civil society organisations (CSOs), media, the academic community, international institutions and committed political leaders are essential to implement these strategies.

In South Asia, the role of CSOs becomes even more important in voicing the demands and aspirations of ordinary citizens. A strong and independent media can act as an invaluable tool for raising peoples' awareness of governance issues. Similarly, the academic community, independent policy think tanks, and the intelligentsia can mobilise lobbies for change by initiating debate on important governance issues. As globalisation brings to the fore the importance of basic international precepts, like transparency and accountability, international and regional organisations have gained increased importance in governance reforms. A committed leadership, with a clear and long-term vision, is undoubtedly the most important factor in this frame work for change.

REFERENCES

1. Noronha, Frederick, 'Human Development: Indian Story', *The Tribuze*, April 7, 1997.
2. Ibid.
3. World Bank, *World Development Report*, 1995.
4. 'International Trade Statistics', *Yearbook,* United Nations, 1995.
5. 'Direction of Trade Statistics', *Yearbook*, IMF, 1996.
6. Ibid.
7. Ibid.
8. *Economic Survey*, 1996-97, Government of India, Ministry of Finance, New Delhi.
9. *SAARC SCAN*, November 1996.
10. Ibid.
11. *Economic and Political Weekly, Vol. XXXII,* No. 19, May 10-16, 1997.
12. Ibid.
13. Ibid.

14. *Economic Times*, May 19, 1997.
15. Ibid.
16. Ibid.
17. 'International Trade Statistics' *Yearbook*, United Nations, 1995.
18. Ibid.
19. Ibid.
20. World Bank, *World Development Report*, 1995.
21. Hossain, A.R.M.A, *Migration of Labour from Bangladesh, Bureau of Manpower Employment and Training,* 1979.
22. Tinker, H., *The Banyan Tree: Overseas Emigration from India, Pakistan and Bangladesh*, Oxford University Press, 1997.

Copenhagen Declaration on Social Development

1. For the first time in history, at the invitation of the United Nations, we gather as heads of state and government to recognise the significance of social development and human well-being for all and to give to these goals the highest priority both now and into the twenty-first century.

2. We acknowledge that the people of the world have shown in different ways an urgent need to address profound social problems, especially poverty, unemployment and social exclusion, that affect every country. It is our task to address both their underlying and structural causes and their distressing consequences in order to reduce uncertainty and insecurity in the life of people.

3. We acknowledge that our societies must respond more effectively to the material and spiritual needs of individuals, their families and the communities in which they live throughout our diverse countries and regions. We must do so not only as a matter of urgency but also as a matter of sustained and unshakeable commitment through the years ahead.

4. We are convinced that democracy and transparent and accountable governance and administration in all sectors of society are indispensable foundations for the

realisation of social and people centred sustainable development.

5. We share the conviction that social development and social justice are indispensable for the achievement and maintenance of peace and security within and among our nations. In turn, social development and social justice cannot be attained in the absence of peace and security or in the absence of respect for all human rights and fundamental freedoms. This essential interdependence was recognised 50 years ago in the Charter of the United Nations and has since grown ever stronger.
6. We are deeply convinced that economic development, social development and environmental protection are interdependent and mutually reinforcing components of sustainable development, which is the framework for our efforts to achieve a higher quality of life for all people. Equitable social development that recognises empowering the poor to utilise environmental resources sustainability is a necessary foundation for sustainable development. We also recognise that broadbased and sustained economic growth in the context of sustainable development is necessary to sustain social development and social justice.
7. We recognise, therefore, that social development is central to the needs and aspirations of people throughout the world and to the responsibilities of governments and all sectors of civil society. We affirm that, in both economic and social terms, the most productive policies and investments are those that empower people to maximise their capacities, resources and opportunities. We acknowledge that social and economic development cannot be secured in a sustainable way without the full participation of women and that equality and equity between women and men is a priority for the international community and as such must be at the centre of economic and social development.

8. We acknowledge that people are at the centre of our concerns for sustainable development and that they are entitled to a healthy and productive life in harmony with the environment.

9. We gather here to commit ourselves, our governments and our nations to enhancing social development throughout the world so that all men and women, especially those living in poverty, may exercise the rights, utilise the resources and share the responsibilities that enable them to lead satisfying lives and to contribute to the well-being of their families, their communities and humankind. To support and promote these efforts must be the overriding goals of the international community, especially with respect to people suffering from poverty, unemployment and social exclusion.

10. We make this solemn commitment on the eve of the fiftieth anniversary of the United Nations, with a determination to capture the unique possibilities offered by the end of the cold war to promote social development and social justice. We reaffirm and are guided by the principles of the Charter of the United Nations and by agreements reached at relevant international conferences, including the World Summit for Children, held at New York in 1990; the United Nations Conference on Environment and Development, held at Rio de Janeiro in 1992; the World Conference on Human Rights, held at Vienna in 1993; the Global Conference on the Sustainable Development of Small Island Developing States, held at Bridgetown, Barbados in 1994; and the International Conference on Population and Development, held at Cairo in 1994. By this Summit we launch a new commitment to social development in each of our countries and a new era of international cooperation between governments and peoples based on a spirit of partnership that puts the needs, rights and

aspirations of people at the centre of our decisions and joint actions.

11. We gather here in Copenhagen in a Summit of hope, commitment and action. We gather with full awareness of the difficulty of the tasks that lie ahead but with a conviction that major progress can be achieved, must be achieved and will be achieved.

12. We commit ourselves to this Declaration and Programme of Action for enhancing social development and ensuring human well-being for all throughout the world now and into the twenty-first century. We invite all people in all countries and in all walks of life, as well as the international community, to join us in our common cause.

CURRENT SOCIAL SITUATION AND REASONS FOR CONVENING THE SUMMIT

13. We are witnessing in countries throughout the world the expansion of prosperity for some, unfortunately accompanied by an expansion of unspeakable poverty for others. This glaring contradiction is unacceptable and needs to be corrected through urgent actions.

14. Globalisation, which is a consequence of increased human mobility, enhanced communications, greatly increased trade and capital flows, and technological developments, opens new opportunities for sustained economic growth and development of the world economy, particularly in developing countries. Globalisation also permits countries to share experiences and to learn from one another's achievements and difficulties, and promotes a cross-fertilisation of ideals, cultural values and aspirations. At the same time, the rapid processes of change and adjustment have been accompanied by intensified poverty, unemployment and social

disintegration. Threats to human well-being, such as environmental risks, have also been globalised. Furthermore, the global transformations of the world economy are profoundly changing the parameters of social development in all countries. The challenge is how to manage these processes and threats so as to enhance their benefits and mitigate their negative effects upon people.

15. There has been progress in some areas of social and economic development:

    a) The global wealth of nations has multiplied sevenfold in the past 50 years and international trade has grown even more dramatically;

    b) Life expectancy, literacy and primary education, and access to basic health care, including family planning, have increased in the majority of countries and average infant mortality has been reduced, including in developing countries;

    c) Democratic pluralism, democratic institutions and fundamental civil liberties have expanded. Decolonisation efforts have achieved much progress, while the elimination of apartheid is a historic achievement.

16. Yet we recognise that far too many people, particularly women and children, are vulnerable to stress and deprivation. Poverty, unemployment and social disintegration too often result in isolation, marginalisation and violence. The insecurity that many people, in particular vulnerable people, face about the future—their own and their children's—is intensifying:

    a) Within many societies, both in developed and developing countries, the gap between the rich and the poor has increased. Furthermore, despite the fact that some developing countries are growing rapidly. The gap between developed and many developing countries, particularly the least developed countries, has widened;

b. More than one billion people in the world live in abject poverty, most of whom go hungry every day. A large proportion, the majority of whom are women, have very limited access to income, resources, education, health care or nutrition, particularly in Africa and the least developed countries;

c. There are also serious social problems of a different nature and magnitude in countries with economies in transition and countries experiencing fundamental political, economic and social transformations;

d. The major cause of the continued deterioration of the global environment is the unsustainable pattern of consumption and production, particularly in industrialised countries, which is a matter of grave concern, aggravating poverty and imbalances;

e. Continued growth in the world's population, its structure and distribution, and its relationship with poverty and social and gender inequality challenge the adaptive capacities of governments, individuals, social institutions and the natural environment;

f. Over 120 million people worldwide are officially unemployed and many more are underemployed. Too many young people, including those with formal education, have little hope of finding productive work;

g. More women than men live in absolute poverty and the imbalance continues to grow, with serious consequences for women and their children. Women carry a disproportionate share of the problems of coping with poverty, social disintegration, unemployment, environmental degradation and the effects of war;

h. One of the world's largest minorities, more than one in 10, are people with disabilities, who are too often forced into poverty, unemployment and social isolation. In addition, in all countries older persons may be particularly vulnerable to social exclusion, poverty and marginalisation;

i. Millions of people worldwide are refugees or internally displaced persons. The tragic social consequences have a critical effect on the social stability and development of their home countries, their host countries and their respective regions.

17. While these problems are global in character and affect all countries, we clearly acknowledge that the situation of most developing countries, and particularly of Africa and the least developed countries, is critical and requires special attention and action. We also acknowledge that these countries, which are undergoing fundamental political, economic and social transformation, including countries in the process of consolidating peace and democracy, require the support of the international community.

18. Countries with economies in transition, which are also undergoing fundamental political, economic and social transformation, require the support of the international community as well.

19. Other countries that are undergoing fundamental political, economic and social transformation require the support of the international community as well.

20. The goals and objectives of social development require continuous efforts to reduce and eliminate major sources of social distress and instability for the family and for society. We pledge to place particular focus on and give priority attention to the fight against the worldwide conditions that pose severe threats to the health, safety, peace, security and well-being of our people. Among these conditions are chronic hunger; malnutrition; illicit

drug problems; organised crime; corruption; foreign occupation; armed conflicts; illicit arms trafficking, terrorism, intolerance and incitement to racial, ethnic, religious and other hatreds; xenophobia; and endemic, communicable and chronic diseases. To this end, coordination and cooperation at the national level and especially at the regional and international levels should be further strengthened.

21. In this context, the negative impact on development of excessive military expenditures, the arms trade, and investment for arms production and acquisition must be addressed.

22. Communicable diseases constitute a serious health problem in all countries and are a major cause of death globally; in many cases, their incidence is increasing. These diseases are a hindrance to social development and are often the cause of poverty and social exclusion. The prevention, treatment and control of these diseases, covering a spectrum from tuberculosis and malaria to the human immunodeficiency virus/acquired immunodeficiency syndrome (HIV/AIDS), must be given the highest priority.

23. We can continue to hold the trust of the people of the world only if we make their needs our priority. We know that poverty, lack of productive employment and social disintegration are an offence to human dignity. We also know that they are negatively reinforcing and represent a waste of human resources and a manifestation of ineffectiveness in the functioning of markets and economic and social institutions and processes.

24. Our challenge is to establish a people-centred framework for social development to guide us now and in the future, to build a culture of cooperation and partnership, and to respond to the immediate needs of those who are most

affected by human distress. We are determined to meet this challenge and promote social development throughout the world.

PRINCIPLES AND GOALS

25. We heads of state and government are committed to a political, economic, ethical and spiritual vision for social development that is based on human dignity, human rights, equality, respect, peace, democracy, mutual responsibility and cooperation, and full respect for the various religious and ethical values and cultural backgrounds of people. Accordingly, we will give the highest priority in national, regional and international policies and actions to the promotion of social progress, justice and the betterment of the human condition, based on full participation by all.

26. To this end, we will create a framework for action to:

    a. Place people at the centre of development and direct our economics to meet human needs more effectively;

    b. Fulfil our responsibility for present and future generations by ensuring equity among generations and protecting the integrity and sustainable use of our environment;

    c. Recognise that, while social development is a national responsibility, it cannot be successfully achieved without the collective commitment and efforts of the international community;

    d. Integrate economic, cultural and social policies so that they become mutually supportive, and acknowledge the interdependence of public and private spheres of activity;

    e. Recognise that the achievement of sustained social development requires sound, broadly based economic policies;

f. Promote democracy, human dignity, social justice and solidarity at the national, regional and international levels; ensure tolerance, non-violence, pluralism and non-discrimination, with full respect for diversity within and among societies;

g. Promote the equitable distribution of income and greater access to resources through equity and equality of opportunity for all;

h. Recognise the family as the basic unit of society, and acknowledge that it plays a key role in social development and as such should be strengthened, with attention to the rights, capabilities and responsibilities of its members. In different cultural, political and social systems various forms of family exist. It is entitled to receive comprehensive protection and support;

i. Ensure that disadvantaged and vulnerable persons and groups are included in social development, and that society acknowledges and responds to the consequences of disability by securing the legal rights of the individual and by making the physical and social environment accessible;

j. Promote universal respect for, and observance and protection of all human rights and fundamental freedoms for all, including the right to development; promote the effective exercise of rights and the discharge of responsibilities at all levels of society; promote equality and equity between women and men; protect the rights of children and youth; and promote the strengthening of social integration and civil society;

k. Reaffirm the right of self-determination of all peoples, in particular of peoples under colonial or other forms of alien domination or foreign occupation, and the importance of the effective realisation of this right, as enunciated, *inter alia,* in the Vienna Declaration and

Programme of Actions adopted at the World Conference on Human Rights;

l. Support progress and security for people and communities whereby every member of society is enabled to satisfy his or her basic human needs and to realise his or her personal dignity, safety and creativity;

m. Recognise and support indigenous people in their pursuit of economic and social development, with full respect for their identity, traditions, forms of social organisation and cultural values;

n. Underline the importance of transparent and accountable governance and administration in all public and private national and international institutions;

o. Recognise that empowering people, particularly women, to strengthen their own capacities is a main objective of development and its principal resource. Empowerment requires the full participation of people in the formulation, implementation and evaluation of decisions determining the functioning and well-being of our societies;

p. Assert the universality of social development and outline a new and strengthened approach to social development, with a renewed impetus for international cooperation and partnership;

q. Improve the possibility of older persons achieving a better life;

r. Recognise that the new information technologies and new approaches to access to and use of technologies by people living in poverty can help in fulfilling social development goals; and therefore recognise the need to facilitate access to such technologies;

s. Strengthen policies and programmes that improve, ensure and broaden the participation of women in all spheres of political, economic, social and cultural life, as equal partners, and improve their access to all resources needed for the full exercise of their fundamental rights;

t. Create the political, legal, material and social conditions that allow for the voluntary repatriation of refugees in safety and dignity to their countries of origin, and the voluntary and safe return of internally displaced persons to their places of origin and their smooth reintegration into their societies;

u. Emphasise the importance of the return of all prisoners of war, persons missing in action and hostages to their families, in accordance with international conventions, in order to reach full social development.

27. We acknowledge that it is the primary responsibility of States to attain these goals. We also acknowledge that these goals cannot be achieved by states alone. The international community, the United Nations, the multilateral financial institutions, all regional organisations and local authorities, and all actors of civil society need to positively contribute their own share of efforts and resources in order to reduce inequalities among people and narrow the gap between developed and developing countries in a global effort to reduce social tensions, and to create greater social and economic stability and security. Radical political, social and economic changes in the countries with economies in transition have been accompanied by a deterioration in their economic and social situation. We invite all people to express their personal commitment to enhancing the human condition through concrete actions in their own fields of activities and through assuming specific civic responsibilities.

COMMITMENTS

28. Our global drive for social development and the recommendations for action contained in the Programme of Action are made in a spirit of consensus and international cooperation, in full conformity with the purposes and principles of the Charter of the United Nations, recognising that the formulation and implementation of strategies, policies, programmes and actions for social development are the responsibility of each country and should take into account the economic, social and environmental diversity of conditions in each country, with full respect for the various religious and ethical values, cultural backgrounds and philosophical convictions of its people, and in conformity with all human rights and fundamental freedoms. In this context, international cooperation is essential for the full implementation of social development programmes and actions.

29. On the basis of our common pursuit of social development, which alms at social justice, solidarity, harmony and equality within and among countries, with full respect for national sovereignty and territorial integrity, as well as policy objectives, development priorities and religious and cultural diversity, and full respect for all human rights and fundamental freedoms, we launch a global drive for social progress and development embodied in the following commitments.

Commitment 1

We commit ourselves to creating an economic, political, social, cultural and legal environment that will enable people to achieve social development.

To this end, at the national level, we will:

a. Provide a stable legal framework, in accordance with our constitutions, laws and procedures, and consistent with international law and obligations, which includes and promotes equality and equity between women and men, full respect for all human rights and fundamental freedoms and the rule of law, access to justice, the elimination of all forms of discrimination, transparent and accountable governance and administration and the encouragement of partnership with free and representative organisations of civil society;

b. Create an enabling economic environment aimed at promoting more equitable access for all to income, resources and social services;

c. Reinforce, as appropriate, the means and capacities for people to participate in the formulation and implementation of social and economic policies and programmes through decentralisation, open management of public institutions and strengthening the abilities and opportunities of civil society and local communities to develop their own organisations, resources and activities;

d. Reinforce peace by promoting tolerance, non-violence and respect for diversity, and by settling disputes by peaceful means;

e. Promote dynamic, open, free markets, while recognising the need to intervene in markets, to the extent necessary, to prevent or counteract market failure, promote stability and long-term investment, ensure fair competition and ethical conduct, and harmonise economic and social development, including the development and implementation of appropriate programmes that would entitle and enable people living in poverty and the disadvantaged, especially women, to participate fully and productively in the economy and society;

f. Reaffirm, promote and strive to ensure the realisation of the rights set out in relevant international instruments and declarations, such as the Universal Declaration of

Human Rights, the Covenant on Economic, Social and Cultural Rights and the Declaration on the Right to Development, including those relating to education, food, shelter, employment, health and information, particularly in order to assist people living in poverty;

g. Create the comprehensive conditions to allow for the voluntary repatriation of refugees in safety and dignity to their countries of origin, and the voluntary and safe return of internally displaced persons to their places of origin and their smooth reintegration into their societies.

At the international level, we will:

h. Promote international peace and security and make and support all efforts to settle international disputes by peaceful means in accordance with the Charter of the United Nations;

i. Strengthen international cooperation for achieving social development;

j. Promote and implement policies to create a supportive external economic environment, through, *inter alia,* cooperation in the formulation and implementation of macroeconomic policies, trade liberalisation, mobilisation and/or provision of new and additional financial resources that are both adequate and predictable and mobilised in a way that maximises the availability of such resources for sustainable development, using all available funding sources and mechanisms, enhanced financial stability, and more equitable access of developing countries to global markets, productive investments and technologies and appropriate knowledge, with due consideration to the needs of countries with economies in transition;

k. Strive to ensure that international agreements relating to trade, investment, technology, debt and official development assistance are implemented in a manner that promotes social development;

l. Support, particularly through technical and financial cooperation, the efforts of developing countries to achieve rapid, broadly based sustainable development. Particular consideration should be given to the special needs of small island and landlocked developing countries and the least developed countries;

m. Support, through appropriate international cooperation, the efforts of countries with economies in transition to achieve rapid broadly based sustainable development;

n. Reaffirm and promote all human rights, which are universal, indivisible, interdependent and interrelated, including the right to development as a universal and inalienable right and an integral part of fundamental human rights, and strive to ensure that they are respected, protected and observed.

Commitment 2

We commit ourselves to the goal of eradicating poverty in the world, through decisive national actions and international cooperation, as an ethical, social, political and economic imperative of humankind.

To this end, at the national level, in partnership with all actors of civil society and in the context of a multidimensional and integrated approach, we will:

a. Formulate or strengthen, as a matter of urgency, and preferably by the year 1996, 'the International Year for the Eradication of Poverty', national policies and strategies geared to substantially reducing overall poverty in the shortest possible time, reducing inequalities and eradicating absolute poverty by a target date to be specified by each country in its national context;

b. Focus our efforts and policies to address the root causes of poverty and to provide for the basic needs of all. These efforts should include the elimination of hunger and malnutrition; the provision of food security, education, employment and livelihood, primary health-care services including reproductive health care, safe drinking water and sanitation, and adequate shelter; and participation in social and cultural life. Special priority will be given to the needs and rights of women and children, who often bear the greatest burden of poverty, and to the needs of vulnerable and disadvantaged groups and persons;

c. Ensure that people living in poverty have access to productive resources, including credit, land, education and training, technology, knowledge and information, as well as to public services, and participate in decision making on a policy and regulatory environment that would enable them to benefit from expanding employment and economic opportunities;

d. Develop and implement policies to ensure that all people have adequate economic and social protection during unemployment, ill health, maternity, child-rearing, widowhood, disability and old age;

e. Ensure that national budgets and policies are oriented, as necessary, to meeting basic needs, reducing inequalities and targeting poverty, as a strategic objective;

f. Seek to reduce inequalities, increase opportunities and access to resources and income, and remove any political, legal, economic and social factors and constraints that foster and sustain inequality.

At the international level, we will:

g. Strive to ensure that the international community and international organisations, particularly the multilateral financial institutions, assist developing countries and all countries in need in their efforts to achieve our overall goal of eradicating poverty and ensuring basic social protection;

h. Encourage all international donors and multilateral development banks to support policies and programmes for the attainment, in a sustained manner, of the specific efforts of the developing countries and all countries in need relating to people-centred sustainable development and to meeting basic needs for all; to assess their existing programmes in consultation with the concerned developing countries to ensure the achievement of the agreed programme objectives; and to seek to ensure that their own policies and programmes will advance the attainment of agreed development goals that focus on meeting basic needs for all and eradicating absolute poverty. Efforts should be made to ensure that participation by the people concerned is an integral part of such programmes;

i. Focus attention on and support the special needs of countries and regions in which there are substantial concentrations of people living in poverty, in particular in South Asia, and which therefore face serious difficulties in achieving social and economic development.

Commitment 3

We commit ourselves to promoting the goal of full employment as a basic priority of our economic and social policies, and to enabling all men and women to attain secure and sustainable livelihoods through freely chosen productive employment and work.

To this end, at the national level, we will:

a. Put the creation of employment, the reduction of unemployment and the promotion of appropriately and adequately remunerated employment at the centre of strategies and policies of governments, with full respect for workers' rights and with the participation of employers, workers and their respective organisations, giving special attention to the problems of structural, long-term unemployment and underemployment of youth, women, people with disabilities, and all other disadvantaged groups and individuals;

b. Develop policies to expand work opportunities and productivity in both rural and urban sectors by achieving economic growth, investing in human resource development, promoting technologies that generate productive employment, and encouraging self-employment, entrepreneurship, and small and medium-sized enterprises; growth and the creation of employment, and exchange experiences on successful policies and programmes aimed at increasing employment and reducing unemployment.

Commitment 4

We commit ourselves to promoting social integration by fostering societies that are stable, safe and just and that are based on the promotion and protection of all human rights, as well as on non-discrimination, tolerance, respect for diversity, equality of opportunity, solidarity, security, and participation of all people, including disadvantaged and vulnerable groups and persons.

To this end, at the national level, we will:

a. Promote respect for democracy, the rule of law, pluralism and diversity, tolerance and responsibility, non-violence and solidarity by encouraging educational systems, communication media and local communities and organisations to raise people's understanding and awareness of all aspects of social integration;

b. Formulate or strengthen policies and strategies geared to the elimination of discrimination in all its forms and the achievement of social integration based on equality and respect for human dignity;

c. Promote access for all to education, information, technology and knowhow as essential means for enhancing communication and participation in civil, political, economic, social and cultural life, and ensure respect for civil, political, economic, social and cultural rights;

d. Ensure the protection and full integration into the economy and society of disadvantaged and vulnerable groups and persons;

e. Formulate or strengthen measures to ensure respect for and protection of the human rights of migrants, migrant workers and their families, to eliminate the increasing acts of racism and xenophobia in sectors of many societies, and to promote greater harmony and tolerance in all societies;

f. Recognise and respect the right of indigenous people to maintain and develop their identity, culture and interests, support their aspirations for social justice and provide an environment that enables them to participate in the social, economic and political life of their country;

g. Foster the social protection and full integration into the economy and society of veterans, including veterans and victims of the Second World War and other wars;

h. Acknowledge and encourage the contribution of people of all age groups as equally and vitally important for the building of a harmonious society, and foster dialogue between generations in all parts of society;

i. Recognise and respect cultural, ethnic and religious diversity, promote and protect the rights of persons belonging to national, ethnic, religious or linguistic minorities, and take measures to facilitate their full participation in all aspects of the political, economic, social, religious and cultural life of their societies and in the economic progress and social development of their countries;

j. Strengthen the ability of local communities and groups with common concerns to develop their own organisations and resources and to propose policies relating to social development, including through the activities of non-governmental organisations;

k. Strengthen institutions that enhance social integration, recognising the central role of the family and providing it with an environment that assures its protection and support. In different cultural, political and social systems, various forms of the family exist;

l. Address the problems of crime, violence and illicit drugs as factors of social disintegration.

At the international level, we will:

m. Encourage the ratification of the avoidance as far as possible of the resort to reservations to, and the implementation of, international instruments and adherence to internationally recognised declarations relevant to the elimination of discrimination and the promotion and protection of all human rights;

n. Further enhance international mechanisms for the provision of humanitarian and financial assistance to refugees and host countries and promote appropriate shared responsibility;

o. Promote international cooperation and partnership on the basis of equality, mutual respect and mutual benefit.

Commitment 5

We commit ourselves to promoting full respect for human dignity and to achieving equality and equity between women and men, and to recognising and enhancing the participation and leadership roles of women in political, civil, economic, social and cultural life and in development.

To this end, at the national level, we will:

a. Promote changes in attitudes, structures, policies, laws and practices in order to eliminate all obstacles to human dignity, equality and equity in the family and in society, and promote full and equal participation of urban and rural women and women with disabilities in social, economic and political life, including in the formulation, implementation and follow-up of public policies and programmes;

b. Establish structures, policies, objectives and measurable goals to ensure gender balance and equity in decision-making processes at all levels, broaden women's political, economic, social and cultural opportunities and independence, and support the empowerment of women, including through their various organisations, especially those of indigenous women, those at the grassroots level, and those of poverty-stricken communities, including through affirmative action, where necessary, and also through measures to integrate a gender perspective in the design and implementation of economic and social policies;

c. Promote full and equal access of women to literacy, education and training, and remove all obstacles to their access to credit and other productive resources and to their ability to buy, hold and sell property and land equally with men;

d. Take appropriate measures to ensure, on the basis of equality of men and women, universal access to the widest range of health-care services, including those relating to reproductive health care, consistent with the Programme of Action of the International Conference on Population and Development;

e. Remove the remaining restrictions on women's rights to own land, inherit property or borrow money, and ensure women's equal right to work;

f. Establish policies, objectives and goals that enhance the equality of status, welfare and opportunity of the girl child, especially in regard to health, nutrition, literacy and education, recognising that gender discrimination starts at the earliest stages of life;

g. Promote equal partnership between women and men in family and community life and society, emphasise the shared responsibility of men and women in the care of children and support for older family members, and emphasise men's shared responsibility and promote their active involvement in responsible parenthood and responsible sexual and reproductive behaviour;

h. Take effective measures, including through the enactment and enforcement of laws, and implement policies to combat and eliminate all forms of discrimination, exploitation, abuse and violence against women and girl children, in accordance with relevant international instruments and declarations;

i. Promote and protect the full and equal enjoyment by women of all human rights and fundamental freedoms;

j. Formulate or strengthen policies and practices to ensure that women are enabled to participate fully in paid work and in employment through such measures as positive action, education, training, appropriate protection under labour legislation, and facilitating the provision of quality child care and other support services.

At the international level, we will:

k. Promote and protect women's human rights and encourage the ratification of, if possible by the year 2000, the avoidance, as far, as possible, of the resort to reservations to, and the implementation of the provisions of the Convention on the Elimination of All Forms of Discrimination against Women and other relevant instruments, as well as the implementation of the Nairobi Forward-looking Strategies for the Advancement of Women, the Geneva Declaration for Rural Women, and the Programme of Action of the International Conference on Population and Development;

l. Give specific attention to the preparations for the Fourth World Conference on Women, to be held at Beijing in

September 1995, and to the implementation and follow-up of the conclusions of that Conference;

m. Promote international cooperation to assist developing countries, at their request, in their efforts to achieve equality and equity and the empowerment of women;

n. Devise suitable means to recognise and make visible the full extent of the work of women and all their contributions to the national economy, including contributions in the unremunerated and domestic sectors.

Commitment 6

We commit ourselves to promoting and attaining the goals of universal and equitable access to quality education, the highest attainable standard of physical and mental health, and the access of all to primary health care, making particular efforts to rectify inequalities relating to social conditions and without distinction as to race, national origin, gender, age or disability; respecting and promoting our common and particular cultures; striving to strengthen the role of culture in development; preserving the essential bases of people-centred sustainable development; and contributing to the full development of human resources and to social development. The purpose of these activities is to eradicate poverty, promote full and productive employment and foster social integration.

To this end, at the national level, we will:

a. Formulate and strengthen timebound national strategies for the eradication of illiteracy and universalisation of basic education, which includes early childhood education, primary education and education for the illiterate, in all communities, in particular for the introduction, if possible, of national languages in the educational system and by support of the various means of non-formal education, striving to attain the highest possible standard of learning;

b. Emphasise lifelong learning by seeking to improve the quality of education to ensure that people of all ages are provided with useful knowledge, reasoning ability, skills, and the ethical and social values required to develop their full capacities in health and dignity and to participate fully in the social, economic and political process of development. In this regard, women and girls should be considered a priority group;

c. Ensure that children, particularly girls, enjoy their rights and promote the exercise of those rights by making education, adequate nutrition and health care accessible to them, consistent with the Convention on the Rights of the Child, and recognising the rights, duties and responsibilities of parents and other persons legally responsible for children;

d. Take appropriate and affirmative steps to enable all children and adolescents to attend and complete school and to close the gender gap in primary, secondary, vocational and higher education;

e. Ensure full and equal access to education for girls and women, recognising that investing in women's education is the key element in achieving social equality, higher productivity and social returns in terms of health, lower infant mortality and the reduced need for high fertility;

f. Ensure equal educational opportunities at all levels for children, youth and adults with disabilities, in integrated settings, taking full account of individual differences and situations;

g. Recognise and support the right of indigenous people to education in a manner that is responsive to their specific needs, aspirations and cultures, and ensure their full access to health care;

h. Develop specific educational policies, with gender perspective, and design appropriate mechanisms at all levels of society in order to accelerate the conversion of general and specific information available worldwide into knowledge, and the conversion of that knowledge into creativity, increased productive capacity and active participation in society;

i. Strengthen the links between labour market and education policies, realising that education and vocational training are vital elements in job creation and in combating unemployment and social exclusion in our societies, and emphasise the role of higher education and scientific research in all plans of social development;

j. Develop broadbased education programmes that promote and strengthen respect for all human rights and fundamental freedoms, including the right to development, promote the values of tolerance, responsibility and respect for the diversity and rights of others, and provide training in peaceful conflict resolution, in recognition of the United Nations Decade for Human Rights Education;

k. Focus on learning acquisition and outcome, broaden the means and scope of basic education, enhance the environment for learning and strengthen partnerships among governments, non-governmental organisations, the private sector, local communities, religious groups and families to achieve the goal of education for all;

l. Establish or strengthen both school-based and community-based health education programmes for children, adolescents and adults, with special attention to girls and women, on a whole range of health issues, as one of the prerequisites for social development, recognising the rights, duties and responsibilities of parents and other persons legally responsible for children consistent with the Convention on the Rights of the Child;

m. Expedite efforts to achieve the goals of national Health-for-All strategies, based on equality and social justice in line with the Alma-Ata Declaration on Primary Health Care, by developing or updating country action plans or programmes to ensure universal, non-discriminatory access to basic health services, including sanitation and drinking water, to protect health, and to promote nutrition education and preventive health programmes;

n. Strive to ensure that persons with disabilities have access to rehabilitation and other independent living services and assistive technology to enable them to maximise their well-being, independence and full participation in society;

o. Ensure an integrated and intersectoral approach so as to provide for the protection and promotion of health for all in economic and social development, taking cognizance of the health dimensions of policies in all sectors;

p. Seek to attain the maternal and child health objectives, especially the objectives of reducing child and maternal mortality, of the World Summit for Children, the United Nations Conference on Environment and Development and the International Conference on Population and Development;

q. Strengthen national efforts to address more effectively the growing HIV/AIDS pandemic by providing necessary education and prevention services, working to ensure that appropriate care and support services are available and accessible to those affected by HIV/AIDS, and taking all necessary steps to eliminate every form of discrimination against and isolation of those living with HIV/AIDS;

r. Promote, in all educational and health policies and programmes, environmental awareness, including awareness of unsustainable patterns of consumption and production.

At the international level, we will:

s. Strive to ensure that international organisations, in particular the international financial institutions, support these objectives, integrating them into their policy programmes and operations as appropriate. This should be complemented by renewed bilateral and regional cooperation;

t. Recognise the importance of the cultural dimension of development to ensure respect for cultural diversity and that of our common human cultural heritage. Creativity should be recognised and promoted;

u. Request the specialised agencies, notably the United Nations Educational, Scientific and Cultural Organisation and the World Health Organisation, as well as other international organisations dedicated to the promotion of education, culture and health, to give greater emphasis to the overriding goals of eradicating poverty, promoting full and productive employment and fostering social integration;

v. Strengthen intergovernmental organisations that utilise various forms of education to promote culture; disseminate information through education and communication media; help spread the use of technologies; and promote technical and professional training and scientific research;

w. Provide support for stronger, better coordinated global actions against major diseases that take a heavy toll of human lives, such as malaria, tuberculosis, cholera, typhoid fever and HIV/AIDS; in this context, continue to support the joint and co-sponsored United Nations programme on HIV/AIDS;

x. Share knowledge, experience and expertise and enhance creativity, for example, by promoting the transfer of technology, in the design and delivery of effective education, training and health programmes and policies, including substance-abuse awareness, prevention and rehabilitation programmes, which will result, *inter alia*, in endogenous capacity- building;

y. Intensify and coordinate international support for education and health programmes based on respect for human dignity and focused on the protection of all women and children, especially against exploitation, trafficking and harmful practices, such as child prostitution, female genital mutilation and child marriages.

Commitment 7

We commit ourselves to accelerating the economic, social and human resource development of Africa and the least developed countries.

To this end, we will:

a. Implement, at the national level, structural adjustment policies, which should include social development goals, as well as effective development strategies that establish a more favourable climate for trade and investment, give priority to human resource development and further promote the development of democratic institutions;

b. Support the domestic efforts of Africa and the least developed countries to implement economic reforms, programmes to increase food security, and commodity diversification efforts through international cooperation, including South-South cooperation and technical and financial assistance, as well as trade and partnership;

c. Find effective, development-oriented and durable solutions to external debt problems, through the immediate implementation of the terms of debt forgiveness agreed upon in the Paris Club in December 1994, which encompass debt reduction, including cancellation or other debt relief measures; invite the international financial institutions to examine innovative approaches to assist low-income countries with a high proportion of multilateral debt, with a view to alleviating their debt burdens; and develop techniques of debt conversion applied to social development programmes and projects in conformity with Summit priorities. These actions should take into account the mid-term review of the United Nations New Agenda for the Development of Africa in the 1990s and the Programme of Action for the Least Developed Countries for the 1990s, and should be implemented as soon as possible;

d. Ensure the implementation of the strategies and measures for the development of Africa decided by the international community, and support the reform efforts, development strategies and programmes decided by the African countries and the least developed countries;

e. Increase official development assistance, both overall and for social programmes, and improve its impact, consistent with countries' economic circumstances and capacities to assist, and consistent with commitments in international agreements;

f. Consider ratifying the United Nations Convention to Combat Desertification in Those Countries Experiencing Serious Drought and/or Desertification, Particularly in Africa, and support African countries in the implementation of urgent action to combat desertification and mitigate the effects of drought;

g. Take all necessary measures to ensure that communicable diseases, particularly HIV/AIDS, malaria and tuberculosis, do not restrict or reverse the progress made in economic and social development.

Commitment 8

We commit ourselves to ensuring that when structural adjustment programmes are agreed to they include social development goals, in particular eradicating poverty, promoting full and productive employment, and enhancing social integration.

To this end, at the national level, we will:

a. Promote basic social programmes and expenditures, in particular those affecting the poor and the vulnerable segments of society, and protect them from budget reductions, while increasing the quality and effectiveness of social expenditures;

b. Review the impact of structural adjustment programmes on social development, including, where appropriate, by means of gender sensitive social impact assessments and other relevant methods, in order to develop policies to reduce their negative effects and improve their positive impact; the cooperation of international financial institutions in the review could be requested by interested countries;

c. Promote, in the countries with economies in transition, an integrated approach to the transformation process, addressing the social consequences of reforms and human resource development needs;

d. Reinforce the social development components of all adjustment policies and programmes, including those resulting from the globalisation of markets and rapid technological change, by designing policies to promote more equitable and enhanced access to income and resources;

e. Ensure that women do not bear a disproportionate burden of the transitional costs of such processes.

At the international level, we will:

f. Work to ensure that multilateral development banks and other donors complement adjustment lending with enhanced targeted social development investment lending;

g. Strive to ensure that structural adjustment programmes respond to the economic and social conditions, concerns and needs of each country;

h. Enlist the support and cooperation of regional and international organisations and the United Nations system, in particular the Bretton Woods institutions, in the design, social management and assessment of structural adjustment policies, and in implementing social development goals and integrating them into their policies, programmes and operations.

Commitment 9

We commit ourselves to increasing significantly and/or utilising more efficiently the resources allocated to social development in order to achieve the goals of the Summit through national action and regional and international cooperation.

a. Develop economic policies to promote and mobilise domestic savings and attract external resources for productive investment, and seek innovative sources of funding, both public and private, for social programmes, while ensuring their effective utilisation;

b. Implement macroeconomic and microeconomic policies to ensure sustained economic growth and sustainable development to support social development;

c. Promote increased access to credit for small and micro-enterprises, including those in the informal sector, with particular emphasis on the disadvantaged sectors of society;

d. Ensure that reliable statistics and statistical indicators are used to develop and assess social policies and programmes so that economic and social resources are used efficiently and effectively;

e. Ensure that, in accordance with national priorities and policies, taxation systems are fair, progressive and economically efficient, cognizant of sustainable development concerns, and ensure effective collection of tax liabilities;

f. In the budgetary process, ensure transparency and accountability in the use of public resources, and give priority to providing and improving basic social services;

g. Undertake to explore new ways of generating new public and private financial resources, *inter alia,* through the appropriate reduction of excessive military expenditures, including global military expenditures and the arms trade, and investments for arms production and acquisition, taking into consideration national security requirements, so as to allow possible allocation of additional funds for social and economic development;

h. Utilise and develop fully the potential and contribution of cooperatives for the attainment of social development goals, in particular the eradication of poverty, the generation of full and productive employment, and the enhancement of social integration.

i. Seek to mobilise new and additional financial resources that are both adequate and predictable and are mobilised in a way that maximises the availability of such resources and uses all available funding sources and mechanisms, *inter alia*, multilateral, bilateral and private sources, including on concessional and grant terms;

j. Facilitate the flow to developing countries of international finance, technology and human skill in order to realise the objective of providing new and additional resources that are both adequate and predictable;

k. Facilitate the flow of international finance, technology and human skill towards the countries with economies in transition;

l. Strive for the fulfilment of the agreed target of 0.7 per cent of gross national product for overall official development assistance as soon as possible, and increase the share of funding for social development programmes, commensurate with the scope and scale of activities required to achieve the objectives and goals of the present Declaration and the Programme of Action of the Summit;

m. Increase the flow of international resources to meet the needs of countries facing problems relating to refugees and displaced persons;

n. Support South-South cooperation, which can take advantage of the experience of developing countries that have overcome similar difficulties;

o. Ensure the urgent implementation of existing debt-relief agreements and negotiate further initiatives, in addition to existing ones, to alleviate the debts of the poorest and heavily indebted low-income countries at an early date, especially through more favourable terms of debt forgiveness, including application of the terms of debt forgiveness agreed upon in the Paris Club in December 1994, which encompass debt reduction, including cancellation or other debt-relief measures; where appropriate, these countries should be given a reduction of their bilateral official debt sufficient to enable them to exit from the rescheduling process and resume growth and development; invite the international financial institutions to examine innovative approaches to assist low-income countries with a high proportion of multilateral debt, with a view to alleviating their debt burdens; develop techniques of debt conversion applied to social development programmes and projects in conformity with Summit priorities;

p. Fully implement the Final Act of the Uruguay Round of multilateral trade negotiations as scheduled, including the complementary provisions specified in the Marrakesh Agreement establishing the World Trade Organisation, in recognition of the fact that broadly based growth in incomes, employment and trade are mutually reinforcing, taking into account the need to assist African countries and the least developed countries in evaluating the impact of the implementation of the Final Act so that they can benefit fully;

q. Monitor the impact of trade liberalisation on the progress made in developing countries to meet basic human needs, giving particular attention to new initiatives to expand their access to international markets;

r. Give attention to the needs of countries with economies in transition with respect to international cooperation and financial and technical assistance, stressing the need for the full integration of economies in transition into the world economy, in particular to improve market access for exports in accordance with multilateral trade rules, taking into account the needs of developing countries;

s. Support United Nations development efforts by a substantial increase in resources for operational activities on a predictable, continuous and assured basis, commensurate with the increasing needs of developing countries, as stated in General Assembly resolution 47/199, and strengthen the capacity of the United Nations and the specialised agencies to fulfil their responsibilities in the implementation of the outcome of the World Summit for Social Development.

Commitment 10

We commit ourselves to an improved and strengthened framework for international, regional and subregional cooperation for social development, in a spirit of partnership, through the United Nations and other multilateral institutions.

To this end, at the national level, we will:

a. Adopt the appropriate measures and mechanisms for implementing and monitoring the outcome of the World Summit for Social Development, with the assistance, upon request, of the specialised agencies, programmes and regional commissions of the United Nations system, with broad participation of all sectors of civil society.

At the regional level, we will:

b. Pursue such mechanisms and measures as are necessary and appropriate in particular regions or subregions. The regional commissions, in cooperation with regional intergovernmental organisations and banks, could convene, on a biennial basis, a meeting at a high political level to evaluate progress made towards fulfilling the outcome of the Summit, exchange views on their respective experiences and adopt appropriate measures. The regional commissions should report, through the appropriate mechanisms, to the Economic and Social Council on the outcome of such meetings.

At the international level, we will:

c. Instruct our representatives to the organisations and bodies of the United Nations system, international development agencies and multilateral development banks to enlist the support and cooperation of these organisations and bodies to take appropriate and coordinated measures for continuous and sustained progress in attaining the goals and commitments agreed to by the Summit. The United Nations and the Bretton Woods institutions should establish regular and substantive dialogue, including at the field level, for more effective and efficient coordination of assistance for social development;

d. Refrain from any unilateral measure not in accordance with international law and the Charter of the United Nations that creates obstacles to trade relations among States;

e. Strengthen the structure, resources and processes of the Economic and Social Council and its subsidiary bodies, and other organisations within the United Nations system that are concerned with economic and social development;

f. Request the Economic and Social Council to review and assess, on the basis of reports of national governments, the regional commissions, relevant functional commissions and specialised agencies, progress made by the international community towards implementing the outcome of the World Summit for Social Development, and to report to the General Assembly, accordingly, for its appropriate consideration and action;

g. Request the General Assembly to hold a special session in the year 2000 for an overall review and appraisal of the implementation of the outcome of the Summit and to consider further actions and initiatives.

AN ENABLING ENVIRONMENT FOR SOCIAL DEVELOPMENT

Basis for Action and Objectives

1. Social development is inseparable from the cultural, ecological, economic, political and spiritual environment in which it takes place. It cannot be pursued as a sectoral initiative. Social development is also clearly linked to the development of peace, freedom, stability and security, both nationally and internationally. To promote social development requires an orientation of values, objectives and priorities towards the well-being of all and the strengthening and promotion of conducive institutions and policies. Human dignity, all human rights and fundamental freedoms, equality, equity and social justice constitute the fundamental values of all societies. The pursuit, promotion and protection of these values, among others, provides the basic legitimacy of all institutions and all exercise of authority and promotes an

environment in which human beings are at the centre of concern for sustainable development. They are entitled to a healthy and productive life in harmony with nature.

2. The economies and societies of the world are becoming increasingly interdependent. Trade and capital flows, migrations, scientific and technological innovations, communications and cultural exchanges are shaping the global community. The same global community is threatened by environmental degradation, severe food crises, epidemics, all forms of racial discrimination, xenophobia, various forms of intolerance, violence and criminality and the risk of losing the richness of cultural diversity. Governments increasingly recognise that their responses to changing circumstances and their desires to achieve sustainable development and social progress will require increased solidarity, expressed through appropriate multilateral programmes and strengthened international cooperation. Such cooperation is particularly crucial to ensure that countries in need of assistance, such as those in Africa and the least developed countries, can benefit from the process of globalisation.

3. Economic activities, through which individuals express their initiative and creativity and which enhance the wealth of communities, are a fundamental basis for social progress. But social progress will not be realised simply through the free interaction of market forces. Public policies are necessary to correct market failures, to complement market mechanisms, to maintain social stability and to create a national and international economic environment that promotes sustainable growth on a global scale. Such growth should promote equity and social justice, tolerance, responsibility and involvement.

4. The ultimate goal of social development is to improve and enhance the quality of life of all people. It requires democratic institutions, respect for all human rights and

fundamental freedoms, increased and equal economic opportunities, the rule of law, the promotion of respect for cultural diversity and the rights of persons belonging to minorities, and an active involvement of civil society. Empowerment and participation are essential for democracy, harmony and social development. All members of society should have the opportunity and be able to exercise the right and responsibility to take an active part in the affairs of the community in which they live. Gender equality and equity and the full participation of women in all economic, social and political activities are essential. The obstacles that have limited the access of women to decision-making, education, health-care services and productive employment must be eliminated and an equitable partnership between men and women established, involving men's full responsibility in family life. It is necessary to change the prevailing social paradigm of gender to usher in a new generation of women and men working together to create a more humane world order.

5. Against this background, we will promote an enabling environment based on a people-centred approach to sustainable development, with the following features:

   a) Broadbased participation and involvement of civil society in the formulation and implementation of decisions determining the functioning and well-being of our societies;

   b) Broadbased patterns of sustained economic growth and sustainable development and the integration of population issues into economic and development strategies, which will speed up the pace of sustainable development and poverty eradication and contribute to the achievement of population objectives and an improved quality of life of the population;

   c) Equitable and nondiscriminatory distribution of the benefits of growth among social groups and countries and expanded access to productive resources for people living in poverty;

d) An interaction of market forces conducive to efficiency and social development;

e) Public policies that seek to overcome socially divisive disparities and that respect pluralism and diversity;

f) A supportive and stable political and legal framework that promotes the mutually reinforcing relationship between democracy, development and all human rights and fundamental freedoms;

g) Political and social processes that avoid exclusion while respecting pluralism and diversity, including religious and cultural diversity;

h) A strengthened role for the family in accordance with the principles, goals and commitments of the Copenhagen Declaration on Social Development and those of the International Conference on Population and Development, as well as for community and civil society;

i) Expanded access to knowledge, technology, education, health-care services and information;

j) Increased solidarity, partnership and cooperation at all levels;

k) Public policies that empower people to enjoy good health and productivity throughout their lives;

l) Protection and conservation of the natural environment in the context of people-centred sustainable development.

ACTIONS

A favourable national and international economic environment

6. The promotion of mutually reinforcing, broad-based, sustained economic growth and sustainable development

on a global scale, as well as growth in production, a non-discriminatory and multilateral rule-based international trading system, employment and incomes, as a basis for social development, requires the following actions:

a) Promoting the establishment of an open, equitable, cooperative and mutually beneficial international economic environment;

b) Implementing sound and stable macro-economic and sectoral policies that encourage broadbased, sustained economic growth and development that is sustainable and equitable, that generate jobs, and that are geared towards eradicating poverty and reducing social and economic inequalities and exclusion;

c) Promoting enterprise, productive investment and expanded access to open and dynamic markets in the context of an open, equitable, secure, non-discriminatory, predictable, transparent and multi-lateral rule-based international trading system, and to technologies for all people, particularly those living in poverty and the disadvantaged, as well as for the least developed countries;

d) Implementing fully and as scheduled the Final Act of the Uruguay Round of multilateral trade negotiations;

e) Refraining from any unilateral measure not in accordance with international law and the Charter of the United Nations that creates obstacles to trade relations among states, impedes the full realisation of social and economic development and hinders the well-being of the population in the affected countries;

f) Increasing food production, through the sustainable development of the agricultural sector and improvement of market opportunities, and improving access to food by low-income people in developing countries, as a means of alleviating poverty, eliminating malnutrition and raising their standards of living;

g) Promoting the coordination of macroeconomic policies at the national, subregional, regional and international levels in order to promote an international financial system that is more conducive to stable and sustained economic growth and sustainable development through, *inter alia,* a higher degree of stability in financial markets, reducing the risk of financial crisis, improving the stability of exchange rates, stabilising and striving for low real interest rates in the long run and reducing the uncertainties of financial flows;

h. Establishing, strengthening or rehabilitating, *inter alia,* through capacity building where necessary, national and international structures, processes and resources available, to ensure appropriate consideration and coordination of economic policy, with special emphasis on social development;

i) Promoting or strengthening capacity building in developing countries, particularly in Africa and the least developed countries, to develop social activities;

j) Ensuring that, in accordance with Agenda 212 and the various consensus agreements, conventions and programmes of action adopted within the framework of the follow-up to the outcome of the United Nations Conference on Environment and Development, broadbased, sustained economic growth and sustainable development respects the need to protect the environment and the interests of future generations;

k) Ensuring that the special needs and vulnerabilities of small island developing States are adequately addressed in order to enable them to achieve sustained economic growth and sustainable development with equity by implementing the Programme of Action for the Sustainable Development of Small Island Developing States.

7. To ensure that the benefits of global economic growth are equitably distributed among countries, the following actions are essential:

   a) Continuing efforts to alleviate the onerous debt and debt-service burdens connected with the various types of debt of many developing countries, on the basis of an equitable and durable approach and, where appropriate, addressing the full stock of debt of the poorest and most indebted developing countries as a matter of priority, reducing trade barriers and promoting expanded access by all countries to markets, in the context of an open, equitable, secure, non-discriminatory, predictable, transparent and multilateral rule-based international trading system, as well as to productive investment, technologies and know-how;

   b) Strengthening and improving technical and financial assistance to developing countries to promote sustainable development and overcome hindrances to their full and effective participation in the world economy;

   c) Changing unsustainable consumption and production patterns, taking into account that the major cause of the continued deterioration of the global environment is the unsustainable pattern of consumption and production, particularly in industrialised countries, which is a matter of grave concern, aggravating poverty and imbalances;

   d) Elaborating policies to enable developing countries to take advantage of expanded international trading opportunities in the context of the full implementation of the Final Act of the Uruguay Round of multilateral trade negotiations; and assisting countries, particularly in Africa, that are not currently in a position to benefit fully from the liberalisation of the world economy;

e) Supporting the efforts of developing countries, particularly those heavily dependent on commodity exports, to diversify their economies.

8. Within the framework of support to developing countries, giving priority to the needs of Africa and the least developed countries, the following actions are necessary at the national and international levels, as appropriate:

a) Implementing effective policies and development strategies that establish a more favourable climate for social development, trade and investments, giving priority to human resource development and promoting the further development of democratic institutions;

b) Supporting African countries and least developed countries in their efforts to create an enabling environment that attracts foreign and domestic direct investment, encourages savings, induces the return of flight capital and promotes the full participation of the private sector, including non-governmental organisations, in the growth and development process;

c) Supporting economic reforms to improve the functioning of commodity markets and commodity diversification efforts through appropriate mechanisms, bilateral and multilateral financing and technical cooperation, including South-South cooperation, as well as through trade and partnership;

d) Continuing to support the commodity diversification efforts of Africa and the least developed countries, *inter alia,* by providing technical and financial assistance for the preparatory phase of their commodity diversification projects and programmes;

e) Finding effective, development-oriented and durable solutions to external debt problems, through the immediate implementation of the terms of debt forgiveness agreed upon in the Paris Club in December 1994, which encompass debt reduction, including cancellation or other debt relief measures; inviting the international financial institutions to examine innovative approaches to assist low-income countries with a high proportion of multilateral debt with a view to alleviating their debt burden; developing techniques of debt conversion applied to social development programmes and projects in conformity with Summit priorities. These actions should take into account the mid-term review of the United Nations New Agenda for the Development of Africa in the 1990 and the Programme of Action for the Least Developed Countries for the 1990 and should be implemented as soon as possible;

f) Supporting the development of strategies adopted by these countries and working in partnership to ensure the implementation of measures for their development;

g) Taking appropriate actions, consistent with the Final Act of the Uruguay Round of multilateral trade negotiations, in particular the decision on measures in favour of the least developed countries and the decision on measures concerning the possible negative effects of the reform programme on the least developed countries and the net food importing developing countries, in order to give these countries special attention, with a view to enhancing their participation in the multilateral trading system and to mitigating any adverse effects of the implementation of the Uruguay Round, while stressing the need to support the African countries so that they can benefit fully from the results of the Uruguay Round;

h) Increasing official development assistance, both in total and for social programmes, and improving its impact, consistent with the countries' economic circumstances and capabilities to assist, and consistent with commitments in international agreements, and striving to attain the agreed upon target of 0.7 per cent of gross national product for official development assistance and 0.15 per cent to the least developed countries, as soon as possible.

9. Making economic growth and the interaction of market forces more conducive to social development requires the following actions:

a) Implementing measures to open market opportunities for all, especially people living in poverty and the disadvantaged, and to encourage individuals and communities to take economic initiatives, innovate and invest in activities that contribute to social development while promoting broad-based sustained economic growth and sustainable development;

b) Improving, broadening and regulating, to the extent necessary, the functioning of markets to promote sustained economic growth and sustainable development, stability and long-term investment, fair competition and ethical conduct; adopting and implementing policies to promote equitable distribution of the benefits of growth and protect crucial social services, *inter alia*, through complementing market mechanisms and mitigating any negative impacts posed by market forces; and implementing complementary policies to foster social development, while dismantling, consistent with the provisions of the Final Act of the Uruguay Round of multilateral trade negotiations, protectionist measures, and to integrate social and economic development;

c) Establishing an open market policy that reduces barriers to entry, promotes transparency of markets through, *inter alia,* better access to information and widens the choices available to consumers;

d) Promoting greater access to technology and technical assistance, as well as corresponding knowhow, especially for micro-enterprises and small and medium-sized enterprises in all countries, particularly in developing countries;

e) Encouraging transnational and national corporations to operate in a framework of respect for the environment while complying with national laws and legislation, and in accordance with international agreements and conventions, and with proper consideration for the social and cultural impact of their activities;

f) Adopting and implementing long-term strategies to ensure substantial, well-directed public and private investment in the construction and renewal of basic infrastructure, which will benefit people living in poverty and generate employment;

g) Ensuring substantial public and private investment in human resource development and in capacity building in health and education, as well as in empowerment and participation, especially for people living in poverty or suffering from social exclusion;

h) Supporting and paying special attention to the development of small-scale and micro-enterprises, particularly in rural areas, as well as subsistence economies, to secure their safe interaction with larger economies;

i) Supporting the economic activities of indigenous people, improving their conditions and development, and securing their safe interaction with larger economies;

j) Supporting institutions, programmes and systems to disseminate practical information to promote social progress.

10. Ensuring that fiscal systems and other public policies are geared towards poverty eradication and that they do not generate socially divisive disparities calls for:

a) Enacting rules and regulations and creating a moral and ethical climate that prevents all forms of corruption and exploitation of individuals, families and groups;

b) Promoting fair competition and ethical responsibility in business activities, and enhancing cooperation and interaction among governments, the private sector and civil society;

c) Ensuring that fiscal and monetary policies promote savings and long-term investment in productive activities in accordance with national priorities and policies;

d) Considering measures to address inequities arising from accumulation of wealth through, *inter alia,* the use of appropriate taxation at the national level, and to reduce inefficiencies and improve stability in financial markets in accordance with national priorities and policies;

e) Re-examining the distribution of subsidies, *inter alia,* between industry and agriculture, urban and rural areas, and private and public consumption, to ensure that subsidy systems benefit people living in poverty, especially the vulnerable, and reduce disparities;

f) Promoting international agreements that address effectively issues of double taxation, as well as cross-border tax evasion, in accordance with the priorities and policies of the States concerned, while improving the efficiency and fairness of tax collection;

g) Assisting developing countries, upon their request, to establish efficient and fair tax systems by strengthening the administrative capacity for tax assessment and collection and tax evader prosecution, and to support a more progressive tax system;

h) Assisting countries with economies in transition to establish fair and effective systems of taxation on a solid legal basis, contributing to the socioeconomic reforms under way in those countries.

A favourable national and international political and legal environment

11. To ensure that the political framework supports the objectives of social development, the following actions are essential:

a) Ensuring that governmental institutions and agencies responsible for the planning and implementation of social policies have the status, resources and information necessary to give high priority to social development in policy making;

b) Ensuring the rule of law and democracy and the existence of rules and processes to create transparency and accountability for all public and private institutions and to prevent and combat all forms of corruption, sustained through education and the development of attitudes and values promoting responsibility, solidarity and a strengthened civil society;

c) Eliminating all forms of discrimination, while developing and encouraging educational programmes and media campaigns to that end;

d) Encouraging decentralisation of public institutions and services to a level that, compatible with the overall responsibilities, priorities and objectives of governments, responds properly to local needs and facilitates local participation;

e) Establishing conditions for the social partners to organise and function with guaranteed freedom of expression and association and the right to engage in collective bargaining and to promote mutual interests, taking due account of national laws and regulations;

f) Establishing similar conditions for professional organisations and organisations of independent workers;

g) Promoting political and social processes inclusive of all members of society and respectful of political pluralism and cultural diversity;

h) Strengthening the capacities and opportunities of all people, especially those who are disadvantaged or vulnerable, to enhance their own economic and social development, to establish and maintain organisations representing their interests and to be involved in the planning and implementation of government policies and programmes by which they will be directly affected;

i) Ensuring full involvement and participation of women at all levels in the decision making and implementation process and in the economic and political mechanisms through which policies are formulated and implemented;

j) Removing all legal impediments to the ownership of all means of production and property by men and women;

k) Taking measures, in cooperation with the international community, as appropriate, in accordance with the Charter of the United Nations, the Universal Declaration of Human Rights, six other international instruments and relevant United Nations resolutions, to create the appropriate political and legal environment to address the root cause of movements of refugees, to allow their voluntary return in safety and dignity. Measures should also be taken at the national level, with international cooperation, as appropriate, in accordance with the Charter of the United Nations, to create conditions for internally displaced persons to voluntarily return to their places of origin.

12. It is essential for social development that all human rights and fundamental freedoms, including the right to development as an integral part of fundamental human rights, be promoted and protected through the following actions:

   a) Encouraging ratification of existing international human rights conventions that have not been ratified; and implementing the provisions of conventions and covenants that have been ratified;

   b) Reaffirming and promoting all human rights and fundamental freedoms, which are universal, indivisible, interdependent and interrelated, including the right to development, and striving to ensure that they are respected, protected and observed through appropriate legislation, dissemination of information, education and training and the provision of effective mechanisms and remedies for enforcement, *inter alia*, through the establishment or strengthening of national institutions responsible for monitoring and enforcement;

   c) Taking measures to ensure that every human person is and all peoples are entitled to participate, to contribute to and to enjoy economic, social, cultural and political development; encouraging all human persons to take responsibility for development, individually and collectively; and recognising that States have the primary responsibility for the creation of national and international conditions favourable for the realisation of the right to development, taking into account the relevant provisions of the Vienna Declaration and Programme of Action;

d) Promoting the realisation of the right to development through strengthening democracy, development and respect for human rights and fundamental freedoms and through effective development policies at the national level, as well as equitable economic relations and a favourable economic environment at the international level, since sustained action is indispensable for fostering a more rapid development of developing countries;

e) Removing obstacles to the realisation of the right of peoples to self-determination, in particular of peoples living under colonial or other forms of alien domination or foreign occupation, which adversely affect their social and economic development;

f) Promoting and protecting the human rights of women and removing all obstacles to full equality and equity between women and men in political, civil, economic, social and cultural life;

g) Giving special attention to promoting and protecting the rights of the child, with particular attention to the rights of the girl child, by, *inter alia,* encouraging the ratification and implementation of the Convention on the Rights of the Child and the Plan of Action for Implementing the World Declaration on the Survival, Protection and Development of Children in the 1990s adopted at the World Summit for Children;

h) Providing all people, in particular the vulnerable and disadvantaged in society, with the benefit of an independent, fair and effective system of justice, and ensuring access by all to competent sources of advice about legal rights and obligations;

i) Taking effective measures to bring to an end all *de lure* and *de facto* discrimination against persons with disabilities;

j) Strengthening the ability of civil society and the community to participate actively in the planning, decision making and implementation of social development programmes, by education and access to resources;

k) Promoting and protecting the rights of individuals in order to prevent and eliminate situations of domestic discrimination and violence.

13. An open political and economic system requires access by all to knowledge, education and information by:

a) Strengthening the educational system at all levels, as well as other means of acquiring skills and knowledge, and ensuring universal access to basic education and lifelong educational opportunities, while removing economic and sociocultural barriers to the exercise of the right to education;

b) Raising public awareness and promoting gender-sensitivity education to eliminate all obstacles to full gender equality and equity;

c) Enabling and encouraging access by all to a wide range of information and opinion on matters of general interest through the mass media and other means;

d) Encouraging education systems and, to the extent consistent with freedom of expression, communication media to raise people's understanding and awareness of all aspects of social integration, including gender sensitivity, non-violence, tolerance and solidarity and respect for the diversity of cultures and interests, and to discourage the exhibition of pornography and the gratuitous depiction of explicit violence and cruelty in the media;

e) Improving the reliability, validity, utility and public availability of statistical and other information on social development and gender issues, including the effective use of gender-disaggregated statistics collected at the national, regional and international levels, including through support to academic and research institutions.

14. International support for national efforts to promote a favourable political and legal environment must be in conformity with the Charter of the United Nations and principles of international law and consistent with the Declaration on Principles of International Law concerning Friendly Relations and Cooperation among States in accordance with the Charter of the United Nations. Support calls for the following actions:

    a) Making use, as appropriate, of the capacity of the United Nations and other relevant international, regional and subregional organisations to prevent and resolve armed conflicts and promote social progress and better standards of life in larger freedom;

    b) Coordinating policies, actions and legal instruments and/or measures to combat terrorism, all forms of extremist violence, illicit arms trafficking, organised crime and illicit drug problems, money laundering and related crimes, trafficking in women, adolescents, children, migrants, and human organs, and other activities contrary to human rights and human dignity;

    c) States cooperating with one another in ensuring development and eliminating obstacles to development. The international community should promote effective international cooperation, supporting the efforts of developing countries, for the full realisation of the right to development and the elimination of obstacles to development, through, *inter alia*, the implementation of the provisions of the Declaration on the Right to Development as reaffirmed by the Vienna Declaration and Programme of Action Lasting progress towards the implementation of the right to development requires effective development policies at the national level, as well as equitable economic relations and a favourable economic environment at the international level. The right to development should be fulfilled so as to equitably meet the social development and environmental needs of present and future generations;

d) Ensuring that human persons are at the centre of social development and that this is fully reflected in the programmes and activities of subregional, regional and international organisations;

e) Reinforcing the capacity of relevant national, regional and international organisations, within their mandates, to promote the implementation of all human rights and fundamental freedoms and the elimination of all forms of discrimination;

f) Elaborating policies, within the mandates and functions of the various international institutions, that will support the objectives of social development and contribute to institutional development through capacity building and other forms of cooperation;

g) Strengthening the capacities of governments, the private sector and civil society, especially in Africa and the least developed countries, to enable them to meet their specific and global responsibilities;

h) Reinforcing the capacities of governments, the private sector and civil society in the countries with economies in transition, with a view to helping them in the process of transforming their economies from centrally planned to market-oriented ones.

EXPANSION OF PRODUCTIVE EMPLOYMENT AND REDUCTION OF UNEMPLOYMENT

Basis for Action and Objectives

1. Productive work and employment are central elements of development as well as decisive elements of human identity, sustained economic growth and sustainable development as well as the expansion of productive employment should go hand in hand. Full and adequately and appropriately remunerated employment is an effective method of combating poverty and promoting social integration, The goal of full employment requires that the State, the social partners and all the other parts of civil society at all levels cooperate to create conditions that enable everyone to participate in and benefit from productive work. In a world of increasing globalisation and interdependence among countries, national efforts need to be buttressed by international cooperation.
2. Globalisation and rapid technological development give rise to increased labour mobility, bringing new employment opportunities as well as new uncertainties. There has been an increase in part-time, casual and other forms of atypical employment. In addition to requiring the creation of new employment opportunities on an unprecedented scale, such an environment calls for expanded efforts to enhance human resource development for sustainable development by, *inter alia*, enhancing the knowledge and skills necessary for people, particularly for women and youth, to work productively and adapt to changing requirements.
3. In many developed countries, growth in employment 'is currently great in small and medium-sized enterprises and in self-employment. In many developing countries, informal sector activities are often the leading source of

employment opportunities for people with limited access to formal-sector wage employment, in particular for women. The removal of obstacles to the operation of such enterprises and the provision of support for their creation and expansion must be accompanied by protection of the basic rights, health and safety of workers and the progressive improvement of overall working conditions, together with the strengthening of efforts to make some enterprises part of the formal sector.

4. While all groups can benefit from more employment opportunities, specific needs and changing demographic patterns and trends call for appropriate measures. Particular efforts by the public and private sectors are required in all spheres of employment policy to ensure gender equality, equal opportunity and nondiscrimination on the basis of race/ethnic group, religion, age, health and disability, and with full respect for applicable international instruments. Special attention must also be paid to the needs of groups who face particular disadvantages in their access to the labour market so as to ensure their integration into productive activities, including through the promotion of effective support mechanisms.

5. Much unremunerated productive work, such as caring for children and older persons, producing and preparing food for the family, protecting the environment and providing voluntary assistance to vulnerable and disadvantaged individuals and groups, is of great social importance. Worldwide, most of this work is done by women who often face the double burden of remunerated and unremunerated work. Efforts are needed to acknowledge the social and economic importance and value of unremunerated work, to facilitate labour-force participation in combination with such work through flexible working arrangements, encouraging voluntary

social activities as well as broadening the very conception of productive work, and to accord social recognition for such work, including by developing methods for reflecting its value in quantitative terms for possible reflection in accounts that may be produced separately from, but consistent with, core national accounts.

6. There is therefore an urgent need, in the overall context of promoting sustained economic growth and sustainable development, for:

   a) Placing the creation of employment at the centre of national strategies and policies, with the full participation of employers and trade unions and other parts of civil society;

   b) Policies to expand work opportunities and increase productivity in both rural and urban sectors;

   c) Education and training that enable workers and entrepreneurs to adapt to changing technologies and economic conditions;

   d) Quality jobs, with full respect for the basic rights of workers as defined by relevant International Labour Organisation and other international instruments;

   e) Giving special priority, in the design of policies, to the problems of structural, long-term unemployment and underemployment of youth, women, persons with disabilities and all other disadvantaged groups and individuals;

   f) Empowerment of women, gender balance in decision-making processes at all levels and gender analysis in policy development to ensure equal employment opportunities and wage rates for women and to enhance harmonious and mutually beneficial partnerships between women and men in sharing family and employment responsibilities;

g) Empowerment of members of vulnerable and disadvantaged groups, including through the provision of education and training;

h) A broader recognition and understanding of work and employment and greater flexibility in working time arrangements for both men and women.

ACTIONS

The centrality of employment in policy formulation

7. Placing the expansion of productive employment at the centre of sustainable development strategies and economic and social policies requires:

   a) Promoting and pursuing active policies for full, productive, appropriately remunerated and freely chosen employment;

   b) Giving priority at the national and international levels to the policies that can address the problems of unemployment and underemployment.

8. Minimising the negative impact on jobs of measures for macroeconomic stability requires:

   a) Pursuing the coordination of macro-economic policies so that they are mutually reinforcing and conducive to broad based and sustained economic growth and sustainable development, as well as to substantial increases in productive employment expansion and a decline in unemployment worldwide;

   b) Giving priority to programmes that most directly promote viable and long-term job growth when budgetary adjustments are required;

   c) Removing structural constraints to economic growth and employment creation as a part of stabilisation policies;

d) Enabling competing claims on resources to be resolved in a non-inflationary manner through the development and use of sound industrial relations systems;

e) Monitoring, analysing and disseminating information on the impact of trade and investment liberalisation on the economy, especially on employment;

f) Exchanging information on different employment promotion measures and their consequences, and monitoring the development of global employment trends;

g) Establishing appropriate social safety mechanisms to minimise the adverse effects of structural adjustment, stabilisation or reform programmes on the workforce, especially the vulnerable, and for those who lose their jobs, creating conditions for their re-entry through, *inter alia*, continuing education and retraining.

9. Promoting patterns of economic growth that maximise employment creation requires:

a) Encouraging, as appropriate, labour-intensive investments in economic and social infrastructure that use local resources and create, maintain and rehabilitate community assets in both rural and urban areas;

b) Promoting technological innovations and industrial policies that have the potential to stimulate short and long-term employment creation, and considering their impact on vulnerable and disadvantage groups;

c) Giving developing countries the capacity to select specific and able technologies;

d) Providing technical assistance and expanded transfer of technology to developing countries to integrate technology and employment policies with other social objectives, and to establish and strengthen national and local technology institutions;

e) Encouraging the realisation in the countries with economic transition of programmes for on-the-job personnel training, facilitating their adaptation to market-oriented reforms and reducing mass unemployment;

f) Promoting mutually supportive improvements in rural farm and non-farm production, including animal husbandry, forestry, fisheries and agro-processing industries, aiming to expand and diversify environmentally sound, sustained economic activity and productive employment in the rural sector;

g) Encouraging community economic development strategies that build on partnerships among Governments and members of civil society to create jobs and address the social circumstances of individuals, families and communities;

h) Introducing sound policies to mobilise savings and stimulate investment in capital-short areas;

i) Maximising the job creation potential inherent in the agenda through the conservation and management of natural resources, the promotion of alternative livelihoods in fragile ecosystems, and the rehabilitation and regeneration of critically affected and vulnerable land areas and natural resources;

j) Encouraging the utilisation of renewable energy, based on local employment-intensive resources, in particular in rural areas.

10. Enhancing opportunities for the creation and growth of private-sector enterprises that would generate additional employment requires:

a) Removing obstacles faced by small and medium-sized enterprises and easing regulations that discourage private initiative;

b) Facilitating access by small and medium-sized enterprises to create national and international markets, management training and technological information;

c) Facilitating arrangements between large and small enterprises, such as subcontracting programmes, with full respect for workers' rights;

d) Improving opportunities and working conditions for women and youth entrepreneurs by eliminating discrimination in access to credit, productive resources and social security protection, and providing and increasing, as appropriate, family benefits and social support, such as health care and child care;

e) Promoting, supporting and establishing legal frameworks to foster the development of cooperative enterprises, and encouraging them to mobilise capital, develop innovative lending programmes and promote entrepreneurship;

f) Assisting informal sectors and local enterprises to become more productive and progressively integrated into the formal economy through access to affordable credit, information, wider markets, new technology and appropriate technological and management skills, opportunities to upgrade technical and management skills, and improved premises and other physical infrastructure, as well as by progressively extending labour standards and social protection without destroying the ability of informal sectors to generate employment;

g) Promoting the creation and development of independent organisations, such as chambers of commerce and other associations or self-help institutions of small formal and informal enterprises;

h) Facilitating the expansion of the training and employment generating opportunities of industries.

Education, training and labour policies

11. Facilitating people's access to productive employment in today's rapidly changing global environment and developing better quality jobs requires:

    a) Establishing well-defined educational priorities and investing effectively in education and training systems;

    b) Introducing new and revitalised partnerships between education and other government departments, including labour, and communications and partnerships between governments and non-governmental organisations, the private sector, local communities, religious groups and families;

    c) Ensuring broad basic education, especially literacy, and promoting general education, including the analytical and critical thinking that is essential to improve learning skills. This is the foundation for acquiring specialised skills and for renewing, adapting and upgrading them rapidly to facilitate horizontal and vertical occupational mobility;

    d) Promoting the active participation of youth and adult learners in the design of literacy campaigns, education and training programmes to ensure that the labour force and social realities of diverse groups are taken into account;

    e) Promoting lifelong learning to ensure that education and training programmes respond to changes in the economy, provide full and equal access to training opportunities, secure the access of women to training programmes, offer incentives for public and private sectors to provide and for workers to acquire training on a continuous basis, and stimulate entrepreneurial skills;

    f) Encouraging and supporting through technical assistance programmes, including those of the United

Nations systems well-designed and adaptable vocational training and apprenticeship programmes to enhance productivity and productive employment;

g) Promoting and strengthening training programmes for the employment of new entrants to the job market and retraining programmes for displaced and retrenched workers;

h) Developing an enhanced capacity for research and knowledge dissemination by encouraging national and international exchanges of information on innovative models and best practices;

i) Developing, in the area of vocational and continuing education, innovative methods of teaching and learning, including interactive technologies and inductive methods involving close coordination between working experience and training.

12. Helping workers to adapt and to enhance their employment opportunities under changing economic conditions requires:

a) Designing, developing, implementing, analysing and monitoring active labour policies to stimulate the demand for labour in order to ensure that the burden of indirect labour costs on employers does not constitute a disincentive to hiring workers, identifying skill shortages and surpluses, providing vocational guidance and counselling services and active help in job searches, promoting occupational choice and mobility, offering advisory services and support to enterprises, particularly small enterprises, for the more effective use and development of their workforce, and establishing institutions and processes that prevent all forms of discrimination and improve the employment opportunities of groups that are vulnerable and disadvantaged;

b) Improving employment opportunities and increasing ways and means of helping youth and persons with disabilities to develop the skills they need to enable them to find employment;

c) Promoting access by women and girls to traditionally male dominated occupations;

d) Developing strategies to address the needs of people engaged in various forms of atypical employment;

e) Promoting labour mobility, retraining and maintenance of adequate levels of social protection to facilitate worker redeployment when there is phasing out of production or closure of an enterprise, giving special attention to vulnerable and disadvantaged groups;

f) Facilitating the integration or reintegration of women into the workforce by developing adequate child care, care for older persons and other support services and facilities;

g) Encouraging cooperation between employers and workers to prepare for the introduction of new technologies and to plan for their employment effects as far in advance as possible, while ensuring adequate protection and adjustment;

h) Strengthening public and private employment services to assist workers to adapt to changing job markets and provide social safety mechanisms, occupational guidance, employment and job search counselling, training, placement, apprenticeships and the sharing of information;

i) Strengthening labour market information systems, particularly through development of appropriate data and indicators on employment, underemployment, unemployment and earnings, as well as dissemination of information concerning labour markets, including, as far as possible, work situations outside formal markets. All such data should be disaggregated by gender in order to monitor the status of women relative to men.

Enhanced quality of work and employment

13. Governments should enhance the quality of work and employment by:

   a) Observing and fully implementing the human rights obligations that they have assumed;

   b) Safeguarding and promoting respect for basic workers' rights, including the prohibition of forced labour and child labour, freedom of association and the right to organise and bargain collectively, equal remuneration for men and women for work of equal value, and nondiscrimination in employment, fully implementing the conventions of the International Labour Organisation (ILO) in the case of States parties to those conventions, and taking into account the principles embodied in those conventions in the case of those countries that are not States parties to thus achieve truly sustained economic growth and sustainable development;

   c) Strongly considering ratification and full implementation of ILO conventions in these areas, as well as those relating to the employment rights of minors, women, youth, persons with disabilities and indigenous people;

   d) Using existing international labour standards to guide the formulation of national labour legislation and policies;

   e) Promoting the role of ILO, particularly as regards improving the level of employment and the quality of work;

   f) Encouraging, where appropriate, employers and workers to find ways and means for enhancing the sharing of work in the productivity of enterprises and promoting cooperation between workers and employers in the decisions of enterprises.

14. To achieve a healthy and safe working environment, remove exploitation, abolish child labour, raise productivity and enhance the quality of life requires:

    a) Developing and implementing policies designed to promote improved working conditions, including health and safety conditions;

    b) Improving health policies that reduce, with a view to eliminating, environmental health hazards and provide for occupational health and safety, in conformity with the relevant conventions, and providing informal sector enterprises and all workers with accessible information and guidance on how to enhance occupational safety and reduce health risks;

    c) Promoting, in accordance with national laws and regulations, sound labour relations based on tripartite cooperation and full respect for freedom of association and the right to organise and bargain collectively;

    d) Setting specific target dates for eliminating all forms of child labour that are contrary to accepted international standards and ensuring the full enforcement of relevant existing laws, and, where appropriate, enacting the legislation necessary to implement the Convention on the Rights of the Child and ILO standards, ensuring the protection of working children, in particular of street children, through the provision of appropriate health, education and other social services;

    e) Designing labour policies and programmes to help eradicate family poverty, which is a main cause of child labour, eliminating child labour and encouraging parents to send their children to school through, *inter alia*, the provision of social services and other incentives;

f) Establishing policies and programmes to protect workers, especially women, from sexual harassment and violence;

g) Encouraging incentives to public and private enterprises to develop, transfer and adopt technologies and know how that improve the working environment, enhance occupational safety and reduce, with a view to eliminating, health risks.

15. The full participation of women in the labour market their equal access to employment opportunities require:

a) Establishing the principle of equality between men and women as basis for employment policy and promoting gender-sensitivity training to eliminate prejudice against the employment of women;

b) Eliminating gender discrimination, including by taking positive action, where appropriate, in hiring, wages, access to credit, benefit promotion, training, career development, job assignment, working conditions, job security and social security benefits;

c) Improving women's access to technologies that facilitate their occupational and domestic work, encourage self-support, generate income transform gender-prescribed roles within the productive process an enable them to move out of stereotyped, low-paying jobs;

d) Changing those policies and attitudes that reinforce the division of labour based on gender, and providing institutional support, such a social protection for maternity, parental leave, technologies that facilitate the sharing and reduce the burden of domestic chores, and flexible working arrangements, including parental voluntary part-time employment and work-sharing, as well as accessible and affordable quality child-care facilities, to enable working parents to reconcile work with family responsibilities, paying particular attention to the needs of single-parent households;

e) Encouraging men to take an active part in all areas of family and household responsibilities, including the sharing of child-rearing and housework.

Enhanced employment opportunities for groups with specific needs

16. The improvement of the design of policies and programmes requires:

    a) Identifying and reflecting the specific needs of particular groups, and ensuring that programmes are equitable and non-discriminatory, efficient and effective in meeting the needs of those groups;

    b) Actively involving representatives of these groups in planning, design and management, and monitoring, evaluating and reorienting these programmes by providing access to accurate information and sufficient resources to ensure that they reach their intended beneficiaries.

17. Employment policies can better address the problem of short- and long-term unemployment by:

    a) Incorporating, with the involvement of the unemployed and/or their associations, a comprehensive set of measures, Including employment planning, re-education and training programmes, literacy, skills upgrading, counselling and job-search assistance, temporary work schemes, frequent contact with employment service offices and preparing for entry and re-entry into the labour market;

    b) Analysing the underlying causes of long-term unemployment and their effect on different groups, including older workers and single parents, and designing employment and other supporting policies that address specific situations and needs;

c) Promoting social security schemes that reduce barriers and disincentives to employment so as to enable the unemployed to improve their capacity to participate actively in society, to maintain an adequate standard of living and to be able to take advantage of employment opportunities.

18. Programmes for entry or re-entry into the labour market aimed at vulnerable and disadvantaged groups can effectively combat the causes of exclusion on the labour market by:

   a) Complementing literacy actions, general education or vocational training by work experience that may include support and instruction on business management and training so as to give better knowledge of the value of entrepreneurship and other private-sector contributions to society;

   b) Increasing the level of skills, and also improving the ability to get a job through improvements in housing, health and family life.

19. Policies should seek to guarantee all youth constructive options for their future by:

   a) Providing equal access to education at the primary and secondary levels, with literacy as a priority and with special attention to girls;

   b) Encouraging the struggle against illiteracy and promoting literacy training in national languages in developing countries, in particular in Africa;

   c) Encouraging various actors to join forces in designing and carrying out comprehensive and coordinated programmes that stimulate the resourcefulness of youth, preparing them for durable employment or self-employment, and providing them with guidance, vocational and managerial training, social skills, work experience and education in social values;

d) Ensuring the participation of youth, commensurate with their age and responsibility, in planning and decision making with regard to their future.

20. The full participation of indigenous people in the labour market and their equal access to employment opportunities requires developing comprehensive employment, education and training programmes that take account of the particular needs of indigenous people.

21. Broadening the range of employment opportunity for persons with disabilities requires:

a) Ensuring that laws and regulations do not discriminate against persons with disabilities;

b) Taking proactive measures, such as organising support services, devising incentive schemes and supporting self-help schemes and small businesses;

c) Making appropriate adjustments in the workplace to accommodate persons with disabilities, including in that respect the promotion of innovative technologies;

d) Developing alternative forms of employment, such as supported employment, for persons with disabilities who need these services

e) Promoting public awareness within society regarding the impact of the negative stereotyping of persons with disabilities on their participation in the labour market.

22. There is need for intensified international cooperational and national attention on to the situation of migrant workers and their families. To that end:

a) Governments are invited to consider ratifying existing instruments pertaining to migrant workers, particularly the International Convention on the Protection of the Rights of All Migrant Workers and Members of Their Families;

b) In accordance with national legislation, governments of receiving countries are urged to consider extending to documented migrants who meet appropriate length-of-stay requirements and to members of their families whose stay in the receiving country is regular, treatment equal to that accorded their own nationals with regard to the enjoyment of basic human rights, including equality of opportunity and treatment in respect of religious practices, working conditions, social security, participation in trade unions and access to health, education, cultural and other social services, as well as equal access to the judicial system and equal treatment before the law;

c) Governments of countries of origin, transit countries and countries of destination are urged to cooperate in reducing the causes of undocumented migration, safeguarding the basic human rights of undocumented migrants and preventing their exploitation;

d) Governments of both receiving countries and countries of origin should adopt effective sanctions against those who organise undocumented migration, exploit undocumented migrants or engage in trafficking in undocumented migrants;

e) Governments of countries of origin are urged to facilitate the return of migrants and their reintegration into their home communities and to devise ways of using their skills. Governments of countries of origin should consider collaborating with countries of destination and engaging the support of appropriate international organisations in promoting the return on a voluntary basis of qualified migrants who can play a crucial role in the transfer of knowledge, skills and technology. Countries of destination are encouraged to facilitate return migration on a voluntary basis by adopting flexible policies, such as the transferability of pensions and other work benefits.

f) A broader recognition and understanding of work and employment.

23. A broader recognition and understanding of work an employment requires:

a) Acknowledging the important contribution of unremunerated work to societal well-being and bringing respect, dignity and value to society perceptions of such work and the people who do it;

b) Developing a more comprehensive knowledge of work and employment through, *inter alia,* efforts to measure and better understand the type, extent and distribution of unremunerated work, particularly work in caring for dependants and unremunerated work done for family farms or businesses, and encouraging, sharing and disseminating information, studies and experience in this field, including on the development of methods for assessing its value in quantitative terms, for possible reflection in accounts that may be produced separately from, but are consistent with, core national accounts;

c) Recognising the relationship between remunerated employment and unremunerated work in developing strategies to expand productive employment, to ensure equal access by women and men to employment, and to ensure the care and well-being of children an other dependants, as well as to combat poverty and promote social integration;

d) Encouraging an open dialogue on the possibilities and institutional requirements for a broader understanding of various forms of work and employment;

e) Examining a range of policies and programmes, including social security legislation, and taxation systems, in accordance with national priorities and policies, to ascertain how to facilitate flexibility in the way people divide their time between education and training paid employment, family responsibilities, volunteer activity and other socially useful forms of work, leisure and retirement, giving particular attention to the situation of women, especially in female-maintained households;

f) Promoting socially useful volunteer work and allocating appropriate resources to support such work without diluting the objective regarding employment expansion;

g) Intensifying international exchange of experience on various aspects of change in the recognition and understanding of work and employment and on new forms of flexible working time arrangements over the lifetime.

24. The development of additional socially useful new types of employment and work requires, *inter alia:*

a) Helping vulnerable and disadvantaged groups to integrate better into society and thus participate more effectively in economic and social development;

b) Helping older persons who are dependent or providing support for families in need of educational assistance or social support;

c) Strengthening social ties through these forms of employment and work, which represents an important achievement of social development policy.

SOCIAL INTEGRATION

Basis for Action and Objectives

1. The aim of social integration is to create 'a society for all', in which every individual, each with rights and responsibilities has an active role to play. Such an

inclusive society must be based on respect for all human rights and fundamental freedoms, cultural and religious diversity, social justice and the special needs of vulnerable and disadvantaged groups, democratic participation and the rule of law the pluralistic nature of most societies has at times resulted it, problems for the different groups to achieve and maintain harmony and cooperation, and to have equal access to all resources in society. For recognition of each individual's rights in the context of the rule of law has not always been fully guaranteed. Since the founding of the United Nations, this quest for humane, stable, safe, tolerant and just societies has shown a mixed record at best.

2. Nevertheless, progress has been noted, as shown in the continuation of the ongoing process of decolonisation; the elimination of apartheid; the spread of democracy; wider recognition of the need to respect human dignity, all human rights and fundamental freedoms and cultural diversity; the unacceptability of discrimination; increasing recognition of the unique concerns of indigenous people in the world; an expanded notion of collective responsibility for all members of a society; expanded economic and educational opportunities and the globalisation of communication; and greater possibilities for social mobility, choice and autonomy of action.

3. Notwithstanding the instances of progress, there ate negative developments that include social polarisation and fragmentation widening disparities and inequalities of income and wealth within among nations; problems arising from uncontrolled urban development and the degradation of the environment; marginalisation of People families, social groups, communities and even entire countries; an strains on individuals, families, communities and institutions as a result of the rapid pace

of social change, economic transformation, migration and major dislocations of population, particularly in the areas of armed conflict.

4. Furthermore, violence, in its many manifestations, including domestic violence, especially against women, children, older persons and people with disabilities, is a growing threat to the security of individuals, families and communities everywhere. Total social breakdown is an all too real contemporary experience. Organised crime, illegal drugs, the illicit arms trade, trafficking in women and children, ethnic and religious conflict, civil war, terrorism, all forms of extremist violence, xenophobia, and politically motivated killing and even genocide present fundamental threats to societies and the global social order. These are compelling and urgent reasons for action by governments individually and, as appropriate, jointly to foster social cohesion while recognising, protecting and valuing diversity.

5. There is therefore an urgent need for:

   a) Transparent and accountable public institutions that are accessible to people on an equal basis and are responsive to their needs;

   b) Opportunities for all to participate in all spheres of public life;

   c) Strengthened participation and involvement of civil society in the formulation, implementation and evaluation of decisions determining the functioning and well-being of societies;

   d) Publicly available objective data to enable people to make informed decisions;

   e) Maintenance of social stability and promotion of social justice and progress;

   f) Promotion of nondiscrimination, tolerance and mutual respect for and the value of diversity;

g) Equity and equality of opportunity and social mobility;

h) Gender equality and equity and empowerment of women;

i) Elimination of physical and social barriers with the aim of creating a society accessible for all, with special emphasis on measures to meet the needs and interests of those who face obstacles in participating fully in society;

j) Giving special attention to the right to the enjoyment of the highest attainable standard of physical and mental health, and to health as a factor of development;

k) Promoting the principle of caring for one another's well, being and fostering the spirit of mutual support, within the context of human rights education;

l) While acknowledging legitimate national defence needs, recognising and addressing the dangers to society of armed conflict, and the negative effect of excessive military expenditures, trade in arms, especially of those arms that are particularly injurious or have indiscriminate effects, and excessive investment for arms production and acquisition. Similarly, the need to combat illicit arms trafficking, violence, crime, the production, use and trafficking of illicit drugs, and trafficking in women and children should be recognised and addressed;

m) The elimination of all forms of violence and the full implementation of the Declaration on the Elimination of Violence against Women.

ACTIONS

Responsive government and full participation in society

6. Governments should promote and protect all human right, and fundamental freedoms, including the right to development, bearing in mind the interdependent and mutually reinforcing relationship between democracy, development and respect for human rights, and should make public institutions more responsive to people's needs by:

   a) Ensuring that decisions are based on accurate data and are taken with the participation of those who will be affected, keeping under review, within each country's constitutional framework, the responsibilities of the different levels of government and the administrative arrangements for organising and delivering services;

   b) Keeping under review, within each country's constitutional framework, the national, provincial, municipal and local capacity and capability in raising revenue, and allocating resources to promote local initiatives in maintaining and increasing community cohesion;

   c) Simplifying administrative regulations, disseminating information about public policy issues and initiatives for collective interests, and facilitating maximum access to information;

   d) Opening channels and promoting full confidence between citizens and government agencies, and developing affordable recourse procedures accessible to all people, especially those who have no access to channels and agencies of communication to seek redress of grievances;

e) Encouraging the production of relevant studies/ research to assess the consequences of global and technological changes on social integration and the production of evaluations of the policies and programmes put in place to achieve the various components of social integration; and encouraging national and international exchanges and dissemination of information on innovative models and successful practices;

f) Requiring accountability for the honest, just and equitable delivery of public services to the people from all public officials;

g) Making their services accessible to all citizens and taking special care to ensure that the services are provided to all persons in need;

h) Strengthening popular political participation, and promoting the transparency and accountability of political groupings at the local and national levels;

i) Encouraging the ratification of, the avoidance as far as possible of the resort to reservations to and the implementation of international human rights instruments aiming to eliminate barriers to the full enjoyment of all human rights.

7. Encouraging the fullest participation in society requires:

a) Strengthening the capacities and opportunities for all people, especially those who are vulnerable and disadvantaged, to establish and maintain independent organisations representing their interests, within each country's constitutional framework;

b) Enabling institutions of civil society, with special attention to those representing vulnerable and disadvantaged groups, to participate in the formulation, on a consultative basis, implementation and evaluation of policies related to social development;

c) Giving community organisations greater involvement in the design and implementation of local projects, particularly in the areas of education, health care, resource management and social protection;

d) Ensuring a legal framework and a support structure that encourage the formation of and constructive contributions from community organisations and voluntary associations of individuals;

e) Encouraging all members of society to exercise their rights, fulfil their responsibilities and participate fully in their societies, recognising that governments alone cannot meet all needs in society;

f) Establishing a universal and flexible social safety net that takes into account available economic resources and encourages rehabilitation and active participation in society;

g) Facilitating the access of disadvantaged and marginalised people to education and information, as well as their participation in social and cultural life;

h) Promoting equality and social integration through sports and cultural activities.

Nondiscrimination, tolerance and mutual respect for and value of diversity

8. Eliminating discrimination and promoting tolerance and mutual respect for and the value of diversity at the national and international levels requires:

a) Enacting and implementing appropriate laws and other regulating to combat racism, racial discrimination, religious intolerance in all it various forms, xenophobia and all forms of discrimination in all walks of life in societies;

b) Encouraging the ratification of, the avoidance as far as possible of the resort to reservations, and the implementation of international instruments, including the International Convention on the Elimination of All Forms of Racial Discrimination 17 and the Convention on the Elimination of All Forms of Discrimination against Women.

c) Taking specific measures, in the context of the implementation of the Nairobi Forward-looking Strategies for the Advancement of Women to remove long-standing legal and social barriers to employment, education, productive resources and public services; assist women in becoming aware of and realising their rights; and ensure the elimination of intra-family discrimination for the girl child, especially in regard to health, nutrition and education;

d) Ensuring gender equality and equity through changes in attitudes, policies and practices, encouraging the full participation and empowerment of women in social, economic and political life, and enhancing gender balance in decision-making processes at all levels;

e) Reviewing with a view to changing legislation, public codes and practices that perpetuate discriminatory practices;

f) Disseminating information in plain language to all groups in society about people's rights and the means available to redress complaints;

9. Strengthening or establishing machinery for monitoring and resolving disputes and conflicts related to discriminatory practices, and developing arbitration and conciliation procedures at the local and national levels;

a) Setting an example through state institutions and the educational system to promote and protect respect for freedom of expression; democracy; political pluralism;

diversity of heritage, cultures and values; religious tolerance and principles; and the national traditions on which a country has been built;

b) Recognising that the languages spoken or used in the world should be respected and protected;

c) Recognising that it is of utmost importance for all people to live in cooperation and harmony, and ensuring that the traditions and cultural heritage of nations are fully protected;

d) Encouraging independent communication media that promote people's understanding and awareness, of all aspects of social integration, with full respect for freedom of expression.

Equality and social justice

10. Governments should promote equality and social justice by:

 a) Ensuring that all people are equal before the law;

 b) Carrying out a regular review of public policy, including health and education policies, and public spending from a social and gender equality and equity perspective, and promoting their positive contribution to equalising opportunities;

 c) Expanding and improving access to basic services with the aim of ensuring universal coverage;

 d) Providing equal opportunities in public-sector employment and providing guidance, information and, as appropriate, incentives to private employers to do the same;

 e) Encouraging the free formation of cooperatives, community and other grassroots organisations, mutual support groups, recreational/sports associations and similar institutions that tend to strengthen social integration, paying particular attention to police that assist families in their support, educational, socialising and nurturing roles;

f) Ensuring that structural adjustment programmes are so designed as to minimise their negative effects on vulnerable and disadvantaged groups and communities while ensuring their positive effects on them by preventing their marginalisation in economic and social activities, and devising measures to ensure that such groups and communities gain access to and control over economic resources and economic and social activities. Actions should be taken to reduce inequality and economic disparity;

g) Promoting full access to preventive and curative health care to improve the quality of life, especially by the vulnerable and disadvantaged groups, in particular women and children;

h) Expanding basic education by developing special measures to provide schooling for children and youth living in sparsely populated and remote areas, for children and youth of nomadic, pastoral, migrant or indigenous parents, and for street children, children and youth working or looking after younger siblings and disabled or aged parents, and disabled children and youth; establishing, in partnership with indigenous people, educational systems that will meet the unique needs of their cultures;

i) Ensuring that the expansion of basic education is accompanied by improved quality, appropriate attention to children of different abilities, cooperation between family and school, and a close link between the school curriculum and the needs of the workplace;

j) Evaluating school systems on a regular basis by results achieved, and disseminating research findings regarding the appropriateness of different methods of evaluation;

k) Ensuring that all people can have access to a variety of formal and non-formal learning activities throughout their lives that allows them to contribute to and benefit from full participation in society; making use of all forms of education, including non-conventional and experimental means of education, such as telecourses and correspondence courses, through public institutions, the institutions of civil society and the private sector, to provide educational opportunities for those who in childhood missed necessary schooling, for youth in the process of transition from school to work, and for those who wish to continue education and upgrade skills throughout their lives;

l) Providing equal access for girls to all levels of education, including non-traditional and vocational training, and ensuring that measures are taken to address the various cultural and practical barriers that impede their access to education through such measures as the hiring of female teachers, adoption of flexible hours, care of dependants and siblings, and provision of appropriate facilities.

Responses to special social needs

11. Governmental responses to special needs of social groups should include:

a) Identifying specific means to encourage institutions and services to adapt to the special needs of vulnerable and disadvantaged groups;

b) Recognising and promoting the abilities, talents and experience of groups that are vulnerable and identifying ways to prevent isolation and alienation, and enabling them to make a positive contribution to society;

c) Ensuring access to work and social services through such measures as education, language training and technical assistance for people adversely affected by language barriers;

d) Supporting by legislation, incentives and other means, where appropriate, organisations of the vulnerable and disadvantaged groups so that they may promote the interests of the groups concerned and become involved in local and national, economic, social and political decision-making that guides society as a whole;

e) Improving the opportunities for people who are disadvantage or vulnerable to seek positions in legislatures, governments, judiciaries and other positions of public authority or influence;

f) Taking measures to integrate into economic and social life demobilised persons and persons displaced by civil conflict and disaster,;

g) Promoting and protecting the rights of indigenous people and empowering them to make choices that enable them to retain their cultural identity while participating in national, economic and social life, with full respect for their cultural values, languages, tradition, and forms of social organisation;

h) Implementing the Plan of Action adopted by the World Summit for Children in 1990 and ratifying, as appropriate, and implementing the provisions of the Convention on the Rights of the Child;

i) Encouraging youth to participate in discussions and decisions effecting them and in the design, implementation and evaluation of policies and programmes; ensuring that youth acquire the skills to participate in all aspects of life in society and to lead self-sufficient lives thorough the provision of relevant and innovative educational programme and establishing laws and measures that ensure the protection of youth against physical and mental abuse and economic exploitation;

j) Adopting specific measures to equip young people for responsible adulthood, particularly out-of-school youth and street children;

k) Promoting the United Nations Standard Rules on the Equalisation of opportunities for Persons with Disabilities and developing strategies for implementing the Rules. Governments, in collaboration with organisations of people with disabilities and the private sector, should work towards the equalisation of opportunities so that people with disabilities can contribute to and benefit from full participation in society. Policies concerning people with disabilities should focus on their abilities rather than their disabilities and should ensure their dignity as citizens;

l) Within the context of the United Nations Principles for Older Persons and the global targets on ageing for the year 2001, reviewing or developing strategies for implementing the International Plan of Action on Ageing so that older persons can maximise their contribution to society and play their full part in the community;

m) Facilitating the implementation of the guidelines for further planning and suitable follow-up in the field of youth with a view to promoting the integration of youth into societies;

n) Taking measures to enable persons belonging to minorities to participate fully and contribute to the development of their society.

Responses to specific social needs of refugees, displaced persons and asylum-seekers, documented migrants and undocumented migrants

12. In order to address the special needs of refugees, displaced persons and asylum-seekers:

a) Governments are urged to address the root causes of movements of refugees and displaced persons by taking appropriate measures, particularly with respect to conflict resolution; the promotion of peace and reconciliation; respect for human rights, including those of persons belonging to minorities; and respect for the independence, territorial integrity and sovereignty of states. Governments and all other entities should respect and safeguard the right of people to remain in safety in their homes and should refrain from policies or practices that force people to flee,

b) Governments are urged to strengthen their support for international protection and assistance activities on behalf of refugees and, as appropriate, displaced persons, and to promote the search for durable solutions to their plight. In so doing, governments are encouraged to enhance regional and international mechanisms that promote appropriate shared responsibility for the protection and assistance needs of refugees. All necessary measures should be taken to ensure the physical protection of refugees, in particular that of refugee women an refugee children and especially against exploitation, abuse and all form of violence;

c) Adequate international support should be extended to countries of asylum to meet the basic needs of refugees and to assist in the search for durable solutions. Refugee populations should be assisted in achieving self-sufficiency. Refugees, particularly refugee women, should be involved in the planning of refugee assistance activities and in their implementation. In planning and implementing refugee assistance activities, special attention should be given to the specific needs of refugee and displaced women and children. Refugees should be provided with access to adequate accommodation, education, health services, including family planning, and other necessary social services. Refugees should respect the laws and regulations of their countries of asylum;

d) Governments and other relevant actors should create comprehensive conditions that allow for the voluntary repatriation of refugees in safety and dignity, and the voluntary and safe return of internally displaced persons to their homes of origin and their smooth reintegration into society;

e) Governments are urged to abide by international law concerning refugees. States that have not already done so are invited to consider acceding to the international instruments concerning refugees, in particular the 1951 Convention relating to the Status of Refugees and the 1967 Protocol to the Convention. Governments are furthermore urged to respect the principle of non-refoulement, that is, the principle of no forcible return of persons to places where their lives or freedom would be threatened because of race, religion, nationality, membership in a particular social group or political opinion. Governments should ensure that asylum-seekers in the Government's territory have access to a fair hearing and should facilitate the expeditious processing of asylum requests, ensuring that guidelines and procedures for the determination of refugee status are sensitive to the particular situation of women;

f) Governments and relevant actors should respect the right of people to seek and enjoy in other countries asylum from persecution.

13. To promote the equitable treatment and integration of documented migrants, particularly documented migrant workers and members of their families:

a) Governments should ensure that documented migrants receive fair and equal treatment, including full respect of their human rights, protection of the laws of the host society, appropriate access to economic opportunities and social services; protection against racism, ethnocentrism and xenophobia; and protection from violence and exploitation. Language training should be provided, in recognition of the centrality of language acquisition to the effective integration of documented migrants, including those not destined for the labour market, in so far as resources permit. Early integration is the key to allowing documented migrants to contribute their skills, knowledge and potential to the development of countries of destination, and involves mutual understanding by documented migrants and the host society. The former need to know and respect the values, laws, traditions and principles of the host society, which in turn should respect the religions, cultures and traditions of documented migrants;

b) Governments of receiving countries are urged to consider giving to documented migrants having the right to long-term residence, civil and political rights and responsibilities, as appropriate, and facilitating their naturalisation. Special efforts should be made to enhance the integration of the children of long-term migrants by providing them with educational and training opportunities equal to those of nationals, allowing them to exercise an economic activity and facilitating the naturalisation of those who have been raised in the receiving country. Consistent with article 10 of the Convention on the Rights of the Child and all relevant universally recognised human rights instruments, all Governments, particularly those of receiving countries, must recognise the vital importance of family reunification and promote its integration into their national legislation in order to ensure protection of the unity of the families of documented migrants. Governments of receiving countries must ensure the protection of migrants and their families, giving priority to programmes and strategies that combat religious intolerance, racism, ethnocentrism, xenophobia and gender discrimination, and that generate the necessary public sensitivity in that regard;

c) Governments and relevant actors should encourage the international exchange of information on educational and training institutions in order to promote the productive employment of documented migrants through greater recognition of foreign education and credentials;

d) Governments should encourage interracial harmony and cross-cultural understanding through educational programmes, where appropriate, including alternative dispute resolution and conflict prevention training in schools.

14. In order to address the concerns and basic human needs related to undocumented migrants:

a) Governments are urged to cooperate in reducing the causes of undocumented migration, safeguarding the basic human rights of undocumented migrants, preventing their exploitation and offering them appropriate means of appeal according to national legislation, and punishing criminals who organise trafficking in human being;

b) Countries of destination, countries of transit and countries of origin should cooperate, as appropriate, to manage immigration flows, prevent undocumented migration, and, if appropriate, facilitate the return of migrants and their reintegration in their home communities;

c) Governments are urged to cooperate to reduce the effects of undocumented migration on receiving countries, bearing in mind the special circumstances and needs of such countries, in particular developing countries;

d) Governments are urged to promote effective measures to protect all undocumented migrants and members of their families against racism, ethnocentrism and xenophobia.

Violence, crime, the problem of illicit drugs and substance abuse

15. Addressing the problems created by violence, crime, substance abuse and the production, use and trafficking of illicit drugs, and the rehabilitation of addicts requires:
    a) Introducing and implementing specific policies and public health and social service programmes to prevent and eliminate all forms of violence in society, particularly to prevent and eliminate domestic violence and to protect the victims of violence, with particular attention to violence against women, children, older persons and persons with disabilities. In particular, the Declaration on the Elimination of Violence against Women should be implemented and enforced nationally. In addition, the provisions of the Convention on the Rights of the Child should be respected;
    b) Taking full measures to eliminate all forms of exploitation, abuse, harassment and violence against women, in particular domestic violence and rape. Special attention should be given to violence resulting from harmful traditional or customary practices and all forms of extremism, which implies both preventive actions and the rehabilitation of victims;
    c) Implementing programmes that channel the energy and creativity of children and youth towards improving themselves and their communities in order to prevent their participation in crime, violence, and drug abuse and trafficking;
    d) Improving mechanisms for resolving conflicts peacefully and reintegrating society following conflicts, including efforts towards reconciliation and confidence-building between the conflicting groups,

training in nonviolent conflict resolution at all levels of education, the reconstruction of social institutions that have been destroyed, the reintegration of displaced and disabled persons, and the re-establishment of the rule of law and respect for all human rights;

e) Establishing partnerships with nongovernmental organisations and community organisations to make adequate provision for the rehabilitation and reintegration into society of offenders, especially young offenders; measures will include efforts to maintain links with their families during detention and to reintegrate them into productive employment and social life after their release from detention;

f) Strengthening international cooperation and coordination devising strategies, policies, legislation and other measures in combating national and transnational organised crime and the use of violence and terrorism;

g) Adopting effective and environmentally sound national strategies to prevent or substantially reduce the cultivation and processing of crops used for the illegal drug trade, paying particular attention to national and international support for development programmes that create viable economic alternatives to drug production and promote the f integration of the social groups involved in such activities;

h) Combating drug and substance abuse and drug trafficking, corruption and related criminal activities through national and internationally coordinated measures, while strengthening integrated, multi-sector programmes to prevent and reduce the demand for consumption drugs in order to create a society free of illicit drugs. In cooperation with the institutions of civil society and the private sector, drug and prevention should be promoted, as well as preventive education of children and youth, and rehabilitation and education programme for former drug and alcohol addicts, especially children and youth, enable them to obtain productive employment and achieve the independence, dignity and responsibility for a drug-free, crime-free productive life;

i) Working nationally and internationally to identify narcotics trafficking and money laundering networks, prosecuting their leaders are seising assets derived from such criminal activities;

j) Supporting comprehensive drug interdiction strategies and strengthening efforts to control precursor chemicals and firearms, ammunition and explosives in order to prevent their diversion to drug trafficking and terrorist groups;

k) Combating trafficking in women and children through national an internationally coordinated measures, at the same time establishing strengthening institutions for the rehabilitation of the victims of the trafficking of women and children.

Social integration and family responsibilities

16. The family is the basic unit of society and as such should be strengthened. It is entitled to receive comprehensive protection an support. In different cultural, political and social systems, various forms of the family exist. Marriage must be entered into with the free consent of the intending spouses, and husband and wife should be equal partners.

17. Helping the family in its supporting, educating and nurturing roles In contributing to social integration should involve:

    a) Encouraging social and economic policies that are designed to meet the needs of families and their individual members, especially the most disadvantaged and vulnerable members, with particular attention to the care of children;

b) Ensuring opportunities for family members to understand and meet their social responsibilities;

c) Promoting mutual respect, tolerance and cooperation within the family and within society;

d) Promoting equal partnership between women and men in the family.

IMPLEMENTATION AND FOLLOW-UP OF SOCIAL DEVELOPMENT

1. Nothing short of a renewed and massive political will at the national and international levels to invest in people and their wellbeing will achieve the objectives of social development. Social development and the implementation of the Programme of Action of the Summit are primarily the responsibility of governments, although international cooperation and assistance are essential for the full implementation. At all levels of implementation, the crucial an essential requirements are:

   a) The promotion and protection of all human rights and fundamental freedoms, the support for democratic institutions and the empowerment of women;

   b) The integration of goals, programmes and review mechanisms that have developed separately in response to specific problems;

   c) Partnership involving states, local authorities, nongovernmental organisations, especially voluntary organisations, other major groups as defined in Agenda 21, the media, families and individuals;

   d) The recognition of the diversity in the world and the need to take measures geared to achieve the Summit's goals;

e) The empowerment of people, who are to be assisted so that they fully participate in setting goals, designing programmes, implementing activities and evaluating performance;

f) Efforts to mobilise new and additional financial resources that are both adequate and predictable, and are mobilised in a way that maximises the availability of such resources, and uses all available funding sources and mechanisms, *inter alia*, multilateral, bilateral and private Sources, including on concessional and grant terms;

g) Solidarity, extending the concept of partnership and a moral imperative of mutual respect and concern among individuals, communities and nations.

ACTIONS

National strategies, evaluations and reviews

2. The promotion of an integrated approach to the implementation of the Programme of Action at the national level, in accordance with national specificities, requires:

   a) Analysing and reviewing macroeconomic, micro-economic and sectoral policies and their impact on poverty, employment, social integration and social development;

   b) Enhancing government policies and programmes to promote social development by strengthening the coordination of all efforts by national and international actors, strengthening the efficiency and operational capacity of public management structures, and facilitating the effective and transparent use of resources, taking due account of the recommendations and follow-up to Agenda 21;

c) Assessing the extent, distribution and characteristics of poverty, unemployment, social tensions and social exclusion, taking measures aiming at eradicating poverty, increasing productive employment and enhancing social integration;

d) Formulating or strengthening, by 1996, comprehensive cross-sectoral strategies for implementing the Summit outcome and national strategies for social development, including government action, actions by states in cooperation with other governments, international, regional and subregional organisations, and actions taken in partnership and cooperation with actors of civil society, the private sector and cooperatives, with specific responsibilities to be undertaken by each actor and with agreed priorities and time-frames;

e) Integrating social development goals into national development plans, policies and budgets, cutting across traditional sectoral boundaries, with transparency and accountability, and formulated and implemented with the participation of the groups directly affected;

f) Defining time-bound goals and targets for reducing overall poverty and eradicating absolute poverty, expanding employment a reducing unemployment, and enhancing social integration, within e national context;

g) Promoting and strengthening institutional capacity-building inter-ministerial coordination, intersectoral collaboration, the coordinated allocation of resources and vertical integration from national capitals to local districts;

h) Developing quantitative and qualitative indicators of social development, including, where possible, disaggregation by gender, to ass poverty, employment, social integration and other social factors, monitor the impact of social policies and programmes, and to find ways to improve the effectiveness of policies and programmes and introduce new programmes;

i) Strengthening implementation and monitoring mechanisms including arrangements for the participation of civil society in policy making and implementation and collaboration with international organisations;

j) Regularly assessing national progress towards implementing the outcome of the Summit, possibly in the form of periodic nation reports, outlining successes, problems and obstacles. Such report could be considered within the framework of an appropriate consolidated reporting system, taking into account the different reporting procedures in the economic, social and environmental fields.

3. International support for the formulation of nation strategies for social development will require actions by bilateral a multilateral agencies for:

a) Assisting countries to strengthen or rebuild their capacities for formulating, coordinating, implementing and monitoring integrated strategies for social development;

b) Coordinating the assistance provided by different agencies for similar planning processes under other international action plans;

c) Developing improved concepts and programmes for the collection and dissemination of statistics and indicators for social development to facilitate review and policy analysis and provide expertise, advice and support to countries at their request.

Involvement of civil society

4. Effective implementation of the Copenhagen Declaration

on Social Development and the Programme of Action of the Summit requires strengthening community organisations and non-profit nongovernmental organisations in the spheres of education, health, poverty, social integration, human rights, improvement of the quality of life, and relief and rehabilitation, enabling them to participate constructively in policy-making and implementation. This will require:

a) Encouraging and supporting the creation and development of such organisations, particularly among the disadvantaged and vulnerable people;

b) Establishing legislative and regulatory frameworks, institutional arrangements and consultative mechanisms for involving such organisations in the design, implementation and evaluation of social development strategies and programmes;

c) Supporting capacity-building programmes for such organisations in critical areas, such as participatory planning, programme design, implementation and evaluation, economic and financial analysis, credit management, research, information and advocacy;

d) Providing resources through such measures as small grant programmes, and technical and other administrative support for initiatives taken and managed at the community level;

e) Strengthening networking and exchange of expertise and experience among such organisations.

5. The contribution of civil society, including the private sector, to social development can be enhanced by:

a) Developing planning and policy-making procedures that facilitate partnership and cooperation between governments and civil society in social development;

b) Encouraging business enterprises to pursue investment and other policies, including non-commercial activities, that will contribute to social development, especially in relation to the generation of work opportunities, social support services at the workplace, access to productive resources and construction of infrastructure;

c) Enabling and encouraging trade unions to participate in the planning and implementation of social development programmes, especially in relation to the generation of work opportunities under fair conditions, the provision of training, health care and other basic services, and the development of an economic environment that facilitates sustained economic growth and sustainable development;

d) Enabling and encouraging farmers' representative organisations and cooperatives to participate in the formulation and implementation of sustainable agricultural and rural development policies and programmes;

e) Encouraging and facilitating the development of cooperatives, including among people living in poverty or belonging to vulnerable groups;

f) Supporting academic and research institutions, particularly in the developing countries, in their contribution to social development programmes, and facilitating mechanisms for independent, detached, impartial and objective monitoring of social progress, especially through collecting, analysing and disseminating information and ideas about economic and social development;

g) Encouraging educational institutions, the media and other sources of public information and opinion to give special prominence to the challenges of social development and to facilitate widespread and well-informed debate about social policies throughout the community.

Mobilisation of financial resources

6. The implementation of the Copenhagen Declaration and the Programme of Action of the Summit at the national level may require substantial new and additional resources, in both the public and the private sectors. Augmenting the availability of public resources social development requires at the national level:

   a) Implementing macroeconomic and micro-economic policies in accordance with national priorities and policies, aimed at encouraging greater domestic savings and investment required for public spending, through progressive, fair and economically efficient taxes that are cognizant of sustainable development concerns, and through cutting back on subsidies that do not benefit the poor;

   b) Reducing, as appropriate, excessive military expenditures and investments for arms production and acquisition, consistent with national security requirements, in order to increase resources for social and economic development;

   c) Giving high priority to social development in the allocation of public spending and ensuring predictable funding for the relevant programmes;

   d) Ensuring that the resources for social development are available at the level of administration that is responsible for formulating and implementing the relevant programmes;

   e) Increasing the effective and transparent utilisation of public resources, reducing waste and combating corruption, and concentrating on the areas of greatest social need;

   f) Developing innovative sources of funding, both public and private, for social programmes, and creating a supportive environment for the mobilisation of resources by civil society for social development, including beneficiary contributions and individual voluntary contributions.

7. Implementation of the Declaration and the Programme of Action in developing countries, in particular in Africa and the least developed countries, will need additional financial resources and more effective development cooperation and assistance. This will require:
   a) Translating the commitments of the Summit into financial implications for social development programmes in developing countries, particularly Africa and the least developed countries;
   b) Striving for the fulfilment of the agreed target of 0.7 per cent of gross national product for overall official development assistance (ODA) as soon as possible, and increasing the share of funding for social development programmes, common people and scale of activities required to achieve the objectives and goals of the Declaration and Programme of Action;
   c) Agreeing on a mutual commitment between interested developed and developing country partners to allocate, on average, 20 per cent of ODA and 20 per cent of the national budget, respectively, to basic social programmes;
   d) Giving high priority in ODA to the eradication of poverty in developing countries, in particular in Africa, low-income countries in Asia and the Pacific, Latin America and the Caribbean, and the least developed countries;
   e) Providing assistance for social-sector activities, such as the rehabilitation and development of social infrastructure, including in the form of grants or soft loans;
   f) Implementing the commitments of the international community to the special needs and vulnerabilities of the small island developing states, in particular by

providing effective means, including adequate, predictable, new and additional resources for social development programmes, in accordance with the Declaration of Barbados and on the basis of the relevant provisions of the Programme of Action for the Sustainable Development of Small Island Developing States;

g) Providing international support and assistance to the land-locked developing countries in their efforts to implement the outcome of the Summit, taking into account the challenges and problems characteristic to those countries;

h) Giving preference, wherever possible, to the utilisation of competent national experts or, where necessary, of competent experts from within the subregion or region or from other developing countries, in project and programme design, preparation and implementation, and to the building of local expertise where it does not exist;

i) Exploring ways and means to strengthen support and expand South-South cooperation based on partnership between developing and developed countries, as well as enhanced cooperation among developing countries;

j) Maximising project and programme efficiency by keeping overhead cost to a minimum;

k) Developing economic policies to promote and mobilise domestic savings and attract external resources for productive investment, and seeking innovative sources of funding, both public and private, for social programmes, while ensuring their effective utilisation;

l) Monitoring the impact of trade liberalisation on progress made in developing countries to meet basic human needs, giving particular attention to new initiatives to expand the access of developing countries to international markets;

m) Encouraging direct cooperation to promote joint ventures, including in the sector of social programmes and infrastructure;

n) Encouraging recipient Governments to strengthen their national coordination mechanisms for international cooperation in social development and to ensure the effective use of international assistance so as to assist donors to secure commitment to further resources for national action plans;

o) Inviting multilateral and bilateral donors to consult with a view to coordinating their financing policies and planning procedures in order to improve the impact, complementary and cost-effectiveness of their contributions to the achievement of the objectives of social development programmes of developing countries.

8. Implementation of the Copenhagen Declaration and the Programme of Action of the Summit in countries with economies in transition will require continued international cooperation and assistance. To this end, there is a need to:

a) Assess the financial implications of the commitments of the Summit for social development programmes in countries with economies in transition;

b) Enhance technical and financial assistance for the implementation of programmes of macroeconomic stabilisation in order to ensure sustained economic growth and sustainable development;

c) Support and encourage transformations in the field of human resources development;

d) Invite multilateral and bilateral donors to consult with a view to coordinating their financing policies and planning procedures in order to improve the impact of their contribution to the achievement of the objectives of social development programmes of countries with economies in transition.

9. Substantial debt reduction is needed to enable developing countries to implement the Declaration and Programme of Action. Building on, *inter alia*, the momentum from the July 1994 meeting the seven major industrialised countries in Naples and the October 1994 meeting of the governors of the World Bank and the International Monetary Fund, further progress can be made by:

   a) Inviting the international community, including the international financial institutions, to continue to explore ways of implementing additional and innovative measures to alleviate substantially the debt burdens of developing countries, in particular of the highly indebted low-income countries, in order to help them to achieve sustained economic growth and sustainable development without falling into new debt crisis;

   b) Adopting measures to substantially reduce the bilateral debts of the least developed countries, in particular the countries of Africa as soon as possible, and exploring other innovative approaches to managing and alleviating the onerous debts and debt service burdens of other developing countries as soon as possible;

   c) Giving special consideration to those developing countries in which multilateral debt constitutes an important part of their total debt in order to seek a durable solution to this increasing problem;

   d) Encouraging the possibilities of debt swaps for social development, with the resources released by debt cancellation or reduction to be invested in social development programmes, without prejudice to more durable solutions, such as debt reduction and/or cancellation;

e) Mobilising the resources of the Debt Reduction Facility of the International Development Association in order to help eligible developing countries to reduce their commercial debt; considering alternative mechanisms to complement that facility;

f) Inviting creditor countries, private banks and multilateral financial institutions, within their prerogatives, to consider continuing the initiatives and efforts to address the commercial debt problems of the least developed countries and of low and middle-income developing countries; to consider the extension of appropriate new financial support to the low-income countries with substantial debt burdens that continue, at great cost, to service debt and meet their international obligations; to continue to explore ways of implementing additional and innovative measures to substantially alleviate the debt burdens of developing countries, in particular of the highly indebted low-income countries, in order to help them achieve sustained economic growth and sustainable development without falling into a new debt crisis.

10. In order to ensure that structural adjustment programmes include social development goals. In particular the eradication of poverty, the generation of productive employment and the enhancement of social integration, governments, in cooperation with the international financial institutions and other international organisations, should:

a) Protect basic social programmes and expenditures, in particular those affecting the poor and vulnerable segments of society, from budget reductions;

b) Review the impact of structural adjustment programmes on social development by means of gender-sensitive social-impact assessments and other relevant methods, and develop policies to reduce their negative effects and improve their positive impact;

c) Further promote policiės enabling small enterprises, cooperatives and other forms of micro-enterprises to develop their capacities for income generation and employment creation.

11. International financial institutions should contribute to the mobilisation of resources for the implementation of the Declaration and Programme of Action. To this end, the relevant institutions are urged to take the following measures:

    a) The World Bank, the International Monetary Fund, the regional and subregional development banks and funds, and all other international finance organisations should, further integrate social development goals in their policies, programmes and operations, including by giving higher priority to social-sector lending, where applicable, in their lending programmes;

    b) The Bretton Woods institutions and other organisations and bodies of the United Nations system should work together with concerned countries to improve policy develop new initiatives to ensure that structural adjustment programmes promote sustained economic and social development, with particular attention to their impact on people living in poverty and vulnerable groups;

    c) The United Nations, in cooperation with the World Bank, the International Monetary Fund and other multilateral development institutions, should study the impact of structural adjustment programmes on economic and social development and assist adjusting countries creating conditions for economic growth, job creation, poverty eradiate and social development.

12. In addition to augmenting the flow of resources through established channels, relevant United Nations bodies, in particular the Economic and Social Council, should be requested to consider new and innovative ideas for generating funds and, for this purpose, to offer any useful suggestions.

D. The role of the United Nations system

12. A framework for international cooperation must be developed in the context of the agenda for development in order to ensure the integrated and comprehensive implementation, follow-up and assessment of the outcome of the Summit, together with the results of other recent and planned United Nations conferences related to social development, in particular the World Summit for Children, the United Nations Conference on Environment and Development the World Conference on Human Rights, the Global Conference on the Sustainable Development of Small Island Developing States, the International Conference on Population and Development, the Fourth World Conference on Women, and the United Nations Conference Human Settlements (Habitat 11). At the international level, as at the national, the financial and organisational implications of the commitments, goals and targets should be assessed, priorities established, and budgets and work programmes planned.

13. With regard to the consideration of social development at the intergovernmental level, special consideration should be given to the roles of the General Assembly and of the Economic and Social Council. To this end:

 a) The General Assembly, as the highest intergovernmental mechanism is the principal policy-making and appraisal organ on matters relating to the follow-up to the Summit. The Assembly should include the follow-up to the Summit in its agenda as an item entitled "Implementation of the outcome of the World Summit for Social Development". In 1996, it should review the effectiveness of the steps taken to implement the outcome of the Summit with regard to poverty eradication, as part of the activities relating to the International Year for the Eradication of Poverty;

b) The General Assembly should hold a special session in the year 2000 for an overall review and appraisal of the implementation of the outcome of the Summit, and should consider further action and initiatives;

c) The General Assembly, at its fiftieth session, should declare the first United Nations decade for the eradication of poverty, following the International Year for the Eradication of Poverty (1996), with a view to its considering further initiatives on the eradication of poverty;

d) The General Assembly, as well as the Economic and Social Council, could convene meetings of high-level representatives to promote international dialogue on critical social issues and on policies for addressing them through international cooperation;

e) The General Assembly should draw upon the initial work of the agenda for development working group on a common framework for the implementation of the outcome of conferences;

f) The Economic and Social Council, in the context of its role under the Charter of the United Nations vis-a-vis the General Assembly and in accordance with Assembly resolutions 45/264, 46/235 and 48/162, would oversee system-wide coordination in the implementation of the Summit outcome and make recommendations in this regard. It should look at ways to strengthen, consistent with the mandates of the Charter of the United Nations, the role and authority, structures, resources and processes of the Council, bringing specialised agencies into a closer working relationship with the Council so that it can review progress made towards implementing the outcome of the Summit as well as improving the Council's effectiveness. The Council, at its substantive session of 1995, should be invited to review the mandate, agenda and composition of the Commission for Social Development, including considerations of the strengthening of the Commission, taking into account the need for synergy with other related commissions and conference follow up. The Council should also draw upon any initial work competed by that time on a common framework for the implementation of conference outcomes. The Council should also be invited to review the reporting system In the area of social development with a view to establishing a coherent system that would result in clear policy recommendations for governments and international actors;

g) Within the framework of the discussions on an agenda for development and the discussions of the Economic and Social Council at its coordination segment of 1995 on a common framework for the implementation of the outcome of United Nations conferences in the economic and social fields, consideration should be given to the possibility of holding joint meetings of the Council and the Development Committee of the World Bank and the International Monetary Fund. The Secretary-General and the heads of IMF, the World Bank, ILO, the United Nations funds and programmes, and other relevant agencies should consider the possibility of holding joint meetings for the purpose of considering the implementation of the Declaration and the Programme of Action prior to the Development Committee sessions;

h) To promote implementation of the outcomes at the regional and subregional levels, the regional commissions, in cooperation with the regional intergovernmental organisations and banks, could convene, on a biennial basis, a meeting at a high political level to review progress made towards implementing the outcome of the Summit, exchange views on their respective experiences and adopt the appropriate measures. The regional commissions should report to the Council on the outcome of such meetings through the appropriate mechanisms;

i) The important role of the Committee on Economic, Social and Cultural Rights in monitoring those aspects of the Declaration and Programme of Action that relate to compliance, by states parties with the International Covenant on Economic, Social and Cultural Rights should be emphasised.

14. The United Nations system should provide technical cooperation and other forms of assistance to the developing countries, in particular in Africa and the least developed countries, in implementing the Declaration and Programme of Action. To this end:

a) The United Nations system, including the technical and sectoral agencies and the Bretton Woods institutions, should expand and improve their cooperation in the field of social development to ensure that their efforts are complementary and, where possible, should combine resources in joint initiatives for social development built around common objectives of the Summit;

b) In order to improve the efficiency and effectiveness of United Nations organisations in providing support for social development efforts at the national level, and to enhance their capacity to serve the objectives of the Summit, there is a need to renew, reform and revitalise the various parts of the United Nations system, in particular its operational activities. All specialised agencies and related organisations of the United Nations system are invited to strengthen and adjust their activities, programmes and medium-term strategies, as appropriate, to take into account the follow-up to the Summit. Relevant governing bodies should review their policies, programmes, budgets and activities in this regard;

c) The Administrative Committee on Coordination should consider how its participating entities might best coordinate their activities to implement the objectives of the Summit;

d) Regular reports on their plans and programmes related to Implementation should be provided to the appropriate forums by United Nations funds and programmes and the specialised agencies.

15. The United Nations system should consider and provide appropriate technical cooperation and other forms of assistance to the countries with economies In transition. To this end:

a) The respective United Nations bodies should assist the efforts of those countries in designing and implementing social development programmes;

b) The United Nations Development Programme should continue to undertake efforts to support the implementation of the social development programmes, taking into account the specific needs of the countries with economies in transition;

c) The organisations and bodies of the United Nations system, including the technical and sectoral agencies, the International Monetary Fund and the World Bank, should continue their cooperation in the field of social development of countries with economies in transition.

16. The implementation of the Copenhagen Declaration and the Programme of Action of the Summit will involve many entities of the United Nations system. In order to ensure coherence in this effort, the General Assembly should give consideration to:

a) Promoting and strengthening the coordination of United Nations system activities, the Bretton Woods institutions and the World Trade Organisation at the global, regional and national levels in the area of economic and social development programmes, including, *inter alia*, through reports to and meetings in coordination with the Economic and Social Council;

b) Inviting the World Trade Organisation to consider how it might contribute to the implementation on of the Programme of Action, including activities in cooperation with the United Nations system;

c) Requesting the International Labour Organisation, which because of its mandate, tripartite structures and expertise has a special role to play in the field of employment and social development, to contribute to the implementation of the Programme of Action;

d) Requesting the Secretary-General to ensure effective coordination of the implementation of the Declaration and Programme of Action.

17. United Nations operational activities for development should be strengthened in order to implement the Summit outcome, in accordance with relevant resol-

utions, particularly General Assembly resolution 47/199, and to this end:

a) The United Nations Development Programme should organise United Nations system efforts towards capacity-building at the local, national and regional levels, and should support the coordinated implementation of social development programmes through its network of field offices;

b) Coordination at the country level should be improved through the resident coordinator system to take full account of the Copenhagen Declaration and the Programme of Action of the Summit and related international agreements;

c) The United Nations system should encourage and assist South-South cooperation and technical cooperation among developing countries, at all levels, as an important instrument for social development and the implementation of the Programme of Action;

d) United Nations development efforts should be supported by a substantial increase in resources for operational activities for development on a predictable, continuous and assured basis, commensurate with the increasing needs of developing countries, as stated in resolution 47/199;

e) The United Nations system's capacity for gathering and analysing information and developing indicators of social development should be strengthened, taking into account the work carried out by different countries, in particular by developing countries. The capacity of the United Nations system for providing policy and technical support and advice, upon request, to improve national capacities in this regard should also be strengthened.

18. The support and participation of major groups as defined in Agenda 21 are essential to the success of the implementation of the Programme of Action. To ensure the commitment of these groups, they must be involved in planning, elaboration, implementation and evaluation at both the national and the international levels. To this end, mechanisms are needed to support, promote and allow their effective participation in all relevant United Nations bodies, including the mechanisms responsible for reviewing the implementation of the Programme of Action.

Bibliography

Aajad, R.D., *Tarai Jal Rahi Hai* (Hindi), 1992, Kathmandu.

Akhteruzzaman, A.K.M., 1982, *A geographical Analysis of International Migration of Workers,* Department of Geography, University of Dhaka.

Ali S.A. 1981, 'Labour Migration from India', *World Bank Staff Working Paper* No. 454.

Azad A.K., 1989, 'The Cost and Financing of Individual Contract Migration', *Working Paper*, ILO, Bangkok.

B.R. Ambedkar, *Pakistan or the Partition of India,* Ed 3, Bombay, Thacker Co, 1946.

Baral, Lok Raj, *Regional Migrations, Ethnicity and Security: The South Asian Case*, Sterling Publishers Private Limited, New Delhi, 1990.

Bista, Dor Bahadur, *Fatalism and Development: Nepal's Struggle for Modernisation,* Orient Longman Limited, Hyderabad. 1991.

Board of Investment, Guide to Investment in Bangladesh, Prime Minister's Office, Dhaka, March 1998.

C.H. Philips, *The Partition of India,* Leads University Press, 1962.

Census of India, 1991, Series, Paper 2 of 1992.

Central Bank of Sri Lanka, *Annual Report*, Colombo, 1998.

Ch. Khaliquzzaman, *Pathways to Pakistan*, Bombay, Orient Longmans, 1961.

Choudhary Rahmat Ali, *India: The Continent of Disia or the Country of Doom,* Cambridge, The Disia Continental Movement, 1945, pp. 6.

'Direction of Trade Statistics', *Yearbook,* IMF, 1996.

Government of Bangladesh, *The Fifth Five Year Plan,* 1997-2002.

Hamilton Francis, *An Account of the Kingdom of Nepal* Edinburgh, 1819.

Hans J. Morgenthau, *Military Imusions,* The New Republic (Washington D.C.), March 19, 1956.

HMG/N, National Commission on Population, *Inter Regional Migration in Nepal: Problems and Prospects,* Kathmandu. 1984.

HMG/N, National Commission on Population, *Population and Development in Nepal,* Kathmandu, 1988.

Hossain, A.R.M.A., *Migration of Labour from Bangladesh, Bureau of Manpower Employment and Training,* 1979.

International Trade Statistics' *Yearbook,* United Nations, 1995.

Julius Gould William L. Koeb (eds), *A Dictionary of Social Science,* New York, The Free Press, 1967.

Kedia, Shankar Lal, *Madhesiya Samaj aur Uski Utpatti* (Hindi), Nepal Tarai Vidyarthi Bhasa Sanskriti Samanwya Samiti, Kathmandu, 1991.

Kenneth Cragg, *Islamic Survey Vol. III,* Edinburgh University Press, 1965.

Kirkpatrick William, *An Account of the Kingdom of Nepal*, London, 1981.

M.L. Qureshi, *Survey of Economy, Resources and Prospects of South Asia,* Marga Institute, Colombo, 1981.

Mahbub Ul Haq Human Development Centre, Islamabad, *Human Development in South Asia*, 1999.

Marie L. Borgatta and Edgar F. Borgatta (eds), *Encyclopedia of Sociology*, Volume 3, 1984, Macmillan Company, New York.

Maulana A.K. Azad, *India Wins Freedom,* Bombay, Orient Longman, 1961.

Moir Shakir, *Khilafat to Partition*, New Delhi, Kalamkar Prakashan, 1970.

Moran, Keray, *Partnership for Development, 40 Years of American Assistance.* USAID, 1991.

N.H. Mitra, *Indian Annual Register,* July-Dec, 1930, Vol. II: 339.

National Commission on Population, *Nepal ma Antarik Tatha Antarrastriga Basai-Sarai.* (Nepali), Kathmandu, 1989.

Nepal, Department of Land Revenue, *Administrative Regulations for Tarai Districts,* 1810, 5 Volumes, Trans. by Regmi Research Project, 1967.

Nepali, Chittaranjan "Nepal Ma Kariya Mochan Ko Itihas", *Nepali XX* July-September, 1964.

Noronha, Frederick, 'Human Development: Indian Story', *The Tribuze*, April 7, 1997.

P.C. Mathur, Virendra Narain and M.V. Lekhi, 'Intra-Regional Relations: A study in Infrastructural Determinants', in S.P. Verma and K.P. Mishra (Ed.), *Foreign Policies in South Asia* (Jaipur, 1969).

Pant, Shastra Dutta, *Vyabasthit Vasti Ra Gaun Vikas* (Nepali), South Asian Research Centre, Kathmandu, 1992.

Penderel Moon, *Divide and Quit*, London, 1961.

Perera, KKYW, 'Energy Issues and Alternatives', *Economic Review*, People's Bank, August 1996.

Peter Berton, 'International Sub-systems: A Submacro Approach to International Studies', *International Studies Quarterly* (Detroit-Michigan) Vol. 13, No. 4, 1969.

Quarterly Newsletter, December 1995, SAARC Chamber of Commerce and Industry, Karachi.

Rabindranath Tagore, 'Through Indian Eye', *Time of India*, Bombay, April 10, 1924.

Regional Studies, 'Indo-Sri Lanka Relations, Retrospect, Problems and Prospects', April, 1986.

Regional Studies, 'Peace Process in Sri Lanka: Problems and Prospects', November-December, 1996.

Regional Studies, 'Polls and Politics in Sri Lanka', January-February, 1984.

Regional Studies, 'The Agony of Sri Lanka', December, 1987.

Regional Studies, 'The Tamil Factor: Genesis and Prospects of the Indian State in Sri Lanka', November-December, 1982.

Regional Studies, Rohingya Refugees in Bangladesh: Their Impact on Regional Stability, November, 1993.

S.P. Verma, *Problems of Democracy in India*, Delhi, S. Chand, 1946, pp. 64.

SAARC, *Sub-regionalism and Bangladesh, Regional Studies*, September 1997.

Seligman, Edwin R.A. and Alvin Johnson (eds), *Encyclopedia of the Social Sciences*, New York, The Macmillan Company.

Sri Prakash, *Pakistan: Birth and Early Days*, Meerut, Meenakshi Prakashan, 1965.

The Economic Times, New Delhi, December 9, 1997.

The Island, February 27, 'Land, Landlessness and Poverty in Sri Lanka', 1989.

The Island, May 22, 'Growth of NGO Sector in Sri Lanka Due to Open Economy and Ethnic Problems', 1991.

The Political Economy of Bangladesh—Perspective and Trends, Regional Studies, January, 1995.

Tinker, H., *The Banyan Tree: Overseas Emigration from India, Pakistan and Bangladesh*, Oxford University Press, 1997.

Treaty of Peace and Friendship, Kathmandu, July 31, 1950,

Weesing's Contempory Archives, Vol. XIV, 20038.

World Bank, *World Development Report 1991: The challenge of Development*, Oxford University Press, New York, June.

World Bank, *World Development Report*, 1995.

Index